PRECOLONIAL BLACK AFRICA

Cheikh Anta Diop

PRECOLONIAL BLACK AFRICA

A

Comparative Study of the Political and Social Systems of Europe and Black Africa, from Antiquity to the Formation of Modern States

TRANSLATED FROM THE FRENCH BY HAROLD J. SALEMSON

Lawrence Hill Books

Chicago

Library of Congress Cataloging-in-Publication Data

Diop, Cheikh Anta.
  Precolonial Black Africa.

  Translation of: L'Afrique noire pre-coloniale.
  1. Africa, Sub-Saharan—Politics and government.
  2. Social structure—Africa, Sub-Saharan—History.
  3. Africa—History—To 1498. 4. Europe—Politics and
  government. 5. Social structure—Europe—History.
  6. Europe—History—To 1492. I. Title.
  JQ1872.D5613 1986   967   86-22804
  ISBN 0-88208-187-X
  ISBN 1-55652-088-3 (paper)
  previously ISBN 0-88208-188-X

First published in France by Presence Africaine
Translated from the French by Harold Salemson

Published by Lawrence Hill Books
An imprint of Chicago Review Press, Incorporated
814 North Franklin Street
Chicago, Illinois 60610
ISBN 978-1-55652-088-4
Printed in the United States of America
20 19 18 17 16

To my professor Gaston Bachelard,
whose rationalistic teaching
nurtured my mind

To my professors M. André Leroi-Gourhan and Dean
André Aymard, who oversaw my work

All my gratitude

Contents

PREFACE xi

I ANALYSIS OF THE CONCEPT OF CASTE 1
Major Divisions Within the Caste System 1
Conditions of the Slaves 3
The Bâ-dolo 5
Genesis of the Caste System 6
Caste in Egypt 9
Genesis of the Caste System in India 11

II SOCIO-POLITICAL EVOLUTION OF THE
ANCIENT CITY 18
Social Classes 18
Eupatridae 18
The Plebs 20
Priest-Kings 20
The City-State 21
Individualism 23
Aristocratic Revolution 24
Social Revolution 26
Movements of Ideas 30
The Influence of Egypt 31
The Roman Empire 33

III FORMATION OF THE MODERN
EUROPEAN STATES 35
The Political and Social Middle Ages 36
The Intellectual Middle Ages 40

IV POLITICAL ORGANIZATION IN BLACK
AFRICA 43
The Mossi Constitution 43
The Constitution of Cayor 46

Matrilinear Succession: Ghana, Mali   48
Songhai, the Oriental Influence   50
Precedence in Songhai   53
The Case of Cayor   55
Significance of Royalty   *The Vitalist Concept*   59
  Obligations of the King Separation of
  Secular and Religious The Lebou
  "Republic"
Monarchic and Tribal Africa   72
Origin of the Constitutional Regime   75
Crowning of the King and Court Life   77
  Songhai   Cayor   Ghana   Mali

V   POLITICAL ORGANIZATION   89
    Power of the African Empires   89
    Strength and Extent of the Empires   89
      Ghana   Mali   Songhai
    Administrative Organization   99
    Resources of the Royalty and Nobility   104
      Taxes   Customs   Gold Mines
      Royal Treasury   Booty   Fees Connected
      with Assuming Administrative Functions
    Government and Administration   108
      Hostages   Songhai   Various Ministries
      Administrative Unity
    Military Organization   115
      Structure   Knights   Cavalry   Foot Soldiers
      Flotilla   Royal Guard   Strategy
      and Tactics
    Judicial Organization   124

VI ECONOMIC ORGANIZATION   130
    Barter   130
    Modern-type Commerce   131
    Currency   133
    Import-Export   136

Means of Transportation, Roads 137
Economic Wealth 141
Comparison of Socio-economic Structures in
Africa and Europe 142
Navetanism 150
The Taalibé 151
Slave Manpower: Concentration 152
Retribalization 157
Primitive Accumulation 158

VII IDEOLOGICAL SUPERSTRUCTURE: ISLAM
IN BLACK AFRICA 162
Peaceful Penetration 163
The Role of Autochthonous Chiefs 163
Metaphysical Reasons 165
Power of Religious Beliefs 167
Mystical Underpinning of Nationalism 169
Renunciation of the Pre-Islamic Past 171
"Sherifism" 172

VIII INTELLECTUAL LEVEL: TEACHING AND
EDUCATION 176
The University 176
Teaching Method 177
The Program 178
Awarding of Diplomas 179
Intellectual Development 179
Importance of the Sherif 186
Survival of the Black Tradition in Education 190
Historical Reminder: The Moroccan Invasion 192

IX TECHNICAL LEVEL 196
Architecture in Nilotic Sudan 196
Architecture in Zimbabwe 197
Architecture in Ghana and the Niger Bend 199
Metallurgy 204

Glassmaking   205
Medicine and Hygiene   205
Weaving   206
Agriculture   207
Crafts   207
Hunting   207
Nautical Experience   208

MIGRATIONS AND FORMATION OF
PRESENT-DAY AFRICAN PEOPLES   212
Origin of the Yoruba   216
Origin of the Laobé   217
Origin of the Peul   220
Origin of the Tuculor   223
Origin of the Serer   224
Origin of the Agni (Añi)   228
Origin of the Fang and Bamum   228
Formation of the Wolof People   229

Postface   235

Preface

Until now [1960, date of the first edition], the history of Black Africa has always been written with dates as dry as laundry lists, and no one has almost ever tried to find the key that unlocks the door to the intelligence, the understanding of African society.

Failing which, no researcher has ever succeeded in revivifying the African past, in bringing it back to life in our minds, before our very eyes, so to speak, while remaining strictly within the realm of science.

Yet the documents at our disposal allow us to do that practically without any break in continuity for a period of two thousand years, at least insofar as West Africa is concerned.

Therefore, it had become indispensable to unfreeze, in a manner of speaking to defossilize that African history which was there at hand, lifeless, imprisoned in the documents.

However, this work is not properly speaking a book of history; but it is an auxiliary tool indispensable to the historian. It indeed affords him a scientific understanding of all the historical facts hitherto unexplained. In that sense, it is a study in African historical sociology. It permits us no longer to be surprised at the stagnation or rather the relatively stable equilibrium of precolonial African societies: the analysis of their socio-political structures presented in it allowing us to gauge the stabilizing factors in African society.

One thereby understands the technical and other lags to

be the result of a different kind of development based upon absolutely objective fundamental causes. Thus, there is no longer any reason for embarrassment.

Once this awareness achieved, we can immediately and fully in almost every slightest detail relive all the aspects of African national life: the administrative, judicial, economic, and military organizations, that of labor, the technical level, the migrations and formations of peoples and nationalities, thus their ethnic genesis, and consequently almost linguistic genesis, etc.

Upon absorbing any such human experience, we sense deep within ourselves a true reinforcement of our feeling of cultural oneness.

PRECOLONIAL BLACK AFRICA

Chapter One

ANALYSIS OF THE CONCEPT OF CASTE

It seems necessary at the outset to point out the specific features of the caste system, in order more clearly to bring out the difference in social structure which has always existed between Europe and Africa. The originality of the system resides in the fact that the dynamic elements of society, whose discontent might have engendered revolution, are really satisfied with their social condition and do not seek to change it: a man of so-called "inferior caste" would categorically refuse to enter a so-called "superior" one.[1] In Africa, it is not rare for members of the lower caste to refuse to enter into conjugal relations with those of the higher caste, even though the reverse would seem more normal.

MAJOR DIVISIONS WITHIN THE CASTE SYSTEM

Let us proceed to a description of the internal structure of the caste system, before attempting an explanation of its origin. The present territory of Senegal will be used here as a model for study: nevertheless, the conclusions which are drawn from it hold true for the whole of detribalized Sudanese Africa. In Senegal, society is divided into slaves and freemen, the latter being *gor,* including both *gér* and *ñéño.*

The gér comprise the nobles and all freemen with no manual profession other than agriculture, considered a sacred activity.

I

The ñéño comprise all artisans: shoemakers, black-smiths, goldsmiths, etc. These are hereditary professions. The *djam,* or slaves, include the *djam-bur,* who are slaves of the king; the *djam neg nday,* slaves of one's mother; and the *djam neg bây,* slaves of one's father. The *gér* formed the superior caste. But—and herein lay the real originality of the system—unlike the attitude of the nobles toward the bourgeoisie, the lords toward the serfs, or the Brahmans toward the other Indian castes, the *gér* could not materially exploit the lower castes without losing face in the eyes of others, as well as their own. On the contrary, they were obliged to assist lower caste members in every way possible: even if less wealthy, they had to "give" to a man of lower caste if so requested. In exchange, the latter had to allow them social precedence.

The specific feature of this system therefore consisted in the fact that the manual laborer, instead of being deprived of the fruits of his labor, as was the artisan or the serf of the Middle Ages, could, on the contrary, add to it wealth given him by the "lord."

Consequently, if a revolution were to occur, it would be initiated from above and not from below. But that is not all, as we shall see: members of all castes including slaves were closely associated to power, as de facto ministers; which resulted in constitutional monarchies governed by councils of ministers, made up of authentic representatives of all the people. We can understand from this why there were no revolutions in Africa against the regime, but only against those who administered it poorly, i.e., unworthy princes. In addition, there were, of course, also palace revolutions.

For every caste, advantages and disadvantages, deprivations of rights and compensations balanced out. So it is outside of consciences, in material progress and external influences, that the historical motives must be sought. Taking into account their isolation, which however must not be exaggerated, it can be understood why Africa's societies remained relatively stable.

CONDITIONS OF THE SLAVES

The only group that would have an interest in overthrowing the social order were the slaves of the father's household, in alliance with the *bâ-dolo* ("those without power," socially speaking, the poor peasants).[2] Indeed, it is clear from what preceded that the status of the artisans was an enviable one. Their consciences could in no way be bearers of the seeds of revolution: being the principal beneficiaries of the monarchical regime, they defend it up to this day, or regret its passing.

By definition, all slaves should make up the revolutionary class. One can easily imagine the state of mind of a warrior or any freeman whose condition through defeat in war radically changes from one day to the next, as he becomes a slave: as in classical antiquity, prisoners of war were automatically subject to being sold. Persons of rank might be ransomed by their families, who would give in exchange a certain number of slaves. In principle, one could have a nephew serve as a substitute: a man's sister's son, in this matriarchal regime, would be given by his uncle in ransom; whence the two Wolof expressions, *na djây* ("may he sell," i.e., the uncle), and *djar bât* ("he who can buy back," i.e., the nephew). But this is where the slaves come in.

In this aristocratic regime, the nobles formed the cavalry of the army (the chivalry). The infantry was composed of slaves, former prisoners of war taken from outside the national territory. The slaves of the king formed the greater part of his forces and in consequence their condition was greatly improved. They were now slaves in name only. The rancor in their hearts had been lightened by the favors they received: they shared in the booty after an expedition; under protection of the king, during periods of social unrest, they could even indulge in discreet pillage within the national territory, against the poor peasants, the *bâ-dolo*—but never against the artisans who were always able to gain restitution of their confiscated goods. The regime, the social mores obtaining, allowed the artisans to go directly to the prince, without fear, and complain to him. The slaves were commanded by one of their own, the infantry general, who was a pseudo-prince in that he might rule over a fief inhabited by freemen. Such was the case, in the monarchy of Cayor (Senegal), of the *djarâf Bunt Keur*, the representative of the slaves within the government and commander-in-chief of the army. His power and authority were so great that the day of his betrayal brought an end to the kingdom of Cayor. We will return to this matter, under the heading of political constitutions.

However, the ennobling of a slave, even by the king, was impossible in Africa, in contrast to the customs of European courts. Birth appeared to be something intrinsic in the eyes of this society and even the king would have been ill-advised to ennoble anyone at all, even a freeman.

The slaves of the king, by force of circumstance, thus became an element favorable to the preservation of the regime; they were a conservative element.

The slave of the mother's household was the captive of our mother, as opposed to the slave of our father. He might have been bought on the open market, come from an inheritance, or be a gift. Once established in the family he became almost an integral part of it; he was the loyal domestic, respected, feared, and consulted by the children. Due to the matriarchal and polygamous regime, we feel him closer to us, because he belongs to our mother, than the slave of the father, who is at an equal distance, socially speaking, from all the children of the same father and different mothers. As can easily be seen, the slave of the father would become the scapegoat for the society. Therefore, the slave of the mother could not be a revolutionary.

The slave of the father's household, by contrast, considering his anonymous position (our father is everyone's, so to speak, while our mother is truly our own), will be of no interest to anyone and have no special protection in society. He may be disposed of without compensation. However, his condition is not comparable to that of the plebeian of ancient Rome, the thete of Athens, or the sudra of India. The condition of the sudra was based on a religious significance. Contact with them was considered impure; society had been structured without taking their existence into account; they could not even live in the cities nor participate in religious ceremonies, nor at the ouset have a religion of their own. We will return to this matter later. However, the alienation of the slaves of the father's household in Africa was great enough, on the moral and material plane, that their minds could be truly revolutionary. But for reasons connected to the preindustrial nature of Africa, such as the dispersion of the population into villages, for example, they could not effect a revolution. We must also add that they were really intruders in a hostile society which watched them day and night, and would never have allowed them time to plot a rebellion with their peers. It made it even less possible for them to acquire economic position and moral and intellectual education, in short, any social strength comparable to that of the bourgeoisie of the West when it overthrew the aristocracy. Slaves of this category might apparently at best have joined forces with the poor peasants, those *bâ-dolo* ("without power") whose labor actually sustained the nation more than that of the artisans.

THE BÂ-DOLO

The *bâ-dolo* by definition, were not *ñéños*, but *gérs* of modest means, doomed to the cultivation of the earth. As *gérs*, belonging to the same level as the prince, the latter found nothing dishonorable or debasing in pillaging their goods, however small they might be. Since a well-to-do *gér*, finding himself in privileged circumstances, might marry a princess, although of secondary rank to be sure, the *bâ-dolo* being a *gér* without means would have to carry the fiscal burdens of society. Indeed, according to the African concept of honor, it was not those of inferior rank who were to be exploited, should occasion arise, but rather social equals, particularly where the latter did not have the material power to defend themselves, which was the case of the *bâ-dolo*. For reasons of this kind, the possessions of the artisan were spared. In such preindustrial, agricultural regimes, it is true, everyone was involved in the cultivation of the soil, including the king (who, according to Cailliaud, was the foremost farmer of Seennaar).[3] But on closer examination, it was the *bâ-dolo*, more than the artisans, who fed the population and constituted the majority of the laboring class.

Out of caste prejudice, however, as can easily be deduced from the preceding, they could not lower themselves so far as to form an alliance with the malcontent slaves, especially since the latter were disorganized and had no chance of success. If such an alliance had come to be in the course of African history, it would have led to a peasants' and slaves' revolt, a *jacquerie,* of the kind Egypt experienced toward the close of the Middle Kingdom, or the sort common to Western history ever since the Middle Ages—none of which was ever successful. It would have been a revolt and not a revolution such as the French (bourgeois) Revolution. But we shall see that, in precolonial Africa, the length of the periods of prosperity had nothing in common with that of the periods of dearth, which were rather exceptional and ephemeral, and that the general abundance of economic resources and the extraordinary, legendary wealth of the continent in fact foreclosed the birth and growth of any revolutionary spirit in African consciousness.

GENESIS OF THE CASTE SYSTEM

The caste system arose from a division of labor, but under an advanced political regime, which was monarchic (for one never finds castes where there are no nobles). However, it is very probable that the specialization of labor, which led to the hereditary transmission of trades in the caste system, on a family or individual scale, evolved out of the clanic organization. If one looks at the totemic names, all those who practice the same trade, all those who belong to the same caste, are of the same totemic clan. For example, in spite of all the exogamic marriages that may have taken place after detribalization, all *Mârs* are shoemakers, belong to the same clan, and have the same totem, no matter how territorially separated they may have become. Thus, two Mârs who meet for the first time understand that they have a common clan origin.

Be that as it may, at the time of the empires of Ghana and Mali, as evidenced by the testimony of Ibn Khaldun, Ibn Battuta, and the *Tarikh es Sudan,* detribalization had already taken place throughout these great empires.

At the time of the conquest of Northern Africa [by the Muslims], some merchants penetrated into the western part of the land of the Blacks and found among them no king more powerful than the king of Ghana. His states extended westward to the shores of the Atlantic Ocean. Ghana, the capital of this strong, populous nation, was made up of two towns separated by the Niger River, and formed one of the greatest and best populated cities of the world. The author of the *Book of Roger* [Al Bakri] makes special mention of it, as does the author of *Roads and Kingdoms.*[4]

One may suppose that in a city such as Ghana, which in the tenth century was already one of the largest in the world, tribal organization had completely given way to the demands of urban life. At any rate, transmission of the individual name and inheritance, as it was practiced in the empire of Mali, according to Ibn Battuta, leaves us in no doubt about the disappearance of the tribal system in this region in 1352.

They [the Blacks] are named after their maternal uncles, and not after their fathers; it is not the sons who inherit from their fathers, but the nephews, the sons of the father's sister. I have never met with this last custom anywhere else, except among the infidels of Malabar in India.[5]

One fact that has not been sufficiently stressed is that the individual had a first, or given, name but not a family name before the dislocation of the clan. Theretofore, a person bore the name of the clan, but only collectively, so that when asked his name, he would always reply that he was of the clan of the Ba-Pende, Ba-Oulé, Ba-Kongo, etc. He was a member of the community, and only the dispersal of it could afford him individual existence as well as a family name, which remained then, as a sort of recall, the name of the clan. This is therefore one of the reasons we always speak of totemic names. And according to the passage cited from Ibn Battuta, we see that the individual already bore a personal family name, the name of his mother, due to the matriarchal system. This is confirmed by all the family names of important personages transmitted to us by the *Tarikh es Sudan*. This work was written by a learned Black of the sixteenth century, A.D., but relates events the most ancient of which date back to the first centuries after the birth of Christ. The same could be said of the *Tarikh el Fettach*, written in the same period, by another Black from Timbuktu [Kâti].

The stability of the caste system was assured by the hereditary transmission of social occupations, which corresponded, in a certain measure, to a monopoly disguised by a religious prohibition in order to eliminate professional competition. Indeed, religious significance was attached to the inheritance of the trade. According to the current beliefs, a subject from outside a trade, even if he acquired all the skill and science of a calling which was not that of his family, would not be able to practice it efficiently, in the mystical sense, because it was not his ancestors who concluded the initial contract with the spirit who had originally taught it to humanity. Due to an understandable tendency toward generalization, even scientific specializations to which no notions of caste are attached—e.g., eye or ear medicine, etc.—are dominated by this idea. Up to this point in Africa, in the villages, a given family was specialized in the treatment of one particular part of the body only; it is interesting to note that this was also the case in ancient Egypt where, in all probability, there was originally a caste system.

CASTE IN EGYPT

There are seven classes of Egyptians, and of these some are called priests, others warriors, others herdsmen, others swineherds, others trademen, others interpreters, and, lastly, pilots; such are the classes of Egyptians; they take their names from the employments they exercise. Their warriors are called Calasiries or Hermotybies, and they are of the following districts, for all Egypt is divided into districts. The following are the districts of the Hermotybies: Busiris, Sais, Chemmis, Papremis, the island called Prosopitis, and the half of Natho. From these districts are the Hermotybies, being in number, when they are most numerous, a hundred and sixty thousand. None of these learn any mechanical art, but apply themselves wholly to military affairs. These next are the districts of the Calasiries: Thebes, Bubastis, Aphthis, Tanis, Mendes, Sebennys, Athribis, Pharbaethis, Thmuis, Onuphis, Anysis, Mycephoris; this district is situated in an island opposite the city Bubastis. These are the districts of the Calasiries, being in number, when they are most numerous, two hundred and fifty thousand men; neither are these allowed to practise any art, but they devote themselves to military pursuits alone, the son succeeding to his father.[6]

The swineherd caste alone was considered impure in Egypt, because of the prevailing religious notion concerning pork.

The Egyptians consider the pig to be an impure beast, and, therefore, if a man in passing by a pig should touch him only with his garments, he forthwith goes to the river and plunges in: and in the next place, swineherds, although native Egyptians are the only men who are not allowed to enter any of their temples; neither will any man give his daughter in marriage to one of them, nor take a wife from among them; but the swineherds intermarry among themselves. The Egyptians, therefore, do not think it right to sacrifice swine to any other deities; but to the moon and Bacchus they do sacrifice them . . .[7]

The art of medicine is thus divided among them: each physician applies himself to one disease only, and not more. All places abound in physicians; some physicians are for the eyes, others for the head, others for the teeth, others for the parts about the belly, and others for internal disorders.[8]

One might believe that in Egypt as well clanic division corresponded, at least to some extent, with the division of labor, on the word of Herodotus. It is difficult to deny the totemic significance of the *nomes* (districts): with their local flags, they were the first geographical districts occupied by the totemic clans that progressively fused to give birth to the Egyptian nation. But even in the low period, when these territorial divisions no longer had any more than an administrative significance, there remained enough of the effects of the totemic past so that one cannot doubt its existence.

Be that as it may, as evidenced by the preceding, there was a dual bond, religious and economic, which confined each individual within his caste, except in the case of the slave who, not being a native, in reality belonged to a traditional lay category. Society had been conceived without taking his existence into account; he had been forcibly introduced into it, an intruder; a place was made for him somehow or other, without its assuming any religious significance; he was forcibly subjugated, for nothing more nor less than economic and material reasons. No metaphysical concept later arose to justify his condition, as if to ease the consciences of the citizens. We shall see that it was otherwise in India for the pariahs and for the plebeians of antiquity, where the religious systems stipulated the impurity of these inferior classes.

In Africa, slaves belonged to a hierarchy: the social condition of the masters carried over to the slaves. Slaves of a nobleman were superior to those of a simple freeman and "gave" to the latter; and the latter in turn, if the slave of a *gér*, would "give" to the slave of an artisan; an artisan might own slaves, since he was a *gor*.

Nobles and clergy, traditional or Islamic (following the Almoravide movement of the tenth century), belong to the same caste and marry among themselves. But these nobles have the peculiarity of not being landowners, in the sense we give to this term as applied to the Middle Ages in the Western world. The land in Africa does not belong to the conquerors; the mind of the nobles is not concerned with the possession of great landed estates to be cultivated by serfs bound to the soil; in this sense there was no feudal system in Africa. This question will be treated later. In Africa, the nobility never acquired this keen sense of ownership of land. Alongside, the "conqueror," the king, there is in each village a poor old man in tatters, but respected and spared, whom the spirit of the earth is considered to have entrusted with the land. Earth is a divinity: it would be sacrilege actually to appropriate any part of it. It only lends itself to our agricultural activity, in order to make human life possible. Even during the Islamic period, i.e., up to the present day, this religious concept obscurely influences the consciousness of all Africans and it has contributed historically toward stopping or restraining tendencies to form a feudal system.

The concept of privately owned land developed only among the Lebou of the Cape Verde peninsula, as a result of the development of the great port of Dakar, after European penetration. Plots of land there were until very recently more valuable than anywhere else in what was French West Africa.

GENESIS OF THE CASTE SYSTEM IN INDIA

One cannot ignore the case of India, when considering the general question of caste. The notion of caste is so special in that part of the world that a study which did not take it into account would be lacking in consistency and demonstrative vigor, as well as generality. According to Lenormant, this type of social organization was totally alien to the Aryans and Semites. Wherever we find it, in Egypt, Babylon, Africa, or the kingdom of Malabar in India, we can be sure it is due to a southern Cushite influence.

This system is essentially Cushite, and wherever it is found it is not difficult to establish that it stems originally from this race of people. We have seen it flourish in Babylon. The Aryas of India, who adopted it, had borrowed it from the peoples of Cush who preceded them in the Indus and Ganges basins . . .[9]

While this appears to have been the origin of the caste system in India, one can see the transformations that the Aryan invasions occasioned in it.

It has often been maintained, without production of any conclusive historical documents, that it was the Aryans themselves who created the caste system after having subjugated the Black aboriginal Dravidian populace. Had this been the case, the criterion of color should have been at its foundation: there should have been at most three castes, Whites, Blacks, and the gamut of crossbreeds. However, this is not the case, and in India also the castes effectively correspond to a division of labor, without any ethnic connotations. Strabo, in his *Geography*, citing a more ancient author (Megasthenes), reports that there existed in India seven castes corresponding to certain well-defined social functions: Brahmans (philosophers), Kshatriyas (warriors), Farmers, Agents of the King or Ephori (who crisscrossed the country to inform the king of what was going on), Workers and Artisans, Counselors and Courtiers, and Shepherds and Hunters.[10]

Originally the number of castes was smaller: only four, according to the *Laws of Manu*, also corresponding to a division of labor, excluding any idea of ethnic differentiation, since a Dravidian can just as well be a Brahman.

87. But in order to protect this universe He, the most resplendent one, assigned separate (duties and) occupations to those who sprang from his mouth, arms, thighs, and feet.

88. To Brâhma*n*as he assigned teaching and studying (the Veda), sacrificing for their own benefit and for others, giving and accepting (of alms).

89. The Kshatriya he commanded to protect the people, to bestow gifts, to offer sacrifices, to study (the Veda), and to abstain from attaching himself to sensual pleasures;

90. The Vaisya to tend cattle, to bestow gifts, to offer sacrifices, to study (the Veda), to trade, to lend money, and to cultivate land.

91. One occupation only the lord prescribed to the Sûdra, to serve meekly even these (other) three castes.[11]

Giving a divine character to property is an Aryan custom: in Rome, Greece, and India it led to the isolation from society of an entire category of individuals who had no family, had neither hearth nor home, and no right of ownership. They would everywhere constitute the class of the wretched, able to acquire wealth only after the advent of money: profane wealth, which had not been foreseen by the traditional and sacred laws regulating ownership that were made up by the ancestors of the Aryans. It was through its concern with the ownership of material goods that the Aryan spirit or genius impressed its mold upon the caste system.

In the *Laws of Manu* one can follow a meticulous description of the objects that might be possessed by such and such a class and, above all, those objects the possession of which was forbidden to the lowest class and its crossbreeds. This consciousness of material interest, this exclusivism in the domain of possession were the ideas added by the Aryans to the caste system, which at first should not have contained them in India; it would never contain them in Africa. Here it is necessary to recall all the differences between the African slave on the one hand and the plebeian or sudra on the other. The Aryans meant to effect an economic classification of society, in

India as well as in Rome and Greece, and not an ethnic separation.

51. But the dwellings of *Kandâlas* and *Svapakas* shall be outside the village, they must be made Apapâtras, and their wealth (shall be) dogs and donkeys.

52. Their dress (shall be) the garments of the dead, (they shall eat) their food from broken dishes, black iron (shall be) their ornaments, and they must always wander from place to place.

53. A man who fulfills a religious duty, shall not seek intercourse with them; their transactions (shall be) among themselves, and their marriages with their equals.

54. Their food shall be given to them by others (than an Âryan giver) in a broken dish; at night they shall not walk about in villages and in towns.

55. By day they may go about for the purpose of their work, distinguished by marks at the king's command, and they shall carry out the corpses (of persons) who have no relatives; that is a settled rule.

56. By the king's order they shall always execute the criminals, in accordance with the law, and they shall take for themselves the clothes, the beds, and the ornaments of (such) criminals.

57. A man of impure origin, who belongs not to any caste, (varna, but whose character is) not known, who, (though) not an Âryan, has the appearance of an Âryan, one may discover by his acts.[12]

This last paragraph reveals that the "untouchables" of India no more than the plebeians of Rome in principle belonged to a race different from that of the lords. Indeed, the criteria that allowed one to distinguish them were of a moral or material nature, not an ethnic one. The text further elaborates that it is in the behavior of an individual that one can discern the tendencies "unworthy of an Aryan" he inherits from parents of a base class. In the next chapter, we will study the conditions which led to the formation of this class, all of them social. We must stress that this class was totally absent

from the unaltered southern systems in which religious prohibitions might isolate a social category (e.g., the swineherds
of Egypt), yet not affect it in its material interest to the point
expressed in the preceding text. That is one of the fundamental differences between the African and Aryan conceptions.
The swineherds of Egypt could absolutely acquire wealth in
the same manner as others. They were not forbidden the
possession of any goods; but since they raised an animal to
which religious prejudices were attached, these prejudices re-
dounded onto their own condition, and isolated them on a
cultural plane, while leaving intact all their material interests.
All the traditional prohibitions of the rest of Black Africa were
of the same nature and never affected material goods. On the
contrary, we can unquestionably affirm that in every such
instance the possibilities of material gain on the part of subjects of the category concerned were increased by a kind of
sentiment of immanent justice, a kind of compensatory spirit
inherent in the society, for not only can they retain all their
belongings, but they can increase their possessions by "asking" for some of others.

For these material considerations, the *Laws of Manu*
tolerated a certain permeability of the caste system. They
indeed provided for the case in which members of a superior
class could no longer assure their existence solely by the
means that religion recognized as legitimately theirs. In such a
case, they provided a whole series of adaptations and accom-
modations.

83. But a Brâhmana, or a Kshatriya, living by a Vaisya's
mode of subsistence, shall carefully avoid (the pursuit of) agriculture, (which causes) injury to many beings and depends on
others.
84. (Some) declare that agriculture is something excellent,
(but) that means of subsistence is blamed by the virtuous; (for)
the wooden (implement) with iron point injures the earth and
(the beings) living in the earth.[13]

In the domain of marriage, the permeability of the caste system existed, but it was unilateral.

12. For the first marriage of twice-born men (wives) of equal caste are recommended; but for those who through desire proceed (to marry again) the following females, (chosen) according to the (direct) order (of the castes), are most approved.
13. It is declared that a Sûdra woman alone (can be) the wife of a Sûdra, she and one of his own caste (the wives) of a Vaisya, those two and one of his own caste (the wives) of a Kshatriya, those three and one of his own caste (the wives) of a Brâhmana.[14]

The study of the caste system in India holds a wealth of lessons: it allows one to judge the relative importance of racial, economic, and ideological factors. One can see that the Aryan race created Western materialistic and industrial technological civilization wherever the historical and economic circumstances were ripe. It is these factors which must be considered determinant, and not a peculiar set of mind in which the Aryans alone were privileged participants, conferring on them intellectual superiority over all others. Indeed, since it was a branch of this race that actually settled in Iran and India, adopting the social superstructure of the southern peoples—while adapting it—if the racial set of mind were all that counted, one might ask: Why, then, did it not create a civilization of the Western type in there countries? Economic conditions aside, the caste system of social organization assures greater permanemce and stability in society than does the system of classes created by the Aryans in Rome and in Greece—the study of which we will now begin.

NOTES

1. Were it a matter of material interest alone.
2. Ba-dolé, in Tuculor, means "without power." Dolé in Wolof refers to physical or moral strength.

3. Cailliaud, Frédéric, of Nantes, *Voyages à Méroé, au Fleuve blanc, au-delà de Fâzoql, dans le Midi du Royaume de Sennâr*. Printed by authorization of the King, at the Royal Printing Office, 1826.

4. Ibn Khaldun. *Histoire des Berbères et des dynasties musulmanes de l'Afrique Septentrionale* (trans. Baron de Slane). Algiers: Government Printshop, 1954, II, 109.

5. Ibn Battuta. *Voyage au Soudan* (trans. Baron de Slane), p. 12. See also his *Travels in Asia and Africa, 1325–1354*, H.A.R. Gibb, trans.

6. *The Histories of Herodotus* (trans. Henry Cary). New York: Appleton, 1899, Book II, Pars. 164–166.

7. *Idem*, Par. 47.   8. *Idem*, Par. 84.

9. Lenormant. *Histoire ancienne des Phéniciens*. Paris: Ed. Lévy, 1890, p. 384.

10. *The Geography of Strabo* (trans. Horace Leonard Jones). Cambridge: Harvard Univ. Press, Vol. VII, Book XV, I, 67ff., Pars. 39ff.

11. *The Laws of Manu* (trans. from the Sanskrit by Georg Bühler). Oxford: Clarendon Press, 1866; reprinted, New York: Dover Publications, 1969, Book I: "The Creation," 24–25, Secs. 87–91.

12. *Idem*, Book X: "Mixed Castes," 414–415, Secs. 51–57.

13. *Idem*, Book X: "Occupations of the Castes," 420–421, Secs. 83–84.

14. *Idem*, Book III: "Marriage," 14, Secs. 12–13.

Chapter Two

SOCIO-POLITICAL EVOLUTION
OF THE ANCIENT CITY

SOCIAL CLASSES

The facts hereafter related are essentially taken from *The Ancient City* by Fustel de Coulanges. As Grenier remarks in his *Les religions étrusque et romaine* (The Etruscan and Roman Religions), Fustel de Coulanges's work remains the authority. At most, perhaps might one reverse the order of the factors and, contrarily to what he said, explain the religious ideological superstructure by the economic living conditions. But even on this point, it must be recognized that his thought is extremely subtle; for some developments he clearly seems to give precedence to the living conditions.

Originally there were two classes in Greco-Roman society:

     Athens: Eupatridae and Thetes;
     Sparta: Equals and Inferiors;
     Rome: Patricians and Plebeians.

EUPATRIDAE

This first class is that of the "haves." From the very beginning, property had had a divine character and only members of this class could possess the land in the sacred sense of the term. They alone, having ancestors, could have a domestic cult and a god, without which one had no political, judicial, or religious personality and was thus "impure," a plebeian. They alone knew the sacred rites, the prayers which for a long time had remained unwritten and were transmitted orally from father to son. Superstition and conservatism were inherent in them: they alone had an interest in maintaining the order established by their ancestors. If a priest introduced into the cult the slightest innovation, he was punished with death. Thus it is not this class that was responsible for the progressive profanation of religion and the body of traditional beliefs, a profanation inseparable from what we have come to call Greek secular and rational thought. This was the work of the plebs. The owning class alone was patriotic since only it had a "patria," i.e., freedom of the city, while the plebs, without hearth or home, were restricted to the outside or the low parts of the cities, like the untouchables of India. Patriotism, so characteristic of Greco-Roman antiquity, is explained by the fact that society had not allowed for the foreigner, who thereby became enemy number one, without rights, who might be killed with impunity and whose very eyes made the holy objects impure. He was punished with death if he touched a tomb or entered a sacred place. He could protect his life only by voluntarily becoming the slave of a citizen of the city: hence, the class of clients. One can understand why men would defend to the last drop of their blood their city, outside of which they were vile, impure beings, untouchables, worthy at best of slavery. Thus patriotism sprang from the very structure of society. At the start, it did not reflect a sentiment of purely national pride, as was the case in Egypt.

Religious egotism—the gods were first and foremost domestic property—was an obstacle to the existence of a national territory more extensive than the city: houses might not even touch one another, the connecting wall being a sacrilege in antiquity. Even in death, families were not commingled. The boundaries of fields were sacred: the Terminus gods.

Primogeniture, which prevailed, produced among the eupatridae the unprivileged and discontented class of cadets (or younger sons): they would in the end revolt in various cities in order to abolish primogeniture and paternal authority.

THE PLEBS

The lowest class, the plebs, was made up of all those whose hearths had gone out, fatherless children or bastards, onetime clients who now felt freer among the plebs. These could possess no land, married without sacred rites, in other words, profanely, had no sacred prayers, no religion: this is why they were the ones to trample upon tradition and liberate society from its ultra-conservative changelessness, which might otherwise have survived up to our time. In their alienation without any compensation whatsoever, as against the golden rule of African societies, is where we may look for the deeper causes of the transformations and revolutions of the society of antiquity, when they had become the numerically predominant element of the people. The different phases of these revolutions will now be described.

PRIEST-KINGS

At first there existed confusion between priesthood and civil power. The king of the city was at the same time priest, magistrate, and military chief. But kingship was never hereditary in Rome. Kings did not need military force to command obedience: they had neither armies, nor finances, nor police. The confusion of religious and political authority did not end with royalty; the magistrate of the Republic was also a priest; he was designated by rite, that is, by the drawing of lots in Athens. Thus the people had the impression of receiving their magistrates from the gods who had caused them to be so designated. They did not seek the most courageous one, nor the one with the greatest military aptitude or best suited to be chief of state, to invest with power: rather, the man best loved of the gods. All of domestic and political life was dominated by almost unimaginable superstition: a sneeze could cause an undertaking to be stopped; the Senate might meet to make the gravest decisions concerning the security of the city, yet disperse at once when a sign of evil omen appeared. Acts performed with imperfect rites were worthless. As Fustel de Coulanges points out, only at the time of Cicero did people begin not to live their religion, but use it as a political expedient. It was useful to the government, but by then religion was already dead in the people's souls.[1]

THE CITY-STATE

The Aryans, as long as they were relatively isolated in their northern cradle, never had the ability to conceive of a political, judicial, and social state organization extending beyond the limits of the city. The notion of state as a "territory" comprising several cities or that of empire without question came to them from the southern world, and in particular from the example of Egypt.

Two facts we can easily understand: first, that this religion, peculiar to each city, must have established the city in a very strong and almost unchangeable manner; it is, indeed, marvelous how long this social organization lasted, in spite of all its faults and all its chances of ruin; second, that the effect of this religion, during long ages, must have been to render it impossible to establish any other social form than the city.

Every city, even by the requirements of its religion, was independent. It was necessary that each should have its particular code, since each had its own religion, and the law flowed from the religion. Each was required to have its sovereign tribunal, and there could be no judicial tribunal superior to that of the city. Each had its religious festivals and its calendar; the months and the year could not be the same in two cities, as the series of religious acts was different. Each had its own money, which at first was marked with its religious emblem. Each had its weights and measures. It was not admitted that there could be anything common between two cities. The line of demarcation was so profound that one hardly imagined marriage possible between the inhabitants of two different cities. Such a union always appeared strange, and was long considered illegal. The legislation of Rome and that of Athens were visibly averse to admitting it. Nearly everywhere children born of such a marriage were confounded with bastards, and deprived of the rights of citizens . . .

In ancient times there was something more impassable than mountains between two neighboring cities, there were the series of sacred bounds, the difference of worship, and the hatred of the gods towards the foreigner.

For this reason the ancients were never able to establish, or even to conceive of, any other social organization than the city. Neither the Greeks, nor the Latins, nor even the Romans, for a very long time, ever had a thought that several cities might be united, and live on an equal footing under the same government. There might, indeed, be an alliance, or a temporary association, in view of some advantage to be gained, or some danger to be repelled; but there was never a complete union; for religion made of every city a body which could never be joined to another. Isolation was the law of the city.[2]

Under these conditions the annexation of a city or a neighboring territory was unthinkable: one could not govern a conquered city because one was a foreigner in the eyes of its gods. One might massacre the population or deport it in its entirety to be sold. One pillaged towns but always returned home. There could be no question of settling conquered populations on one's own territory and giving them residency, as Merneptah, a Pharaoh of the Nineteenth Dynasty and other Pharaohs of Egypt had done with Aryan peoples each time they conquered them.

Colonization rather had a religious character. The

younger branches without inheritance lighted a torch in the city hearth so as to found another on virgin soil. Thus were founded by Athenian families the dozen towns of Ionia in which for a long time they preserved the priesthood and political power from father to son. Athens was the mother city to these twelve towns which were its "colonies." As can be seen, the bond was purely religious and Athens did not claim in any way to exercise the least political control over the life of these cities. Nevertheless, because of economic necessities, confederations were finally formed to group cities together in a very loose bond. Such were, in particular, the commercial federations of Delos, Thermopylae, Calauria, and Delphi. However, according to Fustel de Coulanges, these associations were for a long time of purely religious significance and it was only under Philip of Macedon that the Amphictyons, as they were called, began to be concerned with political affairs.

INDIVIDUALISM

The individual was totally subordinate to the city. The dictatorship of the city was absolute on people's consciences. Once its power became established, the city-state became responsible for the rearing of the children in the place of the father of the family. It even regulated clothing, the wearing of beards by men, the adornment of women, and went so far as to dictate the sentiments that one should show.

Sparta had just suffered a defeat at Leuctra, and many of its citizens had perished. On the receipt of this news, the relatives of the dead had to show themselves in public with gay countenances. The mother who learned that her son had escaped, and that she should see him again, appeared afflicted and wept. Another, who knew that she should never again see her son, appeared joyous, and went around to the temple to thank the gods. What, then, was the power of the state that could thus order the reversal of the natural sentiments, and be obeyed?[3]

We perceive here one of the causes of Western individualism as opposed to African collectivism. It has often been spoken about without minutely examining how it originated. So, let us inspect the facts available to our analysis. The families of different citizens constituting the city were separate cells, so independent that it was sacrilege for the houses to touch one another, these feelings of independence going back to life on the steppes. But each individual, each family head, each citizen was directly riveted to the dictatorial state by a bond of bronze. The day when this gave way, we would progressively see individuals attempting once again to become absolutely separate, for they had not learned to develop a communal civil life. In contrast, in Africa, the power of the state, although centralized from Egypt to the rest of Black Africa, never subjugated the consciences of citizens in so strong a way. The Pharaoh, considered by Moret to be the most powerful moral figure that ever existed, never dreamed of controlling the sentiments or the dress of his people; the individual always felt dependent upon the state and socially speaking upon his peers within community life. In Africa, there always existed a reciprocal invasion of consciences and individual liberties. In other words, each one felt that he had material and moral rights upon the personalities of others and that they reciprocally had rights on him. This held throughout all political regimes. Even today, on a superficial level the African may display a spirit of independence toward the community; but he is hardly likely to grasp the gap which separates the Western individual from the group.

ARISTOCRATIC REVOLUTION

Turning back to the political regimes of the city-states and following their development, one finds that their legitimacy was questioned as early as the seventh century B.C. The coincidence of the priesthood with political power created a grave problem. The aristocracy formed by the Eupatridae found it to its advantage to disassociate the two factors, leaving in the hands of the king the symbolic ritual and the priesthood, while retaining for itself the political power. A revolution therefore had to break out, a first revolution of only a political but no social character.

The kings wished to be powerful, and the *patres* preferred that they should not be. A struggle then commenced in all the cities, between the aristocracy and the kings. Everywhere the issue of the struggle was the same. Royalty was vanquished. But we must not forget that this primitive royalty was sacred. The king was the man who pronounced the prayers, who offered the sacrifice, who had, in fine, by hereditary right, the power to call down upon the city the protection of the gods. Men could not think, therefore, of doing away with the king; one was necessary to their religion; one was necessary to the safety of the city. . . .

Plutarch [writes]: "As the kings displayed pride and rigor in their commands, the greater part of the Greeks took away their power, and left them only the care of religion."[4]

What was then seen was a curious phenomenon: the kings, kept in place by religion, trampled it as much as they could, for it was the very thing that gave strength to the Eupatridae, the aristocracy. The latter derived all their power from the ancestral religious tradition. The kings then called upon the secular plebeian majority, who were not part of the population, which included only the citizens and the clients. This was what was done by the first seven kings of Rome. Servius, through a series of laws, improved the lot of the plebs, giving them conquered lands which they might own in fact, if not by ritual.

The victory of the Eupatridae was consecrated by the reform of Lycurgus:

Lycurgus had for a moment the power to supress royalty: he took good care not to do this, judging that royalty was necessary, and the royal family inviolable. But he arranged so that the kings were henceforth subordinate to the senate in whatever concerned the government, and that they were no longer anything more than presidents of this assembly, and the executors of its decrees. A century later, royalty was still farther weakened; the executive power was taken away and was entrusted to annual magistrates, who were called *ephors*.[5]

For four centuries, from Codrus to Solon, the Eupatridae governed the city without there having been any striking political events: their authority appeared legitimate throughout this entire period when they were the only ones to know and to transmit the sacred unwritten formulas from father to son. The life of the city, properly speaking, declined because urban activity was incompatible with the patriarchal style of life of the Eupatridae who, after their victory over royalty, all went back to living on their country estates, surrounded by servants: this was a kind of feudal system, in view of the weakening of royal power. There were assemblies in the city only periodically for religious services. Society was steeped in the aristocratic spirit, as evidenced by the importance attached to noble birth. The praise heaped upon members of a noble family within the framework of epic poetry was quite identical to that expressed by African griots.

SOCIAL REVOLUTION

The aristocratic revolution modified the external form of government but not the social structure: the political revolution had forestalled a social and domestic one. However, the latter was not slow in coming: the *gens* came apart as the right of primogeniture disappeared in the wake of the revolt of the younger branches in the cities. The clients peaceably broke away in the course of a long domestic struggle.

At Heraclea, Cnidus, Istros, and Marseilles the younger branches took up arms to destroy at the same time the right of primogeniture and the paternal authority.[6]

True, we do not find in the history of any city mention made of a general insurrection among this class. If there were armed struggles, they were shut up and concealed within the circle of each family. For more than one generation there were on one side energetic efforts for independence, and implacable repression on the other. There took place in each house a long and dramatic series of events which it is impossible to-day to retrace. All that we can say is, that the efforts of the lower classes were not without results. An invincible necessity obliged the masters, little by little, to relinquish some of their omnipotence.[7]

The client, who in some respects could be compared to the slave of the mother's household in Africa, finally disappeared in Athens. This was the result of the legislative work of Solon, who first took a trip to Egypt to draw inspiration from the laws of that country. Before him a client might be sold to pay off a debt and could not own land because of the "sacred boundaries" which institutionalized the ritual ownership by the patron of the soil he cultivated. Solon, according to the time-honored expression, "overturned the sacred boundaries," thus allowing poor peasants to become landowners. He forbade the bonding of oneself to pay off a debt.

The creation of the tribunal, for the defense of the plebs, promoted its unity with the clientele, which then felt secure and freer to fight for its rights. Clientship became voluntary and contractual, as with the "class" of *navetanes* of Black Africa.

Henceforth, there were only two classes: on the one hand, the owners who formed the ruling aristocracy, on the other, the landless of all sorts, comprising both the plebs and the former clientele. All the political and social contradictions being laid bare, a veritable class struggle, harsh and long, was to take place.

Under the aristocracy, plebs and people had regretted the time of the kings, which they considered retrospectively as a Golden Age. At its outbreak, the struggle consisted in strengthening the royalty against the aristocracy, then, from the sixth century on, the people began to take leaders belonging to the master class (lords), but without the sacrosanct character of royalty, who were called tyrants. As Fustel de Coulanges noted, this was an event of supreme importance to the extent that it consecrated, for the first time in ancient history, the obedience of man to man and not that of man to a divinity through an individual.

When the kings had been everywhere overthrown, and the aristocracy had become supreme, the people did not content themselves with regretting the monarchy; they aspired to restore it under a new form. In Greece, during the sixth century, they succeeded generally in procuring leaders; not wishing to call them kings, because this title implied the idea of religious functions, and could only be borne by the sacerdotal families, they called them tyrants.[8]

The invention of money by the Lydians in the sixth century, the progress of commerce, and the new conditions of war allowed the plebs to grow rich and acquire importance. Money was not sacred, anyone might own it, including plebeians, religious tradition not yet having had time to put its stamp upon it. Commerce was no longer forbidden to anyone either: it grew fantastically as Athens looked out toward the sea. Henceforth the plebs entered the army and contributed men to the infantry and the navy; naval operations became progressively more frequent, significant, and decisive than the former land battles which were marked by the chivalry of the patricians, whose members alone were rich enough to afford the necessary armor. The state did not furnish it as it does today. The aristocracy by definition was idle: the manual workers, the artisans were not as in Black Africa free men, belonging to castes, but slaves. As the plebs grew richer and entered into the towns—from which until then they had been excluded—they acquired a faith of their own by adopting foreign beliefs (Egyptian and Asiatic divinities), while gradually the aristocracy became pauperized. The plebs had its own bourgeoisie, its intellectuals, its politicians, its tyrants now emerged from its own ranks and no longer from that of the Eupatridae: they became real tyrants of the people. The real concern of the plebs, as we can see, was not so much to build a regime radically different from that of the aristocracy which had oppressed them, but to become as much as possible like this class by setting up all the institutions and customs they had lacked to be comparable to it.

There then took place a new phenomenon which resembles modern times: a veritable money class having been created, the plebs turned into a financial bourgeoisie and the Eupatridae, like the nobles of the industrial age, married money in the person of a plebeian heiress. Hence a witticism of the times: "What is this man's lineage?"—"He married money!"

When once the lower classes had gained these points; when they had among themselves rich men, soldiers, and priests; when they had gained all that gave man a sense of his own worth and strength; when, in fine, they had compelled the aristocracy to consider them of some account, it was impossible to keep them out of social and political life, and the city could be closed to them no longer.

The entry of this inferior class into the city was a revolution, which from the seventh to the fifth century filled the history of Greece and Italy.

The efforts of the people were everywhere successful, but not everywhere in the same manner, or by the same means. In some cases the people, as soon as they felt themselves to be strong, rose, sword in hand, and forced the gates of the city where they had been forbidden to live. Once masters, they either drove out the nobles and occupied their houses, or contented themselves with proclaiming an equality of rights. This is what happened at Syracuse, at Erythrae, and at Miletus.[9]

Solon's reform coincided with the triumph of the people: it was of a political and social nature. That of Cleisthenes was of a religious nature: its purpose was to give a faith to all those who had none, merely by geographically splitting up the urban population. As against these two legislations, Draco's, which preceded Solon's by thirty years, was drawn up at a time when the Eupatridae had not yet been conquered. It was thus only a more or less precise codification of the interests of that class.

But the poor class was not slow in reacting and naming Pisistratus as dictator. Henceforth the public interest would replace the oldtime religion, universal suffrage would become the form of government, and Athenian democracy would undergo its effects: the unemployed sold their votes in broad daylight and a series of laws was established often confiscating the wealth of the rich. It was a kind of prefiguration of the time of the sharers. Democracy was to suffer from these political blunders to the benefit of the tyrants of the people.

MOVEMENTS OF IDEAS

At that same time, philosophical ideas began to have an effect in the political arena.

> Then philosophy appeared, and overthrew all the rules of the ancient polity. It was impossible to touch the opinions of men without also touching the fundamental principles of their government. Pythagoras, having a vague conception of the Supreme Being, disdained the local worships; and this was sufficient to cause him to reject the old modes of government, and to attempt to found a new order of society.[10]

The ideas of Anaxagoras, of the Sophists who followed, those of Socrates, Plato, and Zeno contributed powerfully to broadening governmental conceptions, and to adapting them to current conditions, rather than allowing them to follow a series of ossified ancestral formulas, no longer meeting any need. Socrates contributed to freeing morals from religions, placing justice above law, and making conscience the guide of man. In this, without meaning to, he opposed the tradition of the city, resulting in the supreme penalty to him.

Anaxagoras had the idea of a God whose principle is pure intelligence; it is He who governs our consciences. He therefore rejected the religious formalism of his time by avoiding assemblies as much as possible and refusing political duties.

The Sophists had great merit not in developing a precise and explicit political philosophy, but in disturbing tradition by questioning it and discussing it publicly. Taste for the dialectic little by little came into existence and people acquired the habit of discussing everything instead of passively accepting ready-made formulas. But until Plato even the boldest of Greek thinkers were not able to go beyond the concept of the city-state; at most they tried to give this framework a new internal structure: Plato's Republic is a City.

It seems that it was Zeno, with the Stoic school, who, having conceived the idea of a universal God, first spread the concept of a government which would bring all men together.

We see from this how far ideas had advanced since the age of Socrates, who thought himself bound to adore, as far as he was able, the gods of the state. Even Plato did not plan any other government than that of a city. Zeno passed beyond these narrow limits of human associations. He disdained the divisions which the religions of ancient ages had established. As he believed in a God of the universe, so he had also the idea of a State into which the whole human race should enter. . . .

Higher ideas prompted men to form more extensive societies. They were attracted towards unity . . .[11]

THE INFLUENCE OF EGYPT

Without any doubt, these universalist ideas derived from the southern world and in particular from Egypt. A thousand years before the Greek thinkers, Socrates, Plato, Zeno, etc., the Egyptians, with the reform of Amenophis IV, had clearly conceived the idea of a universal God responsible for creation, whom all men, without distinction, could adore: He was not the God of any particular tribe, nor of any city, or even any nation, but indeed the God of all humankind. These conceptions which Christianity later adopted were not originally a part of it, it seems. It first appeared as a Jewish sect, dependent on Judaism. It was only after Saint Paul had been ill received by the "Jews" that he turned toward the pagans to convert them. Christianity then became the religion of everyone, instead of being that of a given tribe chosen by God. If it was able to triumph over the other Eastern faiths which coexisted with it in Rome, it was not by its moral superiority, but probably because its first adepts, having been distrusted and sometimes accused of political dissidence (Saint Paul overtly opposed the cult of the Emperor and predicted the end of temporal rule), were treated as martyrs: they were thrown to the wild beasts or beheaded. It was the moral benefit of this repression which Christianity alone suffered that contributed to assuring its triumph over the other faiths which were liturgically better established and morally even more elevated. One cannot too strongly emphasize all that primitive Christianity borrowed from the cult of Isis in Rome, even in the structure of its processions. "Egypt is the country from which contemplative devotion penetrated into Europe."[12]

Concerning the religion of Isis and Osiris the same author wrote: "No religion had yet brought to men so formal a promise of immortality: this above all gave to the Alexandrian mysteries [of Isis] their power of attraction."[13]

We know that Christianity shortly made these conceptions of resurrection and immortality its own.

These foreign religions which made no distinctions among individuals often allowed the disinherited of the plebs to worship. Here again the broadening of religious consciousness manifestly came from the outside. The love of one's neighbor was a moral commonplace in the southern world:

this notion could represent an advance in morals only in the individualistic northern Mediterranean.

The Oriental worships, which began in the sixth century to overrun Greece and Italy, were eagerly received by the plebs; these were forms of worship which, like Buddhism,[14] excluded no caste, or people.[15]

THE ROMAN EMPIRE

Such then were the political and religious ideas which were to permit Rome, allowing for economic conditions, to destroy the municipal regime and establish the empire. At the time of the Peloponnesian War, it had been seen that in all the cities the poor were partisans of Athens and the rich of Sparta. Depending on which faction was victorious in a given city, it became a vassal of Sparta or Athens. Ancient society thus was already divided into two clearly distinct classes, the haves and the have-nots. Their struggle had pushed urban nationalism into the background. It was this situation which in large part allowed the Roman city, so well equipped and enriched by commerce, to conquer the Mediterranean basin.

According to Fustel de Coulanges, Rome was considered a city where a Senate composed of rich patricians governed to the exclusion of the wretched subjugated populace. This idea exerted a very strong influence on the ruling aristocracies of other Mediterranean cities troubled by the class struggle. Therefore at the time of the Roman conquest many of them offered only a semblance of resistance; many declared themselves open cities and their Senates purely and simply turned their cities over to Rome. Such was the course of events that led to the establishment of the Roman Empire.

Municipal patriotism thus became weakened and died out in men's minds. Every man's opinion was more precious to him than his country, and the triumph of his faction became much dearer to him than the grandeur or glory of his city.[16] At Ardea, the aristocracy and the plebs being at enmity, the plebs called the Volscians to their aid, and the aristocracy delivered the city to the Romans.[17]

NOTES

1. Fustel de Coulanges, *La Cité antique* (Paris: Hachette, 1930), p. 257.
2. Fustel de Coulanges, Numa Denis, *The Ancient City* (trans. Willard Small, 1873), (New York: Doubleday Anchor reprint ed., n.d.), pp. 201–203. (This and all succeeding quotations from this work are from this edition.)
3. *Id.*, p. 221.   4. *Id.*, p. 235–236.   5. *Id.*, p. 237.   6. *Id.*, p. 253.
7. *Id.*, p. 259.   8. *Id.*, pp. 270–271.   9. *Id.*, pp. 275–276.   10. *Id.*,p. 355.
11. *Id.*, pp. 358–360.
12. Grenier, *Les Religions étrusque et romaine* (Paris: Ed. P.U.F., Coll. Mana, 1948), tome 3, p. 208.
13. *Id.*, p. 209.
14. Buddhism, by its non-exclusivist character, could not be an Indo-European religious creation.
15. Fustel de Coulanges, *op. cit.*, p. 275.
16. *Id.*, p. 368.   17. *Id.*, p. 370 (citing Livy, VIII, 11.).

Chapter Three

FORMATION OF THE MODERN EUROPEAN STATES

The end of antiquity coincided with the triumph of Christianity. The latter in its hierarchical organization bore the imprint of the temporal organization of the Roman empire: bishoprics, dioceses, etc., which corresponded to the Roman administrative divisions. The bishop of the capital, Rome, was also to have special importance and become Pope. The memory of the Roman empire, perpetuated by the church, is what constantly impelled the barbarian kings to try to rebuild a universal Christian empire. During the High Middle Ages there was true intellectual regression; the West was no longer able to carry forward the achievements of antiquity. This was especially striking in the domain of sculpture and architecture. The culture and knowledge achieved in antiquity vegetated in the monasteries, to emerge from them beginning in the thirteenth century. During this period, the Church played a positive role in social and intellectual development and in the tempering of behavior.

After the failure of the universal empire, national states grew up with the Great Discoveries, the diffusion of ideas, the existence of an insatiable international market for goods, as a consequence of the Portuguese, Spanish, Dutch, and Norman geographical expeditions.

The West was technically less advanced than the East. It was able to overcome its inferiority only with the help of the Arabs who, beginning in the seventh century, wherever they moved spread the achievements of antiquity which had vegetated in Byzantium. Through their philosophers Avicenna and Averroes, Aristotle became known and discussed in the West. They introduced advanced metallurgy (the steelworks of Toledo, Spain). They also introduced the navigator's compass, gunpowder, the use of naval maps, and perhaps the axial helm which made possible the exact determination of a ship's position. Coasting was no longer necessary and long-distance sailing with high-side ships came in. In chemistry and mathematics they also introduced much knowledge derived from the East.

The fact that Spain was the first European country to acquire technical supremacy at the dawn of modern times and for a certain period dominate the world can be explained only by the Arab contribution during the time of its colonization. These two facts are not generally connected as closely as they should be.

In brief, the Catholic Church on one hand, Islam on the other, were the great preservers of the knowledge of antiquity and contributed greatly, over different geographical routes, during the Middle Ages to the transmission of this knowledge to the new modern nations about to emerge.

From the social point of view, the Middle Ages would see the rise of a bourgeois class alongside the wretched serfs. The situations of the serf, the plebeian, and the slave of the father's household were to a certain extent comparable except as concerns their numbers and concentrations. Those of the bourgeois and the African man of caste were not in any way comparable: the former was a once-exploited freedman with a conscience full of revolutionary germs driving toward transformation, whereas the latter was in essence conservative.

THE POLITICAL AND SOCIAL MIDDLE AGES

The Western Empire had been dismembered in the sixth century. There followed a period of chaos and barbarism; in

511, Clovis created the Frankish kingdom with the support of the church. His descendants became the Do-Nothing Kings, the last of whom was eliminated by the Mayor of his Palace: Pépin the Short was crowned and consecrated by the Pope. This was the origin of the sacrosanct royalty of the West, which was to last until the Revolution. Charlemagne was crowned in the year 800. He created the Holy Roman Empire, provided it with a strong centralized administrative organization, and began a movement of rebirth in the arts, literature, and science. His tutor Alcuin played a key role in the unearthing and diffusing of the knowledge of antiquity, especially through his commentary on the works of Aristotle. The transmission to modern man of the Trivium (dialects, rhetoric, grammar) and the Quadrivium (arithmetic, geometry, astronomy, music) was thus assured.

The three grandsons of Charlemagne divided the empire among themselves after his death, since succession to the throne was not yet regulated by any precise tradition. Each kingdom would then start to grow weaker and weaker and finally break apart. In the tenth century, invasions by new barbarians (Normans, Hungarians, etc.) threw Europe into a time of anarchy and political weakness. Most of the kings had only a title without power, and could no longer assure the security of their subjects. This situation forced the subjects to mass around local chiefs strong enough to protect them. The feudal regime was to be born: The lord who would set himself up on a territory, having constructed on it a fortress of either wood or stone capable of protecting the neighboring peasants in case of invasion, would become their real chief, and relationships of dependency would become established, the details of which we will examine.

André Ribard in his book, the only work of Marxist synthesis published in France in the domain of history [as of 1960], gives a rigorous analysis of the formation of this feudal system:

Authority in Europe had not ceased to crumble—kings remained but no states. Too far removed from the immediate peril to be effective against invaders, monarchal power no longer constituted a true central government. The notion of the state was eclipsed by that of security. Populations concentrated at spots favorable for resistance. Escaping from pillage alone was the castle where people and flocks could take refuge while its armed men scoured the countryside in the name of the lord. When the village could no longer be defended, it was abandoned. So this society had to be reorganized around the fortified castle. The effectiveness of the castle dictated a new hierarchy in which the king was merely the nominal suzerain, the essential part being the military caste of lords who decentralized power to their own advantage.

Each man put his trust in one more powerful than he; these bonds of vassalage wove a system of protection and servitude in which the lord was quickly tempted to abuse his authority—danger would often come from the protector himself. A slow historic gestation thus led to a coherent system: feudalism. Its greatest flowering was in France, thick with wooden castle-keeps, battle command posts for military units split up by regions, to fend off the Scandinavian pirates whose penetration was so deep that they supplied the naval terminology of the French language. This organization was just as good as the lord over it: it really assured some security only if he was courageous and well equipped with men and horses. When during two or three generations the same family had devoted itself to this permanent guerrilla warfare, the feudal lord became the suzerain of a number of territories in which, bound together by innumerable traditions of Christian, Germanic, Celtic, or Roman origin, these vassals paid their tributes to him—military service in the case of his companions, agricultural labor in the case of the peasants. These privileged ones had only to fight. They succeeded so well in enriching themselves that the monarchy, whose wealth lay only in landed estates, rapidly saw these dwindle. Forced to transfer ever more estates over to these feudal lords, royalty became pauperized: when it ran out of estates to give, it would no longer be able to command—the feudal system would have devoured its authority. What was left to the monarchy was only the theory of its existence, the fact that it was consecrated and that its rank was still called the first. As for the people, they worked: they fed those who were supposed to protect them and whose exactions had now taken a legal turn; the peasants themselves, their families, and their beasts, had to foot the bill. Man was free, but subject to so many kinds of tributes that his fate would remain atrocious, for it had become hereditary. . . .

The constant dangers threatening this society, its poorly upkept roads, the concentration of population, the isolation of markets guaranteed the stability of the new system: its Law would entrench itself, as would its terms, its customs, and its morals.[1]

The feudal lords invented a series of imposts which became more and more oppressive, as much for free peasants (freeholders) as for serfs who were bound to the land. The latter could be sold with the land, and could transmit nothing by heredity to their descendants, except their condition. When several lords held rights to the same land, they divided among themselves the children of the serfs who cultivated it. Marriage was dependent on the will of the lord whose permission had to obtained.[2] All the apparatus needed for domestic life (mill, oven, etc.) was located at the castle. All the subjects of the lord's domain were required to go and make use of them and pay for the privilege. The technique of the feudal system of exploitation, by its exceptionally inhuman character, explains both the *jacqueries* which marked the Middle Ages and the drive with which the inhabitants of the burgs, better concentrated, were to organize in order to wrest political and economic liberty from the lords. Commerce which was in full bloom (markets, fairs) allowed the artisans and merchants of the cities, despite the condition of the roads, to gain enormous riches.

When the lords fell into debt following the Crusades, they would be more and more obliged to sell some of the political and economic liberties to their subjects: Communes would buy their political autonomy and form commercial confederations, such as the Hanseatic League which grouped nearly eighty German towns with Hamburg as their center. Thus was born the commercial and industrial bourgeoisie which by developing, organizing, and gaining education, would become the preponderant political and economic element of the European society that in short order it would control. Born in shackles and out of struggle, this bourgeoisie had to become essentially revolutionary and lay-minded.

THE INTELLECTUAL MIDDLE AGES

The period of the Middle Ages has been considered in European history as a relatively barbarous epoch of transition during which the achievements of antiquity were absolutely lost. Most certainly, knowledge regressed enormously, but the guiding thread was never totally cut and, as early as the time of Charlemagne, the knowledge which had vegetated in the monasteries began to come out. This intellectual movement, which spread from Ireland and England over the entire continent, is undeniable evidence of intellectual continuity. As the Turks occupied Constantinople, destroying the Eastern Empire, and Greek scholars fled to the West, this intellectual movement gained momentum. The Greek writers who had already been given an introduction by the Arabs were now more widely available. We have seen that thanks to Avicenna and Averroes Aristotle's *Logic* was known and discussed. The intellectual influence of Aristotle, the only Greek philosopher to be studied, was considerable on the thinkers of the Middle Ages. His authority was almost sacrosanct: thanks to him, they little by little familiarized themselves with the rational, scientific manner of thinking. His physics helped the more enlightened minds to grasp the idea of positive science divorced from religion.

Paul Vignaux has pointed out Alcuin's keen awareness of the ties that united his own time to scholarly antiquity.

His praise of the sovereign [Charlemagne] in another letter defines Alcuin's ideal for us: to build in France a new Athens, superior to the earlier one, because taught by Christ. Led by Plato, the earlier one shone with the seven liberal arts. . . . These liberal arts were the culture to be transmitted. Eighty years after the death of Alcuin, one chronicler judged his work a success; the moderns, whether Gauls or Franks, seemed to him the equals of the ancients of Rome and Athens. Chrétien de Troyes was likewise to express the continuity of civilization. . . . At the end of the twelfth century, Paris would seem the new Athens.[3]

In the thirteenth century, following Alhazen, the philosophical school of Oxford with Grosseteste and Roger Bacon clearly conceived the idea of positive physico-mathematical science.

The disciple [Bacon, the disciple of Grosseteste] realized that his master had not followed the path laid out by Aristotle, that having known mathematics and optics, he might have known everything. The mathematicism of Roger Bacon is the sense of *potestas mathematicae*—the ability of this type of knowledge to discipline the mind and explain nature.[4]

In *Le Nombre d'Or* (The Golden Number), Matila Ghyka demonstrated how vast was the influence of antiquity on the esthetic and architectural conceptions of the Renaissance.[5]

In these last two chapters we have rapidly reviewed the politico-social evolution of the European states from antiquity to the formation of the modern nations. The time has come to undertake a detailed comparative study of African politico-social organizations.

NOTES

1. André Ribard, *La prodigieuse histoire de l'humanité* (Paris: Ed. du Myrte, Collection "Pour comprendre l'histoire," 1947), pp. 228–229.

2. So, following Fustel de Coulanges, we must see serfdom and slavery as one.

3. Paul Vignaux, *La Pensée au Moyen Age* (Paris: Lib. A. Colin, Collection Armand Colin, 1938), p. 12.

4. *Idem.*, p. 91.

5. Matila Ghyka, *Le Nombre d'Or: Rites et rythmes pythagoriciens dans le développement de la civilisation européenne* (Paris: Gallimard, new ed., 1976).

Chapter Four

POLITICAL ORGANIZATION IN BLACK AFRICA

The political organization the principles of which we are about to consider is the one which, give or take a few variants, seemingly governed the African states from the first to the nineteenth century. This is what we may assume from the testimony of Al Bakri and Ibn Khaldun concerning the Empire of Ghana (tenth and eleventh centuries) and, more recently, of Battuta on the Empire of Mali (1352–53).

Ghana, Mali, and Songhai were very shortly to become Islamized, beginning in the tenth century, under the influence of the Almoravide movement. In order to come closer to historical truth it seems necessary to take as frame of reference, as example for study, the constitution of an African state contemporary with these, with a parallel history, but which, because of its southern location (Burkina-Faso of today), was not overrun by Islam. It will thus be possible to bring out the modifications of political structure due to external influences.

CONSTITUTION

Mossi is a constitutional monarchy. The emperor, the Moro Naba, comes by heredity from the family of the previous Moro Naba (eleventh century probably), but his nomination is not automatic. He is chosen by an "electoral" college of four dignitaries, presided over by the Prime Minister, the togo naba, as in Ethiopia.[1] He is actually invested with power by the latter who, however, is not a Nakomsé (nobleman), but comes from an ordinary family, and who is, in reality, the representative of the people, of all free men, all the citizens who constitute the Mossi nation.

The emperor is assisted, in addition to the Prime Minister, by three others: the rassam naba, the balum naba, and the kidiranga naba. Each of them governs one region in addition to his more or less specialized functions. The togo naba is in charge of four royal districts: Tziga, Sissamba, Somniaga, and Bissigaï. The togo nabas basically come in turn from three families of commoners residing respectively at Toïsi, Kierga, and Nodé.

After the Prime Minister in order of importance comes the rassam naba or bingo naba, chief of the slaves of the Crown. He is also the Minister of Finances, guardian of the treasury of precious objects, cowries (coin), bracelets, etc. He is the High Executioner, when occasion arises putting to death condemned criminals. He is chief of the blacksmiths and governs them through interposition of the saba naba. He governs the canton of Kindighi. Therefore, although himself a slave, the rassam naba rules over free men, and holds power over full-fledged citizens. We will find the same practice among the Wolofs of Cayor Baol and the Serers of Sine Salum in Senegal.

The balum naba is third in rank: he is Mayor of the Palace, in charge of introducing ambassadors and distinguished visitors. He administers the Zitinga, the Bussu, and the Gursi.

The kidiranga naba, head of the cavalry, comes from one of three ordinary Mossi families.

The rassam naba always comes from the same slave family.

Thus, the ministers who assist the emperor, rather than being members of the high nobility of the Nakomsé, are systematically chosen from outside of it, from among the common people and the slaves. They represent at court, as we shall more clearly see, the different social categories, professions, and castes. "Those without birth," slaves and laborers, organized into professions (castes), far from being kept separated from power in this period which extends far beyond the Occidental Middle Ages (since, very likely, it may go back to the first century and the foundation of Ghana), are associated with it, not in any symbolic but in an organic way. Each profession has its representatives within the government; they will, as needed, present its complaints. That is the spirit of this constitution. In order to comprehend its originality, we would have to imagine, at midpoint of the Middle Ages (1352–53, the time of Ibn Battuta's voyage to the Sudan and of the Hundred Years War), not just some provincial lord, but the King of France or of England, giving a share of his power, with a voice in decisions, to the rural serfs, bound to the soil, the free peasants, the town guildsmen, and the merchants. And beyond all that, imagine the existence of a tradition according to which the king, within the framework of an already-constitutional monarchy, cannot reign, cannot have moral and political authority in the eyes of the people, unless he is invested by a bourgeois who is also chosen from among one or a few traditionally determined families. Neither the bourgeoisie nor the peasantry of the West would then have had the revolutionary virulence that once imbued them, and the course of Western European history would probably have been different.

The non-absolute nature of the monarchy is revealed by the fact that, once invested, the ministers cannot be removed by the king.

Below the ministers come servants of all categories, bureaucrats and military chiefs. The samandé naba is the infantry general: he is not allowed to ride a horse, but at most only an ass, for, since he is a slave, the horse is too noble a steed for him; however, in some cases, he may replace the togo naba, the Prime Minister. The kom naba is leader of the slave soldiers; he cannot command free soldiers. The tom naba is in charge of the "Sand of Investiture." We will return to this ceremony in dealing with the coronation of the King. In its general lines, this is the structure of the council the emperor depends on in order to govern. All details concerning it are to be found in Tauxier.[2] Before analyzing any more deeply the political organization of the African states, we must briefly consider the principles of the Constitution of Cayor. Despite the historical or rather geographic distance separating them, they appear to be a replica of those of the Mossi.

THE CONSTITUTION OF CAYOR

At the height of the power of Ghana, that is, probably from the third to the tenth century, tropical Africa as far as the Atlantic Ocean was ruled by it. Cayor was in all likelihood a former province of Ghana which, in the sixteenth century at the time when the author of the *Tarikh es Sudan* was writing, had already become emancipated into an autonomous kingdom, independent of that of the Djoloff, with a Damel at its head.[3]

The government council which invested the king was constituted as follows:

Lamane Diamatil Botal ub Ndiob Badié Gateigne	representatives of free men, men of castes or without castes, *gor, gér,* or *ñeño*
Eliman of MBalle Sérigne of the village of Kab	representatives of the Muslim clergy
Diawerigne MBul Gallo Diaraf Bunt Ker	representatives of the Tieddos and prisoners of the Crown.

The council was convened and presided over by the Diawerigne MBul Diambur, hereditary representative of free men.

The Tieddos comprised all the individuals attached to the king, whether as soldiers or courtiers. That at least is the meaning of the term retained at the end of the independence of Cayor, engineered by Faidherbe under Napoleon III. This constitution was therefore in effect until 1870. This fact shows that African political constitutions had not appreciably changed with time. Only in the cases where the royal branch became Islamized do we see certain transformations. That was the case of Ghana, Mali, and Songhai.

The seven Cayorian dynasties, to which we will return in discussing succession to the throne, never embraced Islam. It seems that one of the last Damels of Cayor, Latdjor Diop, the very one who had offered such determined resistance to Faidherbe, the symbol of national struggle in Senegal, converted to Islam for diplomatic reasons, in order to find new allies in Salum, such as the Tuculor marabout Ma Ba Diakhu, and in Trarza. It was also customary to oppose the Tieddos to the Domi Sokhna. The latter were the constituent element of the Muslim clergy. They were separate from the traditional priests, and the two groups shared a reciprocal hatred and fought each other without mercy, for there was no possible common ground between them. The Domi Sokhna had the characteristic of being most often members of the nobility; they came from the same social class as the aristocrats, but because of their conversion to Islam were despised and disowned by their blood brothers. It often happened that the latter, because of the matriarchy then in effect, would kidnap their daughters in order to give them in marriage to Tieddos, thus, as they saw it, limiting the damage done.

The Mossi and Cayorian constitutions reflect a political organization which must have been in effect since Ghana, and therefore probably dominated the African states for nearly two thousand years.

Actually, we have fewer details concerning the constitution of Ghana. Bakri relates that the king's interpreters were often chosen from among the Muslims; likewise, the steward of the Treasury and the majority of viziers.[4] There is then every reason to believe that in 1067, at the time Bakri wrote, Islamization of Ghana, though still only very slight, had already influenced its political customs.

The political constitution of Songhai, as it is revealed to us through the text of the *Tarikh es Sudan,* which dates from the sixteenth century, shows an identical situation. The same must also have been true in Mali, and Ibn Khaldun gives the name of its first Islamized king, Bermendana.[5]

MATRILINEAL SUCCESSION: GHANA, MALI

Within the framework of the rites governing succession to the throne and appointment of the various ministers and functionaries of the empires, we can best sense the changes made in the constitutions as a result of foreign influences. In Ghana, the old African tradition was still strictly observed. Bakri is formal on the subject: succession was matrilineal. Only the emperor and his heir apparent, his sister's son, were allowed to wear cut and sewn garments. In 1067, the sovereign of Bakri's time was the Tunka Menin, who had succeeded his maternal uncle Bessi.

> Among this people, custom and rules demand that the successor to the king be his sister's son; for, they say, the sovereign can be sure that his nephew is indeed his sister's son; but nothing can assure him that the son he considers his own in actuality is.[6]

The custom of matrilineal succession can be accepted, without necessarily attaching any importance to the justification given for it, although the latter seems convincing. This explanation, very often heard in Black Africa, considerably postdates the clanic conditions of economic life which gave birth to the matriarchy.[7]

Since the succession to the throne was so strictly regulated, one must suppose that the appointment of the various ministers had not yet become, as it would five centuries later in Songhai, a purely administrative act, made practically without regard to tradition. Ghana was weakened by the Sussu (Sosso) attacks. In 1242, the king of the exterior province of Mali would seize it. He was Sundiata Keita, one of the greatest of all the empire-builders of Black Africa. Mali then would take the place of Ghana by subduing the Sossos. We know that Bermendana was the first of its kings to become Islamized. Ibn Khaldun gives some interesting details on the succession to the throne of Mali: it was still matrilineal. Mari Djata (djata is "lion" in Mandingo; djat, "to ward off the lion" in Wolof) was the first powerful monarch of Mali: It was he who put down the turbulence of the Sossos and deprived them of any type of sovereignty. His son, Mensa Weli, succeeded him, then his brother Wati, and Khalifa, another brother. After the destruction of Ghana, there seems to have been a period of turmoil and political instability, during which the traditional rules of succession were temporarily disregarded. This is confirmed by the reign of Khalifa, an unworthy and bloody prince, who spent his time shooting at passersby with bow and arrow. The people, instead of challenging the monarchy, got rid of him by murdering him and returned to the traditional matrilineal rule of succession.

> Abu-Bekr, the son of Mari-Djata's daughter, succeeded to the throne. He was chosen king according to the principle of the barbaric nations which place the sister (of the deceased monarch) or that sister's son in possession of the throne. We did not learn the paternal genealogy of this prince. At his death by a freedman of the royal family, the usurper Sakura, seized power.[8]

Ibn Battuta, in his voyage to the Sudan, gives precious information about imperial audiences in Mali. The king was assisted by several *ferraris,* each of whom maintained a small court of his own, in the manner of Mossi or Cayorian ministers. However, we have no details about the manner in which they were selected. The author, on the other hand, relates that civil inheritance, on the level of the common people, was matrilineal, and expresses surprise at having come across such a practice only among the Blacks of Africa and India. He also informs us that the child bears the name of his maternal uncle, the one whose heir he is to be. The same method of inheritance thus applied in the case of both the common people and the aristocracy.[9]

SONGHAI, THE ORIENTAL INFLUENCE

Songhai, which belongs to the last phase of the Islamization of sixteenth-century Africa, had political customs less embedded in tradition. They in every way resemble those which applied in the caliphates of Baghdad and the courts of the Arab Orient. The same endless intrigues took place around the throne. Islamic Songhai seems to have recognized only the right of primogeniture; but that was purely theoretical, for the eldest son, if not energetic, or disadvantaged ever so little by circumstances, automatically lost his right to the throne, giving way to another son of the late Askia or any other intriguing personage who succeeded in gaining the support of some influential high functionary. The right of primogeniture was so fragile in the minds and consciences of the royal electors that it seemed normal automatically to disregard the eldest heir if he happened to be away at the time of the election. This was in no way a sanction against a son guilty of the crime of not assisting his father in his dying moments, as one might suppose. Upon the death of the Askia Daud, the eldest of the sons who were at his bedside, El Hadj, took up his arms and mounted his horse as a sign of taking power. As he was more audacious and more energetic than his brothers and all the courtiers feared him, for he knew how to counter their intrigues, they all acquiesced, even adding to his claims. They proclaimed him king (Askia), adding that "El Hadj deserved power and would have been worthy to hold it even in Baghdad."[10] El Hadj, with his entourage, left for Kao Kao, or Gao, the capital of the empire. An incident which occurred on the road, as a result of the intrigues of one of his brothers, Hâmed, allows us to form our own opinion of how they regarded the question of succession. One of the brothers of the new Askia addressed him in the following manner: "We admit only the right of primogeniture. If Mohammed-Benkan [the absent firstborn] had been present this day, the power would not have fallen to you."[11] An Askia deposed by his brother did not have the right to take his sons into exile with him. They automatically went under the "paternal" authority of the victorious ruling brother and were in line to succeed him. That is the reason why the hi-koï who stripped Askia Ishâq II of the royal insignia after his defeat at Djuder pointed out to him that he did not have the right to take his sons with him. To which the Askia answered that he had been defeated by an alien who was succeeding him and not by a brother.[12]

The sons of Benkan were compelled to hide all through the reign of El Hadj, for fear of being murdered as legitimate claimants to the throne. This would continue during the reign of Askia Mohammed Brâno and they would not be seen again until the interregnum which preceded the advent of Askia Ishâq.

It very often happened that a given courtier was responsible for a prince's accession to the throne. According to the *Tarikh es Sudan* (Chapter XV), Askia Ismael was elevated to the throne by the dendi-fâri Mar-Tomzo on the very day his predecessor was deposed; and a dendi-fâri was merely the governor of a province.

Succession to the throne could cause troubles even in

filial relations. Thus, fâri-mondzo Mussa revolted against his father, Askia El-Hadj Mohammed, deposed him, and took his place. After which, he attempted to exterminate his brothers, a certain number of whom escaped to Tendirma and the protection of the kormina-fâri Otsmân-Yubâdo (Chapter XIV). Brothers of the same father, under the African system of polygamous life, were social rivals and did not hesitate to eliminate one another when a matter as important as succession to the throne was involved: Askia Mussa's struggle against his brothers was systematic and unmerciful. Nor was this any longer an isolated case; it became the usual practice in Songhai. All the Askias except Askia Mohammed were sons of "concubines,"[13] according to Kâti (Chapter VI, p. 151). Whereas the reverse was true for the kings of Bara: which would explain the respect that the Askias showed them. The latter were compelled to consider the advice of the bara-koïs. Bara-koï Mansa Kintade, whose mother was a slave, was the only one born of a "concubine."

The administrative organization and its extreme centralism will be described later on. However, we can note here and now that there were provincial governors of varying importance, such as the fâri, the balama, etc.; there were also governors of towns and of border marches such as the koï, mondzo, farba, etc. As against the custom in force in Mossi and Cayor, the Askia appears to have appointed them arbitrarily; he might name to these important positions his son or any other person of his entourage. There was no shortage of intrigues among the candidates; there was often actual bargaining with the Askia, almost a contractual agreement: "Make me the Balama; I will make you the Askia."

Ismael, at his accession, was obliged to give satisfaction to a courtier, by giving him a higher position than the one he had hoped for.

Army generals were no longer—as among the Mossi and Wolofs—chosen systematically from among slaves; they could be any kind of citizens, perhaps even nobles. After having suffered a defeat in the Kanta, Askia Mohammed Benkan wanted to reestablish his prestige by attacking Gurma; to his utter disappointment, his general Dankolko, completely absorbed in a game of chess, remained unaware of the proximity of the enemy who took the field. The king dismissed him, but the general asked for authorization first to name his own successor; the king appeared to give him satisfaction, but did not keep his promise. The spirit in which army chiefs and functionaries were appointed is thus made abundantly clear.[14]

Under the reign of Askia Daud (advent March 24, 1549), the kormina-fâri El-Hâdi revolted against the Askia. The hikoï, Bokar-Chîli-Idji, said to the king, "Appoint me to the office of Dendi-Fâri and I promise to take El-Hâdi and turn him over to you." And it was done.[15]

There was one characteristic object among the royal insignia of the Askias: the *tin-touri* ("kindling wood" in Songhai). It was supposed to be a dead ember from the first fire lit in the country by its first occupants. The members of this family transmitted this emblem from one generation to the next. Thus making them the masters of the soil.

What we have just said about the origins of the Askias shows that they were not the masters of the soil, but usurped this emblem in order themselves to embody the various attributed of sovereignty.[16]

The political customs of Songhai in every way recall those illustrated by the tragic end of the grandson of the Prophet Mohammed, Hussein, who was murdered at Kerbela (Arabia). The custom even spread of cutting off the heads of defeated pretenders to the throne and bringing them to the Askia as a pledge of devotion: this was also the fate of the descendants of the Prophet.

PRECEDENCE IN SONGHAI

Kâti gives details of the greatest importance about the hierarchy of positions in Songhai under Askia Mohammed.

The djina-koï (generalissimo, commander of the "vanguard") was the only one in the entire army entitled to sit on a rug during the audience with the king; he covered himself with flour instead of dust.

The kurmina-fari or kan-fari, whose residence was at Tindirna, was a veritable viceroy. He did not have to take off his headgear or cover his head with dust.

The dendi-fari, governor of one of the most important provinces of the empire, the one bordering on Upper Dahomey, was the only one who could speak frankly to the king without fear.

The bara-koïs alone had the right of veto. It will be recalled that all of them (with one exception) were born of noble women, in contrast to the Askias, all of whom (with one exception) were sons of slaves, of "concubines," according to the same author. The prince was obliged to heed their veto willy-nilly. One gets the impression that the bara-koïs must have been the former legitimate masters of the soil from whom the Askias usurped the *tin-touri,* that emblem of power of the earliest occupants of the land.

The dirma-koï alone could enter the enclosure of the imperial palace on horseback.

Only the cadi could employ the servants of the king. He was entitled to a mat when he came visiting.

The guissiri-donké alone could question the king during an audience.

Only a Sherif could sit next to him on his "platform." Eunuchs (an Oriental custom introduced into Africa with Islam) stood to the left of the Askia, who rose only for scholars and returning pilgrims.

The Askia ate only with Sherifs, scholars, and their children, as well as with the "San," even when these were very young. The latter, whose district in Timbuktu was San-Koré (from which the university got its name), constitute the authentic noble class. It should be remembered that meals were eaten sitting on mats around one common platter.

Kâti attributes all these institutions to Askia Mohammed exclusively, as if they had not existed before his reign and survived him only partially.

In reality, Kâti and Sâdi, being fervent believers, tend excessively to embellish the reign of Askia Mohammed and attribute to him even part of the glory of his predecessors. It is unlikely that institutions so entrenched and so detailed could be of so recent invention.

The attributes of the bara-koï show that they reflect a tradition much older than the advent of the Askias. The explanation suggested by the author concerning these attributes merely confirms this point of view.[17]

The bara-koï who accompanied the Askia on the pilgrimage presumably took advantage of their presence together at the Kaaba to bind the Askia by an oath at the tomb of the Prophet: "Promise me that henceforth you will abide by my counsel," whence the right of veto . . . "I promise you!" . . . and so forth.

The author was not able to show by what necessity the Askia, sovereign of all, voluntarily and so easily allowed himself to be bound by these oaths.

It is notable that, in Mossi country where African tradition remained in effect, only one case of political conflict around succession to the throne is cited, in the whole history of Mossi, although it is longer than that of Songhai. That was the struggle of Tuguri against the *naba* Ba-Ogo, in the nineteenth century, hence in very recent times, at the end of Mossi history.

THE CASE OF CAYOR

The political situation in Cayor was halfway between that of Mossi and that of Songhai. All political positions below that of the king were hereditary. It was impossible arbitrarily to assign one to anyone who did not have a right to it by virtue of belonging to the corresponding caste. Until Faidherbe, the Badié Gateignes, the Botalub NDiobs, the Lamane Diamatils, etc., came exclusively from the same families; apart from competition between family members, there was no intrigue possible regarding these successions. The situation was different in the case of the king. At the end of Cayorian history, there were seven dynasties of *garmis*, or nobles, each with an equal right to the throne. All being of different origins, they were in perpetual rivalry. Unlucky claimants were frequently sent into exile. The *djîn* was a common practice: this consisted of beating the tom-tom and calling out the name of the prince being banished and outlawed. He then emigrated to another more receptive kingdom. If circumstances were favorable, if he could muster forces by buying slaves or getting some from the hospitable king, if he kept in contact with the dissidents in Cayor, if he established sustained relations with the Diaraff N'Diambur, who made and broke Damels, his return to the throne might be assured. It often happened that in utmost secrecy the Diaraff N'Diambur sent for an exiled prince, to place him on the throne, if the reigning king displeased the people. It seems that it was in this way that Maô, one of the bravest princes of the Dorobé dynasty, acceded to the throne. Prior to the Cayorian monarchy, it seems the country was divided into landed "estates" belonging to the Serers: these native lords were called Lamanes, a term which means "successor" in Serer and Tuculor. The kings who, around the fourteenth century, consecrated this organization seem all to have come from outside: they were immigrant kings, rebellious, exiled, hunted princes, perhaps from Mali, Songhai, or Ghana, who had gone to seek their fortune in an outer province of the empire, and willingly led an uprising in it if necessary to gain control. It was common for members of the nobility, who had tasted power at home but lost it, to go and look for it elsewhere. The history of the Macina provides a typical example. One of the early kings of this country, Djâdji, wanted to marry his brother's widow, who turned him down. He began to hate his other brother Maghan, whom he believed responsible for her rejection. Maghan emigrated to the home of the Bâghena-fâri, the governor of the region situated north of the Upper Senegal–Niger. He was welcomed and invited to settle wherever he wished, within the province: in addition, he was recognized as king of all those who had accompanied him into exile, instead of being treated as a prisoner by the Fâri. Some other Peuls of the Termès region from which he came soon joined him. Such, according to the *Tarikh es Sudan*, was the origin of the dynasty that reigned in the Macina, the territory chosen by Maghan.

Generally speaking, these outside kings did not in any way modify the sociopolitical structure they found established in the area. We can then see why the less important traditions remained unchanged while transformation occurred only at the royal level. And one can readily conceive that such kings could not be sacrosanct in the eyes of the people. There was no worship of them; they were just Tieddos embodying brute force. They form a third category of African kings who must be distinguished from both the traditional kings who, with their people, retained their religion (Mossi: Moro Naba; Yoruba: Alafin of Oyo), and the Islamized kings (Songhai, Futa-Toro, Futa-Djallon).

Until the conquest of Senegal, the seven Cayorian dynasties systematically refused to embrace the Islamic religion, whose followers were scorned and often mistreated. These dynasties were: the Muyôy, Sogno, Ouagadou, Guelewar, Dorobé, Guedj, and Bey.

We know very little about the origin of the Muyôys. The Sognos are considered to be Socés. The Ouagadou dynasty was founded by Détié Fu N'Diogu Fall: it was the very first; its name brings to mind the cradle of Ghana; its creator, says tradition, baptized it with this name in remembrance of his mother's native country. The Guelewar were probably a Mandingo aristocracy who went to rule over the Serers of Sine-Salum: a tradition common to the history of both countries tends to confirm this origin. We know with certainty that according to tradition Sudiata Keita, king of the Mandingo, had been helped by his sister to triumph over his enemies; in exchange for this service he instituted a matrilineal succession in the royal branch. The present-day Guelewars of Sine-Salum also claim that matrilineal filiation was introduced among them in the same circumstances. This was confirmed for me by a conversation I had with Fodé Diouf, head of the province of Salum and traditional king of this country, during his visit in Paris in 1956.

As for the Dorobé, although they do not like to admit it, they seem originally to have been Peul, or Tuculor. Indeed, there presently exists, among the Mossi, in Upper Volta (Burkina-Faso), a Peul clan called Torombé. Also at Futa-Toro, there is the Tuculor clan of Torobé, which supported Ousman Dan Fodio. The bé is merely a plural ending in Peul and in Tuculor. Torombé, Torobé, and Dorobé seem to be only variants of the same word derived from Toro. Moreover, the very names of the first ruling princes of this dynasty—Maô, for example—prove that they were Peuls or Tuculor. The Dorobés differed from the other dynasties in that the king actually took command of his army, instead of remaining at the rear and communicating orders; in defeat, he must die at the site. Members of the dynasty who survive a defeat are excluded from it, if not in fact, at least in effect. Such was the case of the Damel Madiodio who, starting in 1861, was defeated several times by Lat-Dior, without committing suicide; since he dared to survive a defeat, in the popular mind he was no longer worthy of being a Dorobé.

The Guedj come from common people. They are distinguished by their adaptive ability and their military genius. The dynasty is named for the country of origin of the first founding Damel's mother. She was a commoner from the seacoast, who married the king; *guedj* meaning "sea" in Wolof. Her son, though he had no right to the throne, succeeded in being crowned, through his energy and mental agility. The Beys were in the beginning merely a good-luck family among whom pretenders to the throne went to select virgins. According to a curious tradition, it was enough to have contact with a virgin daughter of this family for one's chances of accession to the throne to increase seriously. The family, then, progressively became an integral part of royalty.

As can be seen from the above, within each of these dynasties, succession to the throne was matrilineal. The dynastic founders remembered only their mothers or sisters, whose names were sacred; this was also true for the sons of Gongo or Konko Mussa. Gongo Mussa was one of the most powerful emperors of Mali, and Gongo was the name of his mother, according to Kâti.[18] Thus, it was the existence of several parallel, rival dynasties that introduced so many problems into the succession to the throne of Cayor.

SIGNIFICANCE OF ROYALTY

The Vitalist Concept

The African universe was run in a strictly orderly manner, metaphysically speaking. The works of Marcel Griaule, Germaine Dieterlen, and Father Tempels revealed these fundamental ideas to the West.

According to Fr. Tempels, the Universe was ruled by only one set of hierarchic forces: every being, animate or inanimate, could occupy only a specific place according to his or its potential. These forces were cumulative: thus, a living being who had as talisman the fang or claw of a lion, in which the vital force of the animal was concentrated, increased his own power by that much. In order to overcome him in battle, one had to have a sum of forces greater than his own plus the lion's. Therefore, the struggle between two kings was, above all, a magic struggle on the level of these vital forces; it took place long before the physical combat in the arena, around the water jugs and libation stumps set up in the ground, during the night, in the sacred groves. We can be sure that, from the beginning of African history until the conquest by the West, each traditional king before going into combat indulged in these practices, and therefore firmly believed that victory was on his side. Islamization did not change this: it just displaced the center of interest. Instead of turning to the traditional priests who mediated between them and the hidden forces of the universe, the princes now went to the Muslim clergy, the marabouts who practiced Eastern Kabbalah and gave them grigris to assure their victory.

This metaphysics, far from constituting a minor fact in African historical sociology, was a predominant trait. If scientific explanation ignores it, all that it will grasp will be lifeless, external forms with no apparent logical connection. No one has revealed the internal logic of this African society better than Marcel Griaule, as has been pointed out by André Leroi-Gourhan and Jean Poirier:

> All work and human activities . . . remind us of [universal movement]: pottery, cattle breeding, dance, music, decoration, and particularly the prestigious art of the forge—the Monitor was a blacksmith—the rhythm of the bellows and anvil of which inspired the first dance . . . The world is ordered like a vast equation; human animation corresponds to the animation of nature, and each gesture extends back to its mythical precedents. The Black African world which seemed to some so simple is simple indeed, but only because of its internal logic. It is very complicated in appearance; creation takes on a sense that can be called philosophical. The Black Universe had seemed crude; it now turns out to be profoundly elaborate.[19]

Within the framework of this universal harmony, in which each being has his place, the king has a precise function, a definite role: he must be the one with the greatest vital force in the whole kingdom. Only in this way can he serve as mediator—he being sacrosanct—with the superior universe, without creating any break, any catastrophic upheaval within the ontological forces. If he is not a legitimate king, fulfilling these exact conditions of established filiation, and appointed according to the rites of tradition, all of nature will be sterile, drought will overtake the fields, women will no longer bear children, epidemics will strike the people. As long as the tradition was carried on in isolation from external influences, the king fulfilled a function in which no usurper could replace him. The obligations were strict and the succession to the throne was practically without incident, as we have seen among the Mossi. The council which convened to invest the king (Moro Naba) in reality examined the degree of legitimacy of the different claimants: it was not actually an election—the term is improper—for they were compelled after a thorough enlightened examination of each case to appoint, not according to their preferences, but in accordance with tradition, the one who had all the requisite qualities.

Along the same lines, when the level of vital force of even a legitimate king decreased, he was put to death, either actually as was apparently the case in the beginning, or later on, with evolution, symbolically. This was the general practice in Black Africa and ancient Egypt, where the symbolic execution coincided with the festival of Zed. By this means, the king was supposed to die and be born again, revitalized; he regained the vigor of his youth, he was once again fit to rule. This same practice is found among the Yoruba, Dagomba, Tchamba, Djukon, Igara, Songhai, Wuadaï, Haussa of the Gobir, Katsena, and Daoura, the Shillucks, among the Mbum, in Uganda-Ruanda, in what was ancient Meroë.[20]

In Cayor, a king could not rule when wounded, probably

because his vital force was thus decreased. In any case, it was said that it would bring bad luck to the people. The king, and all those who assumed high responsibilities, whether temporal or spiritual leaders, were considered mystically superior, whence the Wolof expression *ep bop* (having more head, in the metaphysical sense). That meant that those who might go against their will, or who tried to contest their authority, might go mad as a result.

The king is truly guarantor of the ontological, and therefore the terrestrial and social, order. It is remarkable that not one African constitution provided for his replacement during the interregnum following his death for the maintenance of material order: whenever the throne was vacant, whatever the reason, social anarchy descended upon the people. The prisons were emptied among the Mossi, without any representative of the law intervening to oppose it. The situation was identical, perhaps worse, in Songhai, even though it was Islamized. The *Tarikh es Sudan* reports that Askia El Hadj (accession: August 7, 1582) had Mohammed Benkan imprisoned at Kanato on the advice of Amar-ben-Ishâq-Bir-Askia. The three sons of Benkan—Bir, Kato, and Binda—stayed in hiding through the entire reign of El Hadj and that of Bâno, his successor. But they took advantage of the interregnum between the death of Bâno and the accession of Askia Ishâq II, to come out of hiding with impunity and do everything they could to kill Amar, who was responsible for their misfortunes. The latter, warned in time, disguised himself in order to escape certain death, which would have gone unpunished. But he shed his disguise immediately after the crowning of the new Askia, "for, the disturbed situation having come to an end, no one could then commit an act of aggression against another."[21]

Most assuredly, in Songhai this was a vestige of a religious past the death of which had not yet been fully incorporated into the existing institutions. The ontological function of the king had not yet been forgotten. Under the Moroccan occupation, Pasha Ali ben Adb-el-Kader on June 19, 1632, launched a surprise attack on the city of Gao; he was defeated by the inhabitants, who seized his treasure and his wife. They also captured Prince Benkan, the descendant of the Askias, who accompanied him. However, the latter was treated with much respect "and the people of Gao asked him to come and live amongst them, so they might thus obtain the blessings of heaven."[22]

Obligations of the King

The Fondoko Borhom, "Lord of the Macina" (1610), thought that any person invested with royal authority was the servant and shepherd of his people.[23]

Although the major figure of the country, the king was therefore no less obliged to lead a life strictly regulated by custom. Among the Mossi, his schedule was planned down to the slightest details. The Moro Naba did not have the right to leave Ouagadougou, his capital, not because of royal pride, but because ritual forbade it; that is no longer true today, as traditions are beginning to fade. However, the Mossi emperor Nasséré, who laid siege to Ghana and fought against Sonni Ali and Askia Mohammed, must have broken this rule because of the great danger which menaced his kingdom. Indeed, he is said to have directed in person the expedition against Ghana.

It may also be that this tradition is recent and was instituted only at the height of the Mossi empire.

The life of the Kaya-Magha of Ghana was as strictly governed by tradition as that of the Pharaoh of Egypt: each morning, he rode around his capital on horseback, followed by his entire court, preceded by giraffes and elephants, according to Idrisi. Anyone who had a complaint could at that time address him and submit his case, which he settled on the spot. In the afternoon, he traveled the same route alone, and no one was allowed to speak to him. These kings were sometimes so conscious of their role that they tried in every way to maintain contact with the people, to investigate grievances directly, so as to feel its political and social pulse, whatever the cost. Thus, the Moro Naba disguised himself at night and went through the lower-class neighborhoods of his capital in absolute anonymity, listening to conversations. So did certain Damels of Cayor, but it must be recognized that they did this as a ruse, to sound out public opinion for personal reasons: to safeguard their power and prevent palace revolutions in this climate of dynastic rivalry, they had to keep constantly informed.

However, the concept of royalty in Diâra or Kaniâga in the Termès region, not far from Upper Senegal, was rather original. The king was obliged to remain in his palace and never leave it. He was surrounded by no pomp at all. Apparently, the people paid very little attention to him, not out of disdain but because they felt a king was great enough in himself not to need all these external signs of majesty. . . . Its inhabitants were not Peuls, and harbored against the nomadic Peuls a hatred typical of sedentary peoples. This kingdom was at first governed hereditarily by the Niakkaté (Diakkaté), then by the Diawara. With its army of two thousand horsemen, it was dependent first on Ghana, then on Mali. The inhabitants revolted and murdered the representative of Mali. But it cannot be affirmed that their concept of royalty grew out of that revolt.[24]

The traditional kings thus governed with minimal constraint, except for such administrative abuses as were committed by civil servants, which will be discussed in chapter VIII. The tax system they established appeared not as exploitation, but as the part of one's goods and crops that ritual decreed must be turned over to the sacrosanct authority who linked the two worlds, so that order might be maintained in the universe and nature continue to be fruitful.

Actually, the historical reality is less sublime: this almost divine order of things must have begun to degenerate from the very start. The description given above reflects an ideal situation which was not always realized because of the need for an administration dependent on an army of civil servants. But, in either case, the evolution of the system never gave rise to a revolution. Ghana probably experienced the reign of a corrupt dynasty between the sixth and the eighth centuries. Kâti tells of an extremely violent revolt of the masses against it. The members of that dynasty were systematically massacred. In order to wipe it out completely, the rebels went so far as to extract fetuses from the wombs of women of the royal family. Yet this did not constitute a revolution, for the monarchy itself was not eliminated; it was apparently not even seriously questioned.

Filiation was matrilineal: the emperor Kanissa-aï, contemporaneous with the prophet Mohammed (sixth century), had chosen as his capital not Ghana but Koranga, the native city of his mother.[25]

The practice of matriarchy from the beginning in the royal succession is an important argument against those who support the theory that Ghana might have been founded by Semites, for the latter recognized only patrilineal filiation.

Whatever our present attitude toward this metaphysics of social positions, this ontology, for more than two thousand years it ruled in an absolute manner the minds and consciences of our ancestors: it explains, to a certain extent, their failure or success when confronted with the tasks of civilization. This is why it cannot be too minor a factor in the historical explanation; we cannot fail to consider it.

Separation of Secular and Religious

In pagan antiquity, as in traditional Africa, secular and religious powers were long identified one with the other. As a consequence of Christianity and Islam, they were separated in both places, in the sense that the king no longer performed religious services even when, with Pépin the Short, he once again became sacrosanct. In Arabia, Islam blotted from the mind of the people the very memory of Sabaism: a new religious order, which seemed to emerge from the absolute, blended with the secular in the social organization. The regime of the caliphates rapidly evolved into a theocratic monarchy. No more Sabean king vegetating, like a fossil, next to the Kaaba. This would obtain in all the Arab kingdoms, of Egypt, North Africa, and Spain. In Black Africa, the social order remained practically as it had been before Islamization; but in those places where the people and the king became Islamized, one particular fact appeared. The king no longer exercised a religious function; he was progressively secularized, and was seen now only as a simple temporal governor of the country. He was not like those Islamic empire builders, propagators of the faith who established themselves as kings after the conquest of a country, thereby becoming sacred beings uniting the two powers in themselves.

He was no longer a preacher; the halo of holiness which surrounded him was progressively to fall onto the shoulders of representatives of the foreign religion (a Muslim clergy of lower-class origin), whereas he, the king, more and more symbolized the secular with its implications of coercion and administrative impositions. Under the influence of religion, he would progressively be discredited and considered the very incarnation of Satan. What had created his spiritual force, was traditional religion; that, along with the cosmogony, justified his place in society. When those were overcome by the "foreign" religion, the same fate would befall the institutions to which they had given rise.

If this analysis is correct with regard to the king who preserved his religion and ruled over an Islamized people (e.g., the Damels of Cayor), and if it is basically correct in the case of those like Sonni-Ali (1464) whose conversion was merely a formality, it proves inadequate in the case of such prophet-kings as the Tuculors of Senegal: El Hadj Omar, Hamadu-Hamadu, etc., whose precursor was the one in Songhai history who might be referred to as His Most Muslim Majesty Askia Mohammed, prince of believers. He carried out a coup d'état by seizing the throne after having defeated the son of Sonni-Ali (Abubaker-Dau—March 3, 1493). He instituted the dynasty of the Askias, a term of unclear etymology. He maintained friendly relations with the Muslim clergy and the scholars of Timbuktu; contrary to Sonni-Ali, he governed by using them, asking their advice on all important decisions. By protecting the believers, he won their praise. He can almost be compared to King Clovis, protected by the Roman church.[26] He made a celebrated pilgrimage to Mecca, accompanied by 1,500 men (500 calvary and 1,000 foot soldiers). He took with him part of the treasure of Sonni-Ali, 300,000 gold pieces which had been stored with the preacher Amar. Upon his arrival, he gave 100,000 as alms to the cities of Mecca and Medina and purchased in Medina a mansion which was to serve as a hostel for pilgrims from the Sudan. This mansion must have been large, for the cost of maintenance came to 100,000 gold pieces. Africa thus opened its doors to international life by way of its Muslim kings.

In the Holy Land the Askia met the fourteenth Abasside caliph of Egypt (April 1479–September 1497) and asked him to appoint him as his representative in the Sudan. It was to a purely spiritual designation. The caliph accepted, asking the Askia for three days to give up his power, mentally speaking, and come back to see him. This was done and the Askia was solemnly proclaimed by the caliph his spiritual lieutenant in the Black countries. He received for this a cap and turban which made him the delegate of Islam. Was this a way of regaining the moral authority the African Kings had been losing since their Islamization? Or was it a profoundly religious act? Whichever, the Askia on his return undertook the first important holy war waged by a Black sovereign. The enemy was the Mossi emperor Naséré (August 1497–August 1498). The Askia fulfilled all the religious requirements to give his enterprise a sacred character.[27]

Askia Mohammed was the monarch whose attitude coincided with completion of the Islamization of the Songhai monarchy. Before him, a king such as Sonni-Ali had tried to resist: he had, beyond any doubt, attempted to dam the Muslim flood which, in his eyes, was growing too serious. His harshness toward the clergy of Timbuktu, his manner of practicing Islam, to which he was theoretically converted, must be considered gestures of self-defense. Seen from this perspective, his conduct seems very consistent, rather than reflecting a "blood-thirsty" temperament. The terms in which the *Tarikh es Sudan* judges the two monarchs are significant. The author, a fervent Muslim, said of Askia Mohammed:

> Thus did God deliver the Muslims from their anguish; he used the new prince to bring to an end their misfortunes and restlessness. Askia Mohammed displayed, indeed, the greatest zeal for strengthening the Muslim community and improving the lot of its members.[28]

On the other hand, he drew a very unfavorable portrait of Sonni-Ali:

> As for this tyrannical master, this infamous villain . . . he was a man endowed with great force and powerful energy. Evil, licentious, unjust, oppressive, blood-thirsty, he caused so many men to perish that God alone knows their number. He persecuted the scholars and the pious by threatening their lives, their honor, or their reputations.[29]

Sonni-Ali had no lack of excuses. The reason he gave for the massacre of certain scholars of Timbuktu was that they were "friends of the Tuaregs, their courtiers, and that he was therefore against them."[30]

Thus, as has been mentioned, his conversion was very

relative, if we are to believe the *Tarikh es Sudan,* which considered him a monarch who made light of religion. He was in the habit of postponing until evening or the following day his five obligatory prayers; when he did decide to say them, he merely sat down, made several gestures while naming the different prayers, then said to them as if they were people: "Now divide all that among you, since you know one another so well."[31]

The struggle for political power against Islam by the native clergy seeking to discredit it colored a whole period of African history. It was characterized in Senegal by the exodus of the marabouts from the city of Koki in the region of Luga Linguère (between Dakar and Saint Louis) toward the peninsula of Cape Verde. This event took place during the reign of the Damel Amari N'Goné Ndella (1791–1810). The contempt between the secular and the religious powers was reciprocal. The marabouts, especially those who were not part of the court, who were not responsible for the mystical defense of the dynasty through the establishment of the grigris and in other ways, made no mystery of their disdain for everything mortal here on earth. The non-Islamized king was just another "Kaffir," an infidel to them. And since they were often of noble blood, and thus imbued with the same pride as the rest of the artistocracy, they often preached civil disobedience, exactly the way Saint Paul preached against the cult of the emperor. This was why the marabouts of Koki were persecuted and forced to go and ally themselves with the Lebous of Dakar. It is interesting to analyze the kind of authority they would set up on the Cape Verde peninsula after the success of their revolution.

The Lebou "Republic"

It would not be outside the framework of our main topic—the meaning of royalty—for us to examine the nature of this new power which has been inaccurately dubbed a "republic." To do this, it is indispensable that we trace the genesis of events and return to the village of Koki-Diop. We cannot be certain of the origins of the Diop clan, for, in the present state of research, it is difficult to trace their migration across Africa by relying on totemic names, for example. There is no doubt, however, that some Diops were to be found in Nubia (cf. map of migrations). Were they fishermen on the Senegal River? *Thiubolo* means fisherman in Tuculor and Peul. And that was the occupation of the Diops in Futa-Toro. Considering the idea that Africans like to have of their birth, such a modest origin would cause indignation among the Diops of Cayor who considered the Diops of the river as only an isolated nucleus, reduced to dependency on the Tuculor majority. That being as it may, they arrived in this area already Islamized and founded all the villages in Senegal called Koki: Koki-Diop, their homeland near Luga, Koki-Kad, Koki-Dakhar, Koki-Gouy (the second terms of the last three names designate the species of trees that grew around each village). We shall later see that there are many indications of a link between Koki and Kukia, the latter word referring to an historic city on the Niger downstream from Gao. In that case, we would have to look toward the East for the origin of the Diops, of whom a few at most would have made a stopover in Futa. In any case, the Diops of Koki were part of the Domisokhnas (Muslim clergy of noble or distinguished origin).

The first chief of the Lebou state, Dial Diop, was the son of one of the marabouts who had emigrated from Koki. He was appointed, after the victory, despite his foreign origin, because he was the one who dared to head the resistance, organize it within the walls of the peninsula, and stand up to the Cayorian Damel whose maneuvers and state of mind he very well knew and, unlike the Lebou, was not intimidated by. That makes clear a capital fact, that must be definitely stressed in order to clarify the political history of the peninsula. Through a now-habitual confusion, the reigning Diop family has become analogized to the general population and thought of as being Lebous. But we have shown that the Diops originated in Koki. The Lebous are a group midway between Wolofs and Serers. They are closer to the latter, whose ethnic names they share: Diagne, Faye, Ngom. They have the same tradition and practice the same libations. They are of the same ethnic type. The homogeneity of totemic names within an infrequently crossbred human group in Africa allows Lebous and Serers, as well as Wolofs, to be certain that Diop is not a typical Serer-Lebou name.

Having clarified this point of history, let us go on to the analysis of the form of power established. It was not a republican power, as all the manuals state. It would indeed be hard to imagine a republic in which power passed from father to son within a single family from its origin to the present day: Dial Diop, 1795–1815, Matar Diop, his son, 1815–1830. Following a dispute over an extradition he refused to agree to, the French intervened and after lengthy negotiations managed to have him replaced by his cousin Elimane Diop, 1830–1852; Momar Diop, son of Matar Diop, was his successor, 1852–1855; Demba Fall Diop, a descendant of Dial Diop, then acceded to the throne, 1855–1861; the French definitively occupied the peninsula during his reign. From then on, they kept a close eye on the succession to the throne, always trying to have it occupied by the Diop most favorable to them. Things continued in this manner until the time of the Seringe El Hadj Ibrahima Diop, chief of the Lebous early in this century.

When the marabouts arrived from Koki, the majority of the Lebous were non-Islamized, as are present-day Serers. Not until the beginning of the twentieth century was there mass conversion of the populations of the interior, brought about by Ahmadu Bamba and El Hadj Malik Sy. So, it was the Diops who Islamized the Lebous and instituted their government, a theocratic monarchy identical in every way to that founded on the Senegal River by the Tuculors in 1776. It is characterized by the existence of a dynasty, as in all monarchies; it is theocratic and Muslim, in that its only code of laws is the Koran. One must not forget that, after Islamization, the cadis of the empires of Ghana, Mali, and Songhai dispensed justice in strict accordance with the laws of the Koran; the Dakar regime, thus, was no more republican than the governments of those empires. The "king" had the same character as the sultans of the Arab Orient: he once again succeeded in uniting within himself the temporal and the religious.

MONARCHIC AND TRIBAL AFRICA

Africans thus never experienced a lay republic, even though the regimes were almost everywhere democratic, with a balance of powers. That is why every African is at heart a hidden aristocrat, just as every French bourgeois was before the Revolution. The deeper reflexes of the present-day African are more closely tied to a monarchic regime than to a republican one. Rich or poor, peasant or urbanite, all dream of being a small or great lord rather than a small or great bourgeois. The quality of their gestures and attitudes, their manner of seeing things, whatever their caste, is lordly and aristocratic in contrast to bourgeois "pettiness." There is still one revolution's distance between African and Western consciences, in terms of instinctive behavior. These aftereffects of aristocratism would have been extirpated only if the African, in the course of his history, had become responsible for his own destiny within the framework of a republican regime. Western colonization, even when republican, could not change these facts. That also explains why many Blacks adjust perfectly to the manners of the British aristocracy. It is hard to trace to this factor a certain aesthetic approach of the Black, although it does seem to be an important trait of the African character.

This judgment, contrary to what one might think, is applicable to all of Black Africa, to different degrees. In the precolonial period the entire continent was indeed covered by monarchies and empires. No spot where man lived, even in the virgin forest, escaped monarchic authority.[32] But we must recognize that not all peoples living under the same political regime had the same cultural level. Some outlying populations still lived in a scarcely shaken or liberalized clanic organization, whereas the large numbers in the cities were detribalized. A striking example of this is the empires of Ghana, Mali, and Songhai. One can indeed contrast, on the basis of the remaining documents (Al Bakri or Khaldun), the teeming city life of Timbuktu, Gao, Ghana, Djenné, or Mali, which contained only isolated individuals, with the collective life that still held sway in the outlying clans of the goldbearing regions to the southwest, located on the Upper Senegal, and even farther south, where detribalization was scarcely even beginning. According to Idrisi,

> Blacks who went about totally naked, got married without dowries, and were prolific goat- and camelherds with tattooed faces, lived to the West of Mali. The other, more highly developed inhabitants of Ghana went slavehunting in this region, which must have covered part of Lower Guinea and the southern part of present-day Senegal.[33]

These clans and tribes were in every way comparable to those who lived at the borders of the Roman Empire at the time of its decline and fall, when the Romans were already completely detribalized. This was the politico-social condition at the time Africa encountered the West at the start of modern times (sixteenth century).

What happened then? The Africans gradually lost their ability to decide their own fates. The local federating authority dissolved, or was at any rate diminished and rendered powerless. Internal evolution was consequently thrown off balance. In the cities where detribalization had already taken place, a return to the past was out of the question: individuals would continue to be united by social bonds. But where clanic organization still predominated, where social limits were still determined by the territory of the clan or tribe, there would be a sort of turning inward, an evolution in reverse, a retribalization reinforced by the new climate of insecurity. Collective life again took precedence over individual life. But, as can well be imagined, such clans were far from being as primitive as one might offhand have thought: They were not without the after-effects of the earlier imperial epoch. They were already developed and complex. That is why ethnologists, to their immense surprise, but without exception, always discover in them traditions that do not correspond to this stage of social organization, but are more advanced; they often do not hesitate to attribute this to a phenomenon of degeneration, supposing that these populations, living today in so primitive a state, had in the past experienced some forgotten great period. We have tried here to demonstrate how they actually reached this point.

At any rate, monarchic vestiges being less prominent within clanic life, we can proceed to these partial conclusions which have a measure of moral and social significance. We can certainly see that there was a monarchic Africa and a tribal Africa. If we tried to state the factors favoring evolution in one direction or another, we would have to recognize that African spiritualism, which we have already mentioned, and aristocratism within monarchic Africa were psychological and intellectual factors unfavorable to a socialistic evolution. But the African was an aristocratic collectivist: all of the foregoing underlines what separated his attitude from that of a proletarian collectivist. In the light of his politico-social life, his solidarity was a lordly one; despite that, he was not loath to share; the reflexes of accumulation of material wealth remained very slight in him. Consequently, his materialistic habits rather favored a socialistic evolution.

Tribal Africa had the same characteristics, with this exception, that the aristocratic, monarchic factor was almost totally absent; clanic collectivism was proletarian. Justice was also more immanent within the clan: the repressive political apparatus had become less crushing, without however reaching the same degree of withering away as in the tribes and clans conceived by Engels.

Such data bespeak an original type of development.

ORIGIN OF THE CONSTITUTIONAL REGIME

In analyzing the significance of royalty, we reviewed the cases of traditional kings, Islamized kings, and emigrant non-Islamized kings. We also analyzed the content of the constitutions. The time has come to suggest what may have brought these about. Many facts would lead us to feel that at the beginning royal power, being sacrosanct, was absolute. The generally accepted idea of African royalty does not allow for supposing that at the very start its authority might have been limited by some kind of constitutional system. On the other hand, it is not conceivable that this authority might have been exercised in an abusive manner, considering its religious character. But within the royal court, design and spontaneity both playing a part, everyone began to serve within the framework of his own profession; a tradition was born, grew stronger, and finally took root with the ideas that the warrior nobility, linked to the development of the monarchy, had toward manual labor. The latter was rather despised, as against the military calling. It would therefore not have been possible, at the start, for a prince, within the framework of life at court, to be assigned work of a manual character: the equerry, the executioner, the head ostler, the guardian of the treasury, and so on, could not be noblemen. For the nobles, when not fighting, indulged their idleness or played at sports, games of skill and courage, hunting, or *yôté* (a local chess game involving strategy). These first professionals, by caste, were the forerunners of the future government ministers, whose functions, considering the emoluments involved, quickly became hereditary. By this natural mechanism, it worked out as if each caste, from the start, had been called upon to designate its own representative at court. No such thing. The system was not born out of idealism. Only a deceptive appearance can lead to such conceptions: it grew out of the local reality based upon the caste system, the division of labor.

But, as time went by, the council so constituted was to take on importance, by the very dialectic of social relationships. No text, no tradition forced the king to take its advice: he did it first voluntarily in order to rule more wisely; then, he was forced more and more to do so, by the effect of an internal social necessity. The freemen, in particular, the grandees of the kingdom, represented by the Prime Minister, soon made their weight felt, discreetly but effectively limiting the power of the king. In reality, this limitation everywhere extended only to the stopping of abuses. The Prime Minister was the one who could initiate the procedure which, in Cayor for instance, would lead to the deposing of the king, if the latter disagreed with him, that is, with the people; if, in fact, he ceased to rule wisely.

This way of conceiving the genesis of monarchal constitutions is confirmed by the tradition within the courts of African marabouts. Members of the masses, often on their own initiative, without having been specifically designated as at the courts of temporal leaders, carry out activities related to their professions. If this proves satisfactory, they are after awhile duly appointed, confirmed in their positions, without this, however, assuming any hereditary family character. That is how it happened with Amadu Bamba, the founder of Muridism in Senegal, with his brother Cheikh Anta, with Cheikh Ibrahima Fall, during the past fifty years. The identity of appearances of the lives of temporal and spiritual leaders was not without its drawbacks for the latter. The French government often thought that hidden behind the religious facade were temporal ambitions for power. As a result, Amadu Bamba was deported to Gabon for seven years and Cheikh Anta to the Sudan, to Segu, from where he returned only in 1935, after intervention of the deputy Galandou Diouf.

Fustel de Coulanges is quite correct in warning historical researchers against the error of imagining the past in terms of the present. But all the earlier developments relating to the stability of African societies, show that the danger of intellectual adventures is negligible in this case.

CROWNING OF THE KING AND COURT LIFE

To the extent that African history, up to now, has been confined to a monotonous succession of dates and events, drily related, it has seemed important to us to try to picture the local color of the past, with maximum intensity, relying nevertheless very closely on available documentation.

Songhai

In the present state of research, we know practically nothing of the enthronement rites of the *Magha* of Ghana. On the other hand, we can trace the details of this ritual for Songhai. The Askia had a throne in the form of a dais, perhaps inspired by those of the Orient; however that may be, there is no doubt of its existence. When the Askia Mussa's brothers formed a coalition to fight and kill him, they all quickly returned to seize the throne. The Châa-Farma Alou found the Kormina-Fari already on the throne: a short bloody fight ensued, resulting in the death of Alou and the accession of the Kormina-Fari, who was none other than Mohammed-Benkan.[34] He thus owed his accession to the vigilant support of his brother Otsmân-Tinfiran.

During the coronation ceremony, a whole group of people, all equally wearing the burnous, surrounded the king right into the throne room, in solemn procession:[35] they were the *souma,* among whom Amar, when pursued by Benkan's sons, had hidden away in disguise, dressing like them in a burnous.[36] The enthronement was followed by the swearing of oaths. Generals, soldiers, all the people, even the clergy, had to swear on the Koran an oath of faithfulness and obedience to the new Askia. It even seems that this ceremony was more important than the actual enthronement, because it obligatorily took place for each new reign, whereas it was not rare for the Askia to be invested with power in some small outlying city where in all likelihood there was no throne at all. The king had to be present at the Friday prayer, which was said in his name. There are some indications that this oath was not purely a matter of form, and that the masses of people, to the extent that they were fervent believers, truly felt themselves bound by it.[37]

Indeed, the Askia Ismael believed that the hemorrhage which struck him on his accession was due to the fact that he had not respected the oath of faithfulness he had sworn on the Koran to his brother, Askia Benkan. The royal audiences in Songhai were strictly regulated; every high dignitary had a set place in the Assembly, corresponding to his official role: each also had its distinctive uniform and insignia. Following the death of the Dendi-Fari Sinbalo, Askia Daud gave that title to the Koï Kamkoli, but he had him take the insignia off his uniform and allowed him to wear only the official headdress during receptions. We must deduce from this that his appointment was not permanent. During an audience shortly thereafter, the Askia claimed to have consulted the Almighty in order to find out whom he should name to lead the people of Dendi, and appointed Ali Dudo, who had presumably received the divine approval. In the Assembly then sitting before the king, Kamkoli was in the place of the Dendi-Fari; he politely, but firmly and with dignity, took note of the hypocrisy of Askia Daud, then left the Fari's place to take that of the Koï. Of course, the king had even more insignia and emblems which were duly removed from him if he was deposed by a coup d'état, which is what happened to Askia Ishâq.[38] Askia Mohammed received from the Abbeside Caliph Mulay Abbas a turban, a green skullcap, and a saber to wear around the neck. Since he inaugurated the reign of the Askias, these objects were thereafter added to the royal insignia, which already included a royal drum, twelve standards, and the aforementioned *tin-toûri*, which made the Askia master of the earth.[39]

The emperor of Ghana, in addition to his crown which was more like a diadem, had several banners and a single flag, according to Idrisi.[40]

The Fari's uniform must have included a double-tailed tunic and a turban. After the death of Fari Abdallah, this was the outfit, apparently corresponding to his functions, that Askia Mussa gave to his brother Ishâq; the Farma, at least of certain regions, was entitled to a drum. When in 1524 the Adiki-Farma Bella, Askia Mohammed's nephew, was named Binka-Farma, he became entitled to a drum, of which all his other brothers were envious. The *Tarikh es Sudan* notes that the position thus held in the governmental hierarchy was a very high one. When his brothers threatened to smash his drum the day he came to Kâgho, Bella had a very African reaction of defiance.[41]

The ceremonial of court life was very strict and seems, give or take a few variants, to have been the same throughout Black Africa. On approaching the king, one had to cover one's head with dust, as a sign of humility. The chief, in Africa, is by definition the one who must not raise his voice: his rank and dignity require him to speak very softly, whether he be a spiritual or a temporal leader. Thus, the Mansa of Mali, like the Askia, and present-day marabouts, all had their heralds who audibly transmitted to the assembly the words of the chief. The herald in Songhai was called the Wanado. Listening to the orders of the king, even when he was not present, one had to remain standing, provided one had recognized his authority.[42] This was how Otsmane had to act toward Askia Mussa, when he finally temporarily recognized his authority, after having been lectured by his mother.[43] Obviously, one also bared one's head in the presence of the king. In traditional African monarchies, the king alone wore a headdress in early times, as was the case with the Pharaoh of Egypt; even the heir apparent of Ghana, the emperor's nephew, wore nothing on his head in his presence.

Askia Benkan (Bunkan) was the one who embellished life at the court of Songhai:

> The prince maintained the royalty in the most remarkable way; he heightened it, embellished it, and adorned his court with more numerous courtiers than before, dressed in more sumptuous outfits. He increased the number of orchestras and singers of both sexes and lavished more favors and gifts. During his reign prosperity spread throughout his empire and an era of wealth began to be established.[44]

According to Kâti, Bunkan had cloth clothes made for himself, decked his servants with bracelets of precious metals, and went accompanied by drummers in canoes. He introduced the trumpet *(fotorifo)* and the deep-toned drum *(gab-tanda)*. Before him, these two instruments had been the exclusive possession of the King of Aïr. Silk bedding was customarily used.[45]

As can be seen from the following, the luxury of Songhai went into real decline, as compared to Ghana and Mali. This would explain the disappointment of Djuder and Leo Africanus on their arrival at Kaoga. The court music was polyphonic, like the music of the griots and the murids of today. On the other hand, there was the main singer (*debékat* in Wolof) and the choir (*avukat*), which might vary in composition. At the courts of temporal chiefs, the singers were of different sexes, but at those of the marabouts, they could be only male.

In 1706, before the time of the Askias, the insignia of the king of Kaoga, according to Al Bakri, were made up of a seal, a sword, and a Koran, all of which were said to have been sent by the Umayyad sovereign of Spain: the dynasty having already become Islamized, the king was always a Muslim. Kaoga at the time was made up of two cities, the king's and a Muslim quarter. The king was then called the Kanda, which is reminiscent of Nubia.

The people dressed in a loincloth and a jacket of skin or other material, the quality of which depended on the individual's means.[46] They had not yet become Islamized and followed the traditional beliefs. While the king took his meals, a drum was beaten, all urban activity stopped, and Black dancing women in wigs portrayed dance scenes around him. At the end of the meal, its remains were thrown into the river: a different drumbeat informed the city, which resumed its activity, and the courtiers who were present shouted and exclaimed with joy. Such was the local color of life at court in the period of the Kandas, according to Al Bakri.[47]

Cayor

The enthronement of the Damel of Cayor, except for the secret religious side of it, was rather rudimentary. The people foregathered, making a huge pile of sand (in this flat country) atop which the king went to be enthroned, comparably in this to a Frankish king being raised on a shield. It was his elevation above the others, his exalted rank, that was thus made tangible by the building of a throne of sand. His distinctive insigne was a circular grigri on the left ankle: *ndombo'g tank;* originally, it would seem to have been a ring: *lam'u tank.* Whence, *laman,* the heir, the landed owner, in Serer, and *lam toro,* the heir to the Toro in Tuculor. Under Damel Meiça Tenda of Cayor, whose reign was a happy one, the temporary capital of "Maka" was lighted by jars of fat in which dipped a narrow strip of material to serve as a wick. They were placed at every street corner.

Ghana

In Ghana, the luxury evident at court, as the documents allow us to reconstitute it in detail, was equaled only by that of the Aegean period. The emperor, his heir apparent, the notables all literally dripped with gold. The pages, horses, and dogs of the Tunkara were equally covered with it. People were literally living in gold, as is shown by an Al Bakri passage about the audiences of the king who was called both Tunkara and Kaya-Magan. According to him, only the king and his sister's son, that is, the nephew who is heir apparent, were allowed to wear tailored clothes. All others following the same religion as the Tunkara—i.e., the tradition—wore loincloths of cotton, silk, or brocade, according to their means. The men were clean shaven and the women shaved their heads. The king's headpiece was made up of several gold caps wrapped in very delicate cotton materials. When he held an audience for the people, to hear their grievances and remedy them, he sat on a throne inside a pavilion around which stood ten horses caparisoned in gold materials. Behind him, stood ten pages carrying shields and swords mounted in gold; the sons of the princes of his empire stood to his right, dressed in magnificent clothes, their braided hair intertwined with gold threads. The governor of the city sat on the ground before the king and, all about, were the viziers, that is, his ministers, in the same position. The door of the pavilion was guarded by dogs of excellent breed who almost never left the king's side: they wore gold and silver collars, from which dangled bells of the same metals. The sound of a drum *(deba)* made of a hollow piece of wood announced the opening of the session. The people came running, clapping hands, poured dust over their heads, and presented their grievances.

Through the description of one of the emperor's audiences, we get an idea of how both the Tunkara and his retinue were dressed, the insignia they wore, how the pages were armed, the women coiffed, and so on. Alongside these audiences, or royal sessions of justice, which were common to Ghana, Mossi, Mali, and Songhai, there were no less general horseback rides through the capital. The Tunkara, like the Moro Naba, rode on horseback, followed by his entire court, through the various neighborhoods of the city, also to hear his subjects' grievances and remedy them.

That, by and large, was the court ceremonial of Ghana, as the documents allow us to reconstitute it.

We must add that the emperor, according to Al Bakri, lived in a stone castle, surrounded by a wall.[48] Idrisi is even more precise: according to him, the emperor lived in a fortified château, built in 1116, decorated with sculptures and paintings, and boasting glass windows. Understandably, Delafosse was reluctant to accept that text too literally.[49]

Idrisi wrote in 1150; he was one of the best Arab geographers of his time. In Sicily, he drew up the first navigational charts that were to be used in modern times. Nevertheless, it is customary to point out that in his "Description of Spain and Africa" he relates facts about this continent on which he was not as well informed as Al Bakri. However that may be, it is hard to believe that so scrupulous and thoughtful a geographer would invent out of whole cloth such precise details in describing the château.

Mali

Ibn Battuta who visited Mali in 1351–1353, under Mansa Soleiman, left testimony which allows us to recreate the local color of the royal audiences. On audience days, the emperor sat in an alcove that had a door leading into the palace: it had three windows made of wood covered in silver foil, and below three others decked with gold plate or vermeil (which leads us to conclude that the palace had at least two stories). These windows had curtains: a handkerchief with Egyptian designs, attached to a silken cord, was slipped through the grillwork that protected them on audience days. The people were summoned by horns and drums. Three hundred soldiers carrying bows and javelins lined up in double columns on either side of the window in which the emperor was to be. Those with the javelins were on the outside and standing, while those with the bows sat in front of them, the four columns facing each other. Two saddled, bridled horses and two rams were brought in: a custom reminiscent of Ghana. Nearly three hundred subjects went looking for Candja Mussa. The ferraris, the emirs, the preacher *(khatib),* and the jurists arrived and took seats, to the right and left in front of the soldiers, in the space between their columns. Dugha, the herald, stood at the door, wearing *zerdkhanan* clothes: on his head a fringed turban, typical of the country; he alone had the privilege of wearing boots on this day; he had a sword in a gold scabbard on his side; and he wore spurs, two gold and silver javelins with iron tips. Soldiers, bureaucrats, pages, Messufites, and all others, remained outside, in a wide tree-lined street. Each of the ferraris was preceded by his subordinates carrying blades, bows, drums, and horns made of elephants' tusks. One of the musical instruments was the balafon, which was made of reeds and gourds and was played with drumsticks. Each ferrari had a quiver of arrows at his back and a bow in his hand; he was mounted, and his subordinates, both foot and horse, stood in front of him. When the emperor arrived behind the window, Dugha served as mouthpiece, transmitting the orders, recovering the grievances and submitting them to the sovereign, who gave his decisions. Sometimes the audience was held inside the palace courtyard. Then a silk-covered seat mounted on three tiers was placed under a tree; this throne was called *ben-bi*. A cushion was placed on it and the whole thing covered by a dome-shaped silken parasol, with a golden bird at the top, as large as a hawk. The Mança came out of the palace with a bow in his hand, a quiver on his back. He wore a turban of gold cloth bound by golden ribbons ending in metal tips more than a palm in length, looking like daggers. He wore a red coat, of European material: the *montenfès*. Singers walked before him, holding in their hands gold and silver vessels; he walked forward slowly, followed closely by three hundred armed soldiers, and stopped from time to time. Before taking his place on his seat, he would make a slow turn around; then the horns, the trumpets, and the drums sounded as soon as he was seated. Once again the two horses and the ram were brought to drive away bad luck. Dugha was at his habitual place near the Mança; the rest of the people were on the outside; the ferraris were called in and the session began in the usual conditions, as in Ghana.[50]

When in October 1559 Askia Daud defeated the Mança of Mali, at the battle of Dibikaralâ, he married his daughter Nâra; she then lived in a luxury comparable to that of Helen of Troy.

> She was covered with jewels, surrounded by numerous slaves, both male and female, and abundantly supplied with furniture and baggage. All of her household utensils were made of gold: dishes, jars, mortars, pestles, and so on.[51]

Obviously, an illustration of African history is possible: there are more documents than generally stated. They allow us to reconstitute, sometimes even in detail, over a period of almost two thousand years, African political and social life. We know how the members of the different classes in Ghana, Mali, Mossi, Songhai, and Cayor were dressed; what they did with their spare time, their daily routines, and so on. We know what social relationships governed society, and thus the behavior of an entire society which we can vividly bring back to life before our eyes, even on the stage or in films. The local color would be authentic.

This description of the different aspects of African life will be fleshed out in succeeding chapters by the addition of facts no less abundant or detailed, concerning the administrative, juridical, and military administration, as well as the intellectual life, and so on. In the course of these developments, we will be able better to see the convergences and divergences between them and the European societies contemporaneous with the period under consideration.

NOTES

1. In Ethiopia, all the pretenders to the throne were locked up in a fortress, to await the decision announced by the Prime Minister after deliberation (Baumann).
2. Tauxier, *Etudes Soudanaises: Le Noir du Yatanga* (Paris: Ed. Emile Larose, 1917), Bk. VII, pp. 339–360.
3. The testimony of Cada Mosto confirms this (1455).
4. Al Bakri, *Description de l'Afrique septentrionale* (trans. Slane) (Algiers: Typographie Adolphe Jourdan, 1913), pp. 327–330: "Description de Ghana et moeurs de ses habitants."
5. Ibn Khaldun, *op. cit.*, p. 110.
6. Al Bakri, *op. cit.*, pp. 327–328.
7. Cf. Diop, *L'Unité culturelle de l'Afrique noire*, esp. ch. III.
8. Ibn Khaldun, *op. cit.*, p. 111.
9. Ibn Battuta, *op. cit.*, pp. 13–15.
10. Sâdi, *Tarikh es-Soudan* (trans. O. Houdas) (Paris: Ed. Ernest Leroux, 1900), ch. XVIII, p. 184. (Reprinted by A. Maisonneuve, 1981.)
11. *Idem.*, p. 185.

12. Mahmoûd Kâti, *Tarikh el-Fettach* (Trans. O. Houdas and M. Delafosse) (Paris: Ed. E. Leroux, 1913), ch. XIV, p. 274. (Reprinted by A. Maisonneuve, 1981.)
13. This term must be understood to mean women of the slave class who were legally married in religion and in law, after the first wife, who was generally a freewoman. They were called *târa* in Wolof.
14. Sâdi, *Tarikh es-Soudan* (hereinafter referred to as *T.S.*), pp. 147–148.
15. *Idem.*, p. 167.
16. Cf. Kâti, *Tarikh el-Fettach* (hereinafter referred to as *T.F.*), XIV, p. 274.
17. *T.F.*, ch. I, pp. 13–44.
18. Cf. *T.F.*, p. 55.
19. André Leroi-Gourhan and Jean Poirier, *Ethnologie de l'Union française*, Vol. I, "Afrique" (Paris: Presses Universitaires de France, 1953), p. 369.
20. Westermann and Baumann, *Les Peuples et les Civilisations de l'Afrique* (trans. L. Homburger) (Paris: Ed. Payot, 1947), p. 328.
21. Sâdi, *T.S.*, ch. XVIII, pp. 187–188.
22. *Idem*, ch. XXXIII, p. 359.
23. *Ibid.*, ch. XXVII, p. 299.
24. Cf. *T.F.*, ch. III, pp. 71–72.
25. *T.F.*, ch. IV, pp. 75–77.
26. Merovingian king of the Franks (481–511), who converted to Christianity in 496 A.D. (Tr. Note).
27. Sâdi, *T.S.*, ch. XIII, pp. 117–122.
28. *Idem.*, ch. XIII, p. 118.
29. *Idem.*, ch. XII, p. 103.
30. *Ibid.*, p. 107.
31. *Ibid.*, p. 110.
32. Cf. Robert Vigondy's map of Africa, 1795.
33. *Idrissi géographe* (trans. Amédée Jaubert) (Paris: Royal Printshop, 1836), I, p. 19.
34. Sâdi, *T.S.*, ch. XIV, p. 144.
35. During ordinary sessions, the Askia sat on a kind of platform or divan which could accommodate several people. Only a Sherif was allowed to sit beside him.
36. Sâdi, *T.S.*, ch. XVIII, p. 188.
37. *Idem.*, p. 185.
38. *Idem.*, ch. XXII, p. 231.
39. Kâti, *T.F.*, ch. XIV, p. 173.
40. *Idrissi géographe, op. cit.*, p. 17.
41. Sâdi, *T.S.*, ch. XIII, p. 131, and ch. XIV, p. 142.
42. Marabouts today are greeted as the kings were greeted, however without covering oneself in dust.

43. *T.S.*, p. 135.
44. *Ibid.*, ch. XIV, p. 145.
45. Cf. Kâti, *T.F.*, chs. VIII–IX, pp. 158, 166. Sonni Ali had several residences (Madugu) at Kaoga, Kabarra, Djenné. Kâti saw the remaining walls of the last of these.
46. And later a loincloth of "windi," held up by a belt and a silver bracelet on the right wrist, according to Kâti, *T.F.*, p. 189.
47. Al Bakri, *op. cit.*, "Route de Ghana à Tademekka," pp. 342–343.
48. *Idem.*, "Description de Ghana et moeurs de ses habitants," pp. 327–330.
49. Delafosse, *Haut-Sénégal–Niger* (Paris: Ed. Larose, 1912), Vol. I, p. 15.
50. Ibn Battuta, *op. cit.*, pp. 23–26.
51. Sâdi, *T.S.*, ch. XVII, p. 170.

Chapter Five

POLITICAL ORGANIZATION

POWER OF THE AFRICAN EMPIRES

Before undertaking a detailed analysis of the political organization of precolonial Africa, we must show the actual power and the extent of the African empires. These factors are often minimized, or left vague. Insofar as there exists a certain persistent tendency to allude to more or less mythical White conquerors to explain African civilizations, it is worthwhile to reestablish the truth strictly based on facts and documents, with regard to the relationship between White and Black cultures toward the close of the First Millennium—when Africa's history was beginning just about everywhere.[1]

Delafosse, quoting Ibn Khaldun, relates that, as early as the eighth century, after the conquest of North Africa by the Umayyads, Arab traders crossed the Sahara as far as the Sudan.

STRENGTH AND EXTENT OF THE EMPIRES

Ghana

Henceforth new connections, never again interrupted, were being forged with the outside, particularly the Arab Orient and the Mediterranean world. These first traders discovered that the Sudan was governed by a Black emperor whose capital was Ghana. The empire at its highest point extended from Djaka on the west of the Niger River to the Atlantic Ocean and, north to south, from the Sahara to the edge of Mali. The gold-rich region of Upper Senegal, centered around Gadiaru, Garentel, and Iresni, belonged to the Empire. In Bakri's day the outlying village of Aluken was an Eastern border territory governed by the son of the late Emperor Bessi, uncle of the reigning Tunka Min. The white populations then inhabiting the land were under the strict authority of the Blacks. In 990 the Berber center of the Lemtunas, Aoudaghast, was governed by a Black *farba* who levied taxes, tariff duties, etc., in the name of the Emperor on the goods and merchandise of the city's population, made up almost exclusively of Berbers and Arabs; these two groups moreover hated each other at the time.

Immediately following the occupation of North Africa, the first Umayyads sent an army to attempt the conquest of the Empire of Ghana. It was defeated, but its survivors were not executed: they were allowed to settle on the land and live there in the same conditions as others. They were known as the El Honneihîn, a portion of whom broke away and settled in the village of Silla, on the Senegal River, where the ruler was already Islamized. In 1067, during Bakri's time, the El Honneihîn minority had practically been assimilated into the Black society whose religion it shared. Those who had settled along the river were called El Faman.[2] Can there possibly be an etymological link between that name and *Laman, Lam-Toro;* heir of the *Toro?* Is that, perhaps, the White origin often claimed by the Tuculors and, in particular, the ruling dynasty of the Lam-Toros? However that may be, it was through peaceful intermarriage that this white minority must have fused with the Black element.

Not until the decline of Ghana did it cease to rule Aoudaghast, after the attacks of the Almoravides in 1076. While the Berbers remained vassals of the Black emperor of Ghana for centuries, the Almoravide revenge on Ghana lasted only ten years; it ended in 1087 with the death of Abubeker-

Ben-Omar, killed by the arrow of a Black warrior inside the borders of present-day Mauritania. The Almoravides displayed extreme cruelty at the time of the taking of Ghana: goods were looted, the inhabitants slaughtered. After this ten-year interruption, Ghana was once again to be attacked by the Sosso vassals but succeeded in holding its own until the siege of the capital by Sundiata Keita in 1240.

The Empire of Ghana, according to Bakri, was defended by two hundred thousand warriors, forty thousand of them archers. Its power and reputation, renowned as far as Baghdad in the East, were no mere legend: it was actually a phenomenon attested to by the fact that for 1250 years a succession of Black emperors occupied the throne of a country as vast as all of Europe, with no enemy from without nor any internal tensions able to dismember it.

The capital was already a cosmopolitan and international city; it had its own Arab quarter where Islam existed alongside the traditional cult, before the conversion of the royal dynasty and the people: in Bakri's time the city already boasted a dozen mosques located in the Arab sector, with their imam, muezzins, and salaried "lectors."[3] It had a large number of jurists and scholars. Ten thousand meals, cooked over a thousand bundles of wood, were served daily. The Emperor himself attended these feasts to which he treated the populace outside his palace.

The Empire first opened itself to the world-at-large through commerce; it already enjoyed international repute, which would be inherited and extended by the future empires of Mali and Songhai. But domestic slavery at this time was rife in African society: one could sell his fellow man to another citizen or a foreigner. Which explains why Berber and Arab merchants, grown rich since settling at Aoudaghast, though still vassals of the Black sovereign, could acquire Black slaves on the open market. Some individuals in the city owned as many as a thousand slaves.

This shows the peaceful means by which the white world

could possess Black slaves.[4] It was not through conquest, as has often been asserted. These empires, defended when necessary by hundreds of thousands of warriors, and having their centralized political and administrative organization, were much too powerful for a single traveler, thousands of miles from home, to try any sort of violence against them. The reality of the matter was much simpler, as evidenced by the preceding; for reasons to be explained later on, slavery would cease to exist in the white world, especially Europe, while still subsisting in the Black. One sees here the complex facts that it has often been very tempting to use so as to obscure certain points of history. All the white minorities living in Africa might own Black slaves, but slaves and white masters alike were all subjects of a Black Emperor: they were all under the same African political power. No historian worth his salt can permit the obscuring of this politico-social context, so that only the one fact of Black slavery emerges from it.

Mali

The boundaries of the Empire of Mali stretched from Kaoga (Gao) all the way to the Atlantic and from the Sahara to the tropical forest. According to Ibn Khaldun, the Emperor of Mali reigned over the entire Sahara: ". . . Mansa Mussa was a powerful sovereign whose authority extended as far as the desert near Uargla."[5]

In Bakri's view, Ifrikya (North Africa) was bounded by a line parallel to the Equator, passing through Sijjilmessa,[6] and had the same universalist tendency, the same cosmopolitan character as Ghana. The capital city, Mali, also had its own Arab quarter, its mosques and jurists, its Muslim cemetery, etc. The Emperor, Mansa Kankan Mussa, made a celebrated pilgrimage to Mecca (1324–1325). He exchanged embassies with Morocco, maintaining commercial and diplomatic ties with Egypt, Portugal, and Bornu.

There were African interpreters in Egypt. Ibn Khaldun, speaking of the frontiers of Mali which extended as far as the Atlantic Ocean, mentions the name of El Hajj Yunos, a Tekrurian interpreter in Cairo.[7] Africans were already in the habit of traveling to North Africa, and sometimes settling there to study. Mali's international activity thus increased. Delafosse was quite right to be impressed by the might of this nation.

Meanwhile, Gao had recovered its independence between the death of Gongo (Kankan) Mussa and the accession of Suleiman Mansa, and approximately one century later, the Mandingo Empire began to decline under the attacks of Songhai, while preserving enough power and prestige so that its sovereign could meet on an equal footing with the King of Portugal, then at the height of his glory.[8]

The might of the Empire was such that the Arabs at times called on it for military aid. Such was the case, according to Khaldun, of El Mamer, who fought the Arabo-Berber tribes from the region of Uargla, in the North Sahara. He appealed to Kankan Mussa, on the latter's return from Mecca, to come to his aid militarily. Khaldun also tells of the size of the Moroccan embassy in Mali and the interest the Sultan of Morocco displayed in it.

The Maghreban sultan even had prepared a selection of the finest products of his realm and entrusted to Ali Ibn-Ghanem, Emir of the Mâkil, the task of transporting this truly royal gift to the sultan of the Blacks. A deputation made up of the highest-ranking individuals in the empire accompanied Ibn-Ghanem.[9]

Contrary to the notions prevailing today, the relationship then existing between Whites and Blacks could not have been those of masters to slaves. A passage from Ibn Battuta, who visited that very Empire of Mali, clearly reveals the state of mind and the pride of Africans of this period (1352). The border regions of the Empire, such as Ualata, at the edge of the

Sahara, were governed by Black *farbas* who levied customs duties and other taxes on caravans bringing merchandise into the country. Upon arrival, the merchants had to clear administrative formalities with them, before being allowed to carry on their trade. It was in such circumstances that Ibn Battuta, accompanying one of these caravans, met the *farba* of Ualata, Hussein.

> Our merchants stood up in his presence and, even though they were close to him, he spoke to them through a third person. This was a mark of the little consideration he had for them and I was so unhappy at this that I regretted bitterly having come to a country whose inhabitants display such bad manners and give evidence of such contempt for white men.[1ʳ]

Ibn Battuta was an eyewitness; it is difficult to contradict him regarding the feelings and attitudes he attributes to the speaker. But, if the pride and dignity of the *farba* are beyond question, the contemptuous intentions attributed to him by Battuta seem to derive from the latter's ignorance of the proper ceremonials governing receptions and audiences of any African chieftain. As we have already seen in chapter IV, the latter addresses a crowd only through a herald; this was how the *farba* must have acted at his own court in Ualata.

The white minorities who lived in the Empire at the time of Ghana were now, in even greater numbers, under the rule of Mali: the Ullimidden, located on the bend of the Niger, the Medeza, near Ras-el-Mâ, and all the Berber tribes living in Mauritania, as evidenced by this passage from Mohammed Hamidullah, in an article entitled "Africa Discovered America before Christopher Columbus," based on a contemporary text:[11]

> Iban Fadallâh al-Umarîy (d.1348) has left us an account of an attempt to reach America from West Africa. Of his voluminous encyclopedia, *Masâlik al-absād*, only a minute fragment has so far been published. What follows is an excerpt from the fourth volume of this work (MS. Asasafia, Istanbul, fol. 18b, 19a, 19b, 23b):

Chapter Ten, concerning Mâli and its dependencies . . .
"In these regions there is no one deserving the name of king,
unless it be the sovereign of Ghânah, who is a kind of viceroy of
the Emperor of Mâli, although in his own domain he is like a
veritable king. To the north of Mâli, there are white Berbers
who live as his subjects. These are the Yantasar, Yantafrâs,
Maddûsah, and Lamtûnah tribes. They have their own cheikhs,
who rule them, except for the Yantasar who have their own
kings, vassals of the Emperor of Mali."

In actuality, when far from their homeland, the Arabs
were often led by their isolation to adapt to the Black African
milieu. Some of them thus traditionally took on the role of
jesters at royal African courts. Though never before emphasized, this aspect of the relations between the two cultures was
no less ancient or general. Khaldun thus relates the story of
two Arab courtiers, Abu-Ishac el Toneijen-El-Mâmer, who
were part of Mansa Mussa's entourage on his return from
Mecca.

We were part of the royal cortège and even outranked the
viziers and heads of the state. His Majesty listened with pleasure to the tales we told him and, at each stopping-place, he
rewarded us with several kinds of foods and sweets.[12]

This tradition extended even to the smaller courts of
Cayor, where it is very much alive. It explains the existence in
this area of Moors who have expediently adopted totemic
names of reigning African princes. Many of the white citizens
of Mauritania are named Fall and Diagne, because the Damel
of Cayor had always to be a Fall, while the Diagnes were the
landed Serer proprietors of the earlier era. Khaldun stresses
the coveted position which Es Sakli must have had at the court
of Mali, in addition to the remuneration he received for building the "mosque" of Kaoga (Gao) for Mansa Mussa.

Songhai

The Songhai Empire extended from east of the Niger
River as far as the Atlantic Ocean and "from the frontiers of

the land of Bindoko as far as Teghezza and its dependencies"[13] under Askia Mohammed. The strength of the army hastily raised to fight Djuder was 12,500 cavalry and 30,000 infantry. Songhai inherited the international renown of Mali. From Kankan Mussa to Askia Mohammed, the memory of the voyages of African princes is recorded in the annals of the East, where the astonishment expressed at the power of the African empires is indescribable.

In their annals the peoples of the Orient told of the voyage of the Prince; they noted their amazement at the power of his Empire, but they did not depict Kankan Mussa as an open-handed, magnanimous individual. For, in fact, despite the extent of his holdings, he gave as alms in the two holy cities only a sum of twenty thousand pieces of gold, whereas Askia-El-Hâjj-Mohammed bestowed upon them one hundred thousand pieces of gold.[14]

Sonni Ali, [15] known also as Ali Ber or Ali the Great, drove out the Tuaregs who had held Timbuktu after the Mandingos, from 1434 to 1468. The Tuareg chief, Akil, fled to Biro (Ualata) without a fight at sight of Sonni Ali; he took with him all the jurists and members of the clergy who were in favor of Tuareg rule. The Tuaregs had committed the worst excesses during the thirty-four years of their domination. In actuality they had never permanently settled in the city; the earlier administration had remained: the city continued to be governed by a Timbuktu-Koï who collected taxes in their name. Only after a series of humiliations, pillages, and massacres did the Timbuktu-Koï call for help from Sonni Ali to free the city. Sonni Ali entered it on January 30, 1468. The Tuaregs had been content to remain nomads, making periodic forays into Timbuktu; their dominion had never extended to the right bank of the river, according to Sâdi. The Tuaregs then became not mercenaries but vassals of the Askias of Kaoga, until the fall of the Empire. Sonni Ali conquered Bara,

the Senhâjja-Nu Berber country governed at the time by
Queen Bikun-Kabi. He seized all the mountain regions where
the Berbers were camped, as well as Kuntaland.[16] The conquered Berbers were assimilated and integrated into the Black
politico-administrative organization; the Askia made their
tribal chiefs into Koïs who owed specified periodic tribute.
Thus, the Maghcharen-Koï and the Andassen-Koï were each

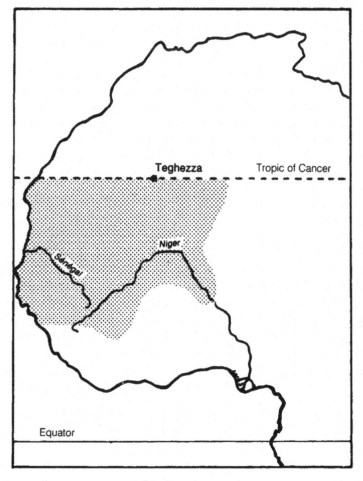

Approximate area of the empires of western Africa.

obliged to provide 12,000 soldiers in case of war. The Tuaregs were at that time far from seeing themselves as members of the same political community as the Arabs. It was with these forces, 24,000 Tuaregs, plus his other men, that Askia Daud campaigned against the Arabs of Bentanba in May 1571.[17] The loyalty of the vassals stood every test; even during the war against Morocco, the Andassen-Koï remained loyal to the Askia, until his death. When Askia Ishâq I, who came to power in 1539, one day received an invitation from Mulay Ahmed, King of Morocco, to cede to him the salt mines of Teghezza, he replied:

> "The Ahmed who listened [to such advice] could not be the present Emperor of Morocco, and as for the Ishâq who would heed him, he is not I; that Ishâq has yet to be born." Then he sent two thousand mounted Tuaregs instructing them to sack the whole end of the region of the Dra'a toward Marrakesh, to kill no one, and then to retrace their steps.[18]

The order was scrupulously carried out; the market of the Beni-Asbih was pillaged, as well as all the wealth of the Draa region. The Askia thus demonstrated his power to the Sultan, who did not react in any way.

This invitation already implicitly raised the question of the frontiers of Black Africa, at least on a political level. All of the foregoing allows us to show that, for more than a thousand years, Black governors administered the border regions of Teghezza on the Tropic of Cancer, Ualata, and Aoudaghast. The belt of the desert situated between the Tropic and a line passing through the Draa and Sijilmesa, was always a no man's land belonging equally to the two countries; it never was subject to precise political authority from one side or the other. An unadministered zone, it was dangerous to cross because of the Messufa Berbers, some of whom did not hesitate to attack caravans unwilling to pay them to serve as guides. One of the last Teghezza-Mondzos, in the service of the Askia, died there in 1557: he was called Mohammed

Ikoma.[19] The universal character and cosmopolitan spirit abroad in this empire are nowhere so well displayed as in the prayer attributed to Konboro, King of Djenné, at the time of his conversion to Islam; he prayed, among other things:

> (1) that he who, driven from his own land by indigence and penury, might come to this city, should in exchange discover here, by the grace of God, wealth and abundance such as to make him forget his old homeland; and (2) that the city be peopled by a number of foreigners greater than that of its citizens.[20]

Aryan Europe during antiquity experienced the self-centered patriotism of the city-state; it experienced universality in the Church of the Middle Ages; it later ended with nationalism and the formation of modern national states. Black Africa was to remain at the level of that universal consciousness politically and sociologically speaking, until its encounter with the West. Then, having undergone the effects of a conquering, expansionist nationalism, it would attempt to retaliate with the same weapons; thus African nationalism would never sink to basic chauvinism: it would consist, at most, in a development of cultural, ethical, and material values which give strength to peoples and assure their survival in the present world, a liberation of the will to transformation latent in the common consciousness.

ADMINISTRATIVE ORGANIZATION

The Empire of Ghana antedated by five hundred years that of Charlemagne, who was crowned Emperior in the year 800. From the dismemberment of the Roman Empire in the fourth century until that date, Europe was nothing but chaos, with no organization comparable to that of the African empire. With Charlemagne commenced the first effort at centralization; but one can say without exaggeration that throughout the Middle Ages Europe never found a form of political organization superior to that of the African states. There is agreement on the fact that the African variety of organization is indigenous: it could not have come from the Aryan or Semitic Mediterranean. If one absolutely had to relate it to some earlier forms, the administrative centralization of Pharaonic Egypt, with its *nomes*, might be brought up. Each provincial governor in Black Africa was an image of the king, with his own small court. All the necessary elements were apparently present to give rise to feudalism. So we can ask ourselves why, up to their disappearance on contact with the West, the African empires did not evolve into a political feudalism through the progressive emancipation of these provincial governors. Yet, among the Mossi, once a governor was appointed, holding rank of minister, the King who had so designated him according to tradition could not dismiss him. We can cite four explanations for this cohesion which was so remarkable, if we except the periodic secessions of certain outlying provinces; but, in these latter cases, it is less a matter of a province becoming detached through the revolt of its governor than of a former small state, recently annexed, but not yet sufficiently assimilated into the Empire, finding enough character to dissociate itself at the slightest weakness of the central organization. This was the case with the Senegalese states vis-à-vis Ghana: Djoloff, El Feruin, Silla, and even Djara.

(A) One of the explanations is of a religious nature. It seems beyond doubt that, in traditional monarchies, such as the Mossi and the Uadai in eastern Chad, the constitution was lived up to by all the people. Those in charge had a religious notion of their functions, which prevented them from taking advantage of internal weaknesses in the political organization. We have seen that, among the Mossi, there was only one case of internal political struggle, and this came very late.

(B) In the Islamized empires, such as Songhai, tradition gave way to a strict administrative control that left very little opportunity for feudal tendencies or possibility for secessionist maneuvers. Everything came from the Askia and everything ended with him. The *Tarikh es Sudan* relates that Askia Mohammed subdued all peoples "as far as Teghezza, by fire and sword," and that he "was docilely obeyed in the various states as in his own palace."[21]

The provincial governors were mere civil servants, dismissable at any moment, in Songhai; but they might remain in office for more than ten years, in fact for life, as long as they did not visibly nurture ambitions above their stations, and their administration was properly conducted.

(C) During the Middle Ages there evolved in European history a situation that has no parallel in Africa: the barbarian invasions. Of course, since prehistoric times, every continent has been invaded by peoples of other races; but, during recorded history, we know of no invasions of Black Africa that compare in suddenness and intensity with those experienced by Europe in the tenth century. The new European society, born of the fusion of Gallo–Romans with the barbarians who invaded in the fourth century, was already established. It had already developed its first political structures, its first tentative administrative centralization in Charlemagne's day. After his death, Europe was eventually divided into three separate kingdoms, ruled by his grandsons. It was then invaded anew by the Norse in the tenth century. As André Ribard has shown, the insecurity which was then prevalent in the rural areas impelled the peasants to organize around a strong protector, a lord, whose authority over those under his protection grew daily more meaningful, whereas that of the King, living in virtual isolation at his capital, was more and more symbolic. It was thus, under the threat of external danger against which protection at any cost was necessary, that European feudalism was born and grew concomitant with the seizure and occupation of the land by the lords.

Much has been made of Arab invasions of Africa: they

occurred in the North, but in Black Africa they are figments of the imagination. While the Arabs did conquer North Africa by force of arms, they quite peaceably entered Black Africa: the desert always served as a protective shield. From the time of the initial Umayyad setbacks in the eighth century, no Arab army ever crossed the Sahara in an attempt to conquer Africa, except for the Moroccan War of the sixteenth century. During the period of our study, from the third to the seventeenth centuries, not one conquest was ever launched by way of the Nile: that of the Sudan, accomplished with the help of England, came only in the nineteenth century. Nor was there ever any Arab conquest of Mozambique or any other East African territory. The Arabs in these areas, who became great religious leaders, arrived as everywhere else individually and settled in peacefully; they owe their influence and later acceptance to spiritual and religious virtues. The Arab conquests dear to sociologists are necessary to their theories but did not exist in reality. To this day no reliable historical documents substantiate such theories. We will cover the question of the later Moroccan occupation of Timbuktu in chapter VII. And we will see that the limited character of this phenomenon could not cause the outbreak of general panic such as took place in Europe, which would have been necessary for the birth of African feudalism. According to Ibn Khaldun, it was rather from Africa, from Ethiopia and Nubia, that an expedition to conquer Yemen took off:

> Beside them [the Demdem], are the Abyssinians, the most powerful of Black nations; they live on the west coast of the [Red] Sea, in the neighborhood of Yemen. It was from their land that the expedition was launched which, at the time of Du Nuas, crossed the sea to seize Yemen.[22]

This is most likely an allusion to the Ethiopian expedition which took place around the time of the birth of Mohammed, which is mentioned in the verse of the Koran entitled "The Elephant Leader."

(D) Whereas during the Middle Ages the entire feudal

system was to be based on possession of the land through progressive despoiling of the protected inhabitants—creating the landed nobility—neither king nor lord in Black Africa ever truly felt he possessed the land. Land possession there never polarized the consciousness of political power. We have seen the religious factors that opposed this. The king and the little local lord knew that they owned slaves and that they ruled the entire country, the extent of which they knew perfectly well, and whose inhabitants paid them a specified tax. Yet they never felt that they owned the land. The African peasant's situation was therefore diametrically opposed to that of the serf bound to the soil and belonging, along with the land he cultivated, to a lord and master. The conditions under which the very first "masters of the soil," such as the Serer Lamans, ceded plots of land were in no way comparable to those in force during feudal times: they could never result in the loss of liberty for a non-slave. Under the worst of them, they called for an annual rental guaranteed by verbal agreement, cancellable at the end of each season. Even the poor worker, the *navetane,* who possessed only the strength of his own arms, could not be reduced to slavery. In the morning he worked for the Laman, and in the afternoon for himself, on the same plot granted to him.

The acute feeling of private ownership that we come across today among the Lebou of Cape Verde is a recent phenomenon connected with the development and exploitation of Dakar since the governorship of Pinet-Laprade (1857). It was he who effected the first subdivision of land and issued authorizations for construction. The economic development of the port of Dakar very quickly gave a special value to all the land on the peninsula, so that the Lebou landowners, who until then had been little concerned about it, now came to appreciate the increased value of their lands.

These are the four causes which seem to explain the absence of a landowning feudal system in the history of Black Africa.

RESOURCES OF THE ROYALTY AND NOBILITY

Taxes

What, then, did this non-landowning nobility live on? What, in particular, were the material resources and the finances of the king? We have seen that the institution of a tax, first conceived of as a tithe, a ritual deduction on the wealth of all subjects, was present in all these empires. As everywhere else, it was at first collected as payment in kind, then later, in Songhai and Mali, in gold currency.

The litigation which opposed the Timbuktu-Koï to the Tuareg chief, Akil, which resulted in the intervention of Ali Ber, arose from the apportionment of the collected taxes. It had been the custom for one-third of the taxes to go to the Koï, but Akil refused to give him a single goldpiece out of the three thousand *mitkâls* he collected.[23] It appears that Askia Ishâq I practically crushed Timbuktu's merchants with taxes. A former singer, Mahmud-Yaza, was his collection agent. Seventy thousand goldpieces were recovered after the death of Ishâq.[24] These two facts prove the ubiquity of both taxation and the use of gold coinage in Songhai.

Customs

The second important source of revenue for the king was made up of customs duties. A strict customs system was established as early as the Ghanaian period; it was retained by the emperors of Mali and Songhai; duty was collected both on imports and on exports. According to Bakri, the Tunkara of Ghana took a fee of one gold dinar for every salt-laden mule entering his country, and two gold dinars for every load of salt exported. For a load of copper the rate was five *mitkâls*, and ten for a load of miscellaneous goods.[25]

Gold Mines

The principal source of revenue for the sovereigns of Black Africa, from antiquity to modern times, from the Indian Ocean to the Atlantic, i.e., from the Nubia of Herodotus and Diodorus Siculus to the Ghana of Bakri and the Mali of Ibn Battuta and Khaldun and the Songhai of Sâdi and Kâti, was gold extracted from mines. According to an anecdote supplied us by Herodotus, the abundance of gold in Nubia was such that even the prisoners' chains were forged of this metal. Of course, this sort of tale cannot be taken literally; nevertheless, it symbolizes an economic reality, a society in which gold seemed more prevalent than all other metals. The established facts conform well enough to this legend: the etymology of Nubia is said to signify "gold." Historically, Nubia was the country from which Egypt acquired all her gold.

Ghana's gold was accumulated, according to Bakri, in the fortified city of Ghiaru, eighteen days distant from the capital on the Upper Senegal. The abundance of this metal was such that the king left to the people all the gold dust they could extract from the empire's mines. The king, however, kept for himself all pieces of native gold found; without this precaution, reasons Bakri,[26] gold would have become so plentiful as to have virtually no more value in the land. Thus, instead of the total product of all the empire's mines, the Tunka kept for himself only that share of the metal that was found formed into chunks. One such chunk, according to Khaldun, weighed fifteen pounds; it had been inherited by and belonged to the Mansa of Mali: it was sold to some Egyptian merchants by Mansa Djata, the grandson of Mansa Mussa, who exhausted the Royal Treasury.[27]

Mali thus inherited the Ghanaian mines situated in Bambuk, the same mines which were known to the Carthaginians and were explored by the Romans after the destruction of

Carthage by Scipio Africanus Minor (Bambuk = the Roman Bambutum).[28]

The region of Gao to the east of the Niger also produced a vast quantity of gold dust and Bakri believes that it was actually the first country to produce this material.[29]

This gold, which was always abundant during the history of the African states, was the currency essential to international trade, first with the Arab Orient, then with Mediterranean Europe (Portugal, Spain). It contributed powerfully to the economic prosperity of the country; it quite certainly meant the sovereigns did not have to overwhelm their respective peoples with taxes and tariffs. In order to grasp the distinction between the economic conditions, the monetary situations of the lower classes in Medieval Europe and Black Africa, we would have to imagine the king and the feudal lords, in 1067, allowing the serfs and the peasants the right to accumulate wealth equivalent to that of this African gold dust from the natural resources of their own countries. It is, therefore, most important to bear in mind this economic factor in explaining the peculiar aspect of Africa's sociopolitical evolution.

Royal Treasury

The treasury of the sovereign thus contained both gold pieces and chunks of gold in the raw state. There were lofts containing taxes in kind such as grains and storerooms for manufactured products: saddles, swords, harnesses, fabrics, etc. A fair share of the treasury of Sonni Ali was deposited with the cadi of Timbuktu, perhaps because the cadis, due to their positions, were traditionally honest men: this treasure did indeed exist, for it was where Askia Mohammed, after his coup and his accession, found the money for his pilgrimage to Mecca.

Booty

Foreign expeditions also were profitable. Whether to secure existing borders or to increase the size of their countries,
the sovereigns undertook military expeditions, outside the
territories inhabited by their own subjects, whom they had to
protect. There was a favorable occasion whenever two con-
tiguous states were not allies: the borders were then vigilantly
guarded and sometimes a defensive reflex might spark a conflict. The properties of the losers would then be appropriated.
Thus, in March 1513, El Hajj Askia Mohammed led an
expedition into Kashena; in February 1514 he began a cam-
paign against El-Odâla, the sultan of Agadez, which ended
February 15, 1515. However, as he gave no share of the booty
to his vassals, one of them, Kotal, the Liki chief, also called
Konta, revolted against him: a battle ensued at the end of
which the Askia's troops were not able decisively to defeat
Konta's. The latter thus freed himself from the Askia's authority. That situation was to last until the end of Songhai. An
unsuccessful attempt at reconquest went on from February 5,
1516 to January 24, 1517.[30]
Three facts should be noted. Contrary to what is sometimes suggested, these expeditions were by principle directed
against foreign territories, for the reasons already given, not
against the sovereign's own subjects living within his realm.
This major political error was only very rarely committed in
desperation, by a few minor émigré kings. This was probably
the case with some of the Damels of Cayor, who were confined
within a relatively small, poor country, beyond whose borders
lay powerful, hostile kingdoms that it would have been out of
the question to attack.
Booty thus acquired was indeed a source of revenue.
Finally, Konta, the chief who won his freedom, was neither a civil servant nor an army leader who might have

mutinied, but the minor king of a foreign region which had
been annexed and thus regained its independence.

The Askia was the center of the administrative system, all
of whose workings were familiar to him. We have seen that he
made the appointments to all offices, some of which might go
to his son. He appointed the cadi, the generals, and so on. He
sometimes asked a functionary promoted to a higher office to
name his own successor. The Askia El Hadj (accession: August 7, 1582), after putting down a palace revolt, elevated the
kala-châ Denkelko, who had remained faithful to him, to the
office of hi-koï, in place of Bokar, who had betrayed him. To
the greatest satisfaction of the kala-châ, he then asked him to
name his successor: the new hi-koï did not hesitate to choose
his own son.[31]

Fees Connected with Assuming Administrative Offices

Appointments to the various offices, in the traditional
kingdoms, entailed the payment of a customary fee, not,
however, necessarily to the king. Thus, among the Mossi, the
"keeper of the sand" confirmed everyone in his respective
office, including the king, by giving him, according to a
religious ritual, a bit of sand from a hole specially prepared for
this purpose: the appointee then had to reward him with
something of value, varying with the importance of the office.
Here once again we see this aspect of the African social
structure, this aspect of the caste system: material wealth often
bypassed the chiefs and notables to pass into the hands of men
of the castes, skilled workers. No comparison with the feudal
system in which the lord kept everything. Later on, with the
profanation of the royal office, its secularization, this fee would
return to the king. Thus, in Songhai, at the time of the conflict
with Morocco, a Fondoko upon appointment was required to
turn over two thousand cows.[32]

GOVERNMENT AND ADMINISTRATION

Hostages

All the sovereigns of the Sudan found it politically and administratively wise to exact of the children of their vassals a variable term of service in the palace. Some of these young princes remained there all their lives as a sort of pages, obviously treated according to their rank, while others returned to their respective provinces after a number of years spent as hostages. Sâdi remarked that this custom lasted from the time of Mali until his own day, and was general throughout the Sudan.[33]

Thus, Ali-Kolon, the future Sonni Ali, was first hostage of the Mansa of Mali at the time his homeland, Songhai, was a vassal of Mali. It is known that, despite the precautions taken by his father's suzerain, he had to make good his escape so as to found the true Kingdom of Kaoga, whose borders, before his accession, did not extend beyond the suburbs of that city. The plan nurtured and executed by Sonni Ali proves, if proof were needed, that the measures taken by the Sudanese kings were not necessary. During this period of raising the sons of their vassals, they hoped to bring them to share their own ideas, to get them to identify closely with the interests of the kingdom, so that they would no longer feel themselves strangers obligated to fight against them out of filial devotion. This was the farsighted pursuit of a policy of strengthening the bonds between the various provinces and the cradle of the realm, an effort at integration after the annexation of a province. In exactly the same way in an earlier period, the Egyptian Pharaohs acted toward the sons of Asiatic princes who were their vassals from the time of the Eighteenth Dynasty onward, after the conquest of Thutmose III. This process of assimilation was thus not the least of the factors in the African governmental and administrative methods.

Songhai

The generals in Songhai were not necessarily slaves; they could be men of any class; likewise, the civil servants. The career of El Amin eloquently illustrates this fact. Under the Askia Mohammed he was only a simple hostler, a member of the royal cortège, one of those who, in turn, were called upon to saddle the king's horse. Askia Ismael promoted him to chief of pedestrians, or routemaster; he pursued these duties until Askia Daud came to power, when the latter made him a Djenné-Monzo or chief of the city of Djenné. Rising from the position of hostler to that of governor of one of the largest trading cities in the empire, can truly be called coming up in the world.[34]

The previously established barriers within the caste system, by division of labor, had now partially given way; we get the impression that one could, therefore, aspire to any position made possible by luck, intrigue, and merit. It must be remembered that the founder of the Askia dynasty, called Mohammed the Great, the Believer Prince, was only a lieutenant of Sonni Ali who usurped the throne after defeating his son, Bekr Dau (March 3, 1493). One important notion would seem to have vanished: that of legitimacy.[35] Any victorious leader is legitimate, as the facts prove: the numerous coups d'état throughout the history of Songhai. The people immediately recognized his authority; they held no rancor toward him. A royal branch was thus born and developed from a very lowly common stock; at the end of one generation it had acquired almost the same prestige as the other already-existing royal families. We thus witness the parallel development of several dynasties, rivals insofar as they are confined to certain relatively distinct families: a situation exactly identical to the one in Cayor in the seventeenth century, which may have been inherited from Songhai. The existence of the Kharejjite sect of Islam may not be unconnected to this state of affairs; this sect is characterized by its refusal to recognize any supreme authority for all Islam, any *caliph*, any sort of Muslim Pope, and by the fact that any believer, however modest his social origins, might be elevated to the rank of king if he otherwise possesses the requisite qualities. Sonni Ali nominally belonged to this sect.[36]

Various Ministries

The hierarchy of offices in Songhai was inflexible. The country was divided into provinces, cantons, villages, large cities of commercial character such as Djenné and Timbuktu, border areas which were strongholds such as Teghezza, Ualata, Nema, etc. A sultan or *fari* governed certain provinces, as might a *châ:* there was the Dendi-fari, the Kormina-fari, the Kala-châ. A *farba*, a *mondzo*, or a *koï* governed cities of different types and their immediate environs. There was the Timbuktu-koï, the Hi-koï, the Dirma-koï, the Hombori-koï, etc. The governor of the Ualata border area, with its dependencies, was a *farba* in the days of Mali: the equivalent term for *farba* in Songhai was *farma*. The border area of Teghezza on the Tropic was governed by a *mondzo*. The *balama* was a kind of supply officer; the title itself was older than that of Askia, according to Kâti.

The *assara-mundio* was a kind of police commissioner: viz., the *assara-mundio* of the city of Djenné or the city of Timbuktu.

The *anfara-kuma* was the traditional judge in pre-Islamic times. It was a hereditary office always held by members of the Kuma clan. They were *anfaras*, or judges, whence the term *anfara-kuma* which came to mean the cadi in Songhai. Kâti insists on the point that this is the inevitable adaptation of the traditional expression for an equivalent Arabic term after Islamization.

The *kan-fari* or *kormina-fari*, was a new office created by Askia Mohammed and occupied for the first time by his own brother, Amar Komdiago, who was *tondi-farma* under Ali

Ber: it corresponded to a veritable viceregency with Tendirma as its capital.

The *tunkoï, kuran,* and *soira* were subaltern military positions that might exist in a city such as Djenné.

The *Djenné-koï, Bani-koï,* and *Kora-koï,* were administrative and military chiefs of cities and regions; they thus had under their command a territorial guard.

The *Guimi-koï,* or *Gumei-koï,* was the port director.

The *Hi-koï* was responsible for ships and smaller craft.

The *Yobu-koï* was in charge of the market.

The *gari-tia* repaired saddles.

The *berbuchi-mundio,* or *mondzo,* was the administrator in charge of affairs concerning the Berabic Arabs.

The *koïra-banda mundio* was a suburban administrator of a city.

The *barei-koï* was the chief of etiquette and protocol.

The *uanei-farma* was the minister of property.

The *sao-farma* was the superintendent of forests.

The *lari-farma* was the superintendent of waterways.

The *koreï-farma* was in charge of affairs concerning the white minorities inhabiting the country.

The *tara-farma* was the cavalry chief.

The *tari-mundio* was the inspector of agriculture.

Certain offices could be held at the same time: one might be a *fari-mondzo.* The *fari* was above the *koï;* the *Hi-koï,* Ali Dudu, provisionally named *dendi-fari,* was obliged to go back to his old seat in the Assembly when he lost this title (as we have already seen). But the *koï* was above the *châ;* we have observed that naming a *kala châ* to the post of *koï* corresponded to a promotion. We will not repeat the description of official insignia and uniforms connected with these offices. The identity of the terms designating the administrative offices of Western Sudan would give evidence, if this were needed, of the earlier administrative unification of this region.

Administrative Unity

Delafosse pointed out that

in many parts of the Sudan the following terms were and still are in use: Fari, Farima, Farhama, Fama (Mande), Faran (Songhai), Fara (Haussa), Far-Ba (Wolof), all of which may derive from the root *Far,* meaning summit, apex, chief, prince, from which also derives the title of the Pharaohs.[37]

In Wolof, in fact, there exists beside the term *farba* that of *fari,* which is an imperial ephithet: *bur* meaning King; *bur-fari* meaning the supreme king, the emperor, the one whose power and greatness cannot be surpassed. The Egyptian term is not etymologically what Dalafosse suggests; it is formed from the plural of *per:* the wall of the house, and by extension the house of the Pharaoh. The meaning of *per* in modern Wolof is identical to that of *per* in ancient Etyptian. In Wolof, words beginning with *p* form their plurals by alteration to *f: Peul bi*—the Peul; *Feul yi*—the Peuls; *per mi*—the wall; *fer yi*—the walls; whence *fari.* We recall that if Pharaoh was derived from the Egyptian plural of *per,* it was because the king was customarily identified with the name of his house, which was a double house. Would this then suggest that the creators of the first West African states recollected an earlier political organization which, by way of Nubia, leads us back to Egypt? The ubiquity of this term in all African languages, the etymological explanations that can be offered, leave little room for doubt. If that were the case, a new light would be shed on this initial period of African history; it would no longer be a question of an absolute beginning, but rather of a continuation following emigration; there would then be nothing surprising in these monarchies' being constitutional from the start: their originators, instead of being creators *ex nihilo,* would have had the benefit of an earlier political experience. Thus it would be equally comprehensible that the forms of sociopolitical organization of the African states were related only to those of Pharaonic Egypt, and could finally be understood only in terms of them.

No insurmountable objections are raised by supposing it would be materially impossible to govern an empire the size of Europe or administer it without a minimum of bureaucracy. It is difficult to realize that, for fifteen hundred years, the Tunkas, Mansas, and Askias simply issued verbal orders and got verbal accounts and reports in return. The customs activities of the border areas, based on what we have just said, would presuppose some kind of precise accounting, just as the payment of taxes and other fees would seem to imply the issuing of receipts, especially to the peripatetic merchants at the markets of Timbuktu, Djenné, etc. The same held true with regard to relations of all sorts between the central authority and the various provinces, to allow administrative coordination. We shall see, in chapter VII, that writing had already long been part of daily life and that intellectual activity had reached a level barely conjecturable today. Epistolary correspondence was common: when Askia Mussa came to power, he wrote two letters, one to his brother Otsman, the other to the latter's mother, so as to avoid any eventual conflict.[38] The Askias who thus carried on private correspondence, did as much on the administrative and political levels. Sâdi and Kâti allow us to be sure of it. The concept of documentation and records clearly existed in the people's consciousness: the author of the *Tarikh es Sudan* stresses that he saw the original of the document addressed by the Sultan of Morocco to Askia Ishâq II, concerning the salt mines of Teghezza.[39] It was customary to accompany these missives with some token of authenticity, if they did not bear an inimitable seal: thus, when the Timbuktu-Koî decided to open the gates of his city to Sonni Ali, he made sure to send one of this boots with the messenger so that Sonni Ali might have proof positive of the authenticity and sincerity of the mission.[40] The existence of African archives will be confirmed by further data when we discuss education and child-rearing.

MILITARY ORGANIZATION

In mentioning above the numbers of men in the armies of Ghana and Songhai, we showed only the size of the imperial forces. The time has come to analyze the structure of these armies, their components, their weapons, their strategy, and even their tactics.

Structure

In Mali and Songhai, we know for certain, the king who appointed the generals was himself the commander-in-chief of the army and personally directed military operations, as would later the Dorobé Damels of Cayor. The *Tarikh es Sudan* points out that Askia El Hadj was never able to undertake an expedition during his entire reign, because at the time of his accession he contracted a disease that kept him from riding a horse. He was an exception, in sharp contrast to all the other Askias.[41]

In each kingdom, each nation, the army was divided into several corps assigned to the defense of different provinces, although under command of the civil authority. Thus, each provincial governor had at his disposal a part of this army to which he could assign tasks under the orders of a general whose powers were purely military. On the lower level, below the king, in political or administrative affairs, the distinction between civil and military powers was thus very clear. The king of Mali, when he conquered Songhai, Timbuktu, Zâgha, Mima, the Baghena, and the environs of that region as far as the Atlantic Ocean, had two generals under his command. One was responsible for the defense of the southern part of the empire, on the Mossi border, the other of the northern part at the edge of the desert. Their respective names were Sankar-Zuma and Faran-Sura. These were the titles corresponding to their military functions. Each of them had under his command a certain number of officers and troops.[42] The western borders of the state of Djenné, before the conquest of the city by Sonni Ali, were defended by the commanders of twelve army corps deployed in the country of Sana: they were specifically assigned to surveillance of the movements of Mali. The Sana-faran was their general-in-chief. We even know the family names of some of the officers under his orders: Yausoro, Soasoro, Mâtigho, Karimu, etc. Likewise, twelve commanders of army corps were assigned to the east of the Niger toward Titili.[43]

Among the Mossi, the Moro Naba whom tradition prohibited from leaving his capital, could not personally direct military expeditions: as a result, this became the task of the active generals. The Mossi conscripted everyone. When the danger had passed, each citizen returned to his home, his village; the army was then demobilized, except for a few security units.

In Songhai, beginning with the reign of Askia Mohammed, a distinction began being made between the people and the army. Instead of mass conscription, a permanent army was created; civilians who were not part of it could go about their business. During the reign of Sonni Ali, all able-bodied nationals were subject to enlistment.[44] The major divisions of the army were: knights, cavalry, foot soldiers, auxiliary bodies of Tuaregs, élite infantry regiments, the royal guard, and an armed flotilla.

Knights

The princes of Black Africa who could afford to outfitted themselves in complete or partial armor like that of the knights of the Western Middle Ages. After the accession of

Askia El Hadj, the *kormina-fari* El Hadj, on February 13, 1584, started a revolt with intent to seize power. But he failed: the Askia, who was well informed, made him take off the flowing boubous he was wearing; beneath he wore a coat of mail.[45] When *balama* Mohammed es-Sâdek revolted against Askia Mohammed Bano and in March 1588 attempted to march on Kaoga, the Askia, who came forth to challenge him to battle, wore an iron breastplate.[46] As it was extremely hot and the Askia was very fat, he died of the effects of his armor. The rebellious balama wore an iron helmet; when Omar-Kato threw a javelin at his head, it ricocheted off the helmet.[47]

Another sultan of Morocco, Mulay Ahmed, in December 1589–January 1590, renewed the request made by one of his predecessors about the mines of the Teghezza. Ishâq II, who was then Askia, reacted violently, and as a sign of defiance and a show of force sent the sultan an offensive letter, some javelins, and two iron boots.[48]

Complete knight's armor was thus in use, as we have seen: coat of mail and iron breastplate, helmet, boots, javelin . . . all of it. The African princes of Songhai were armed as knights. This practice was certainly not as widespread as in Europe, if only because of the climate, as shown by the death of Askia Bano, who died of suffocation.[49] The explorer Barth saw such knights in the kingdom of Bornu in more recent times, about 1850. It is likely that such armor came from Europe, as did certain fabrics; but no documents exist to prove it. It might have come into Africa from Spain. We may suppose that African blacksmiths made replicas from these models, better adapted to the climate, which could be worn either inside or outside clothing. The use of iron armor was common in Benin; the subjects appearing on the bronzes of the time as decoration were in the first instance real armor.

Cavalry

All other mounted soldiers of more modest birth and fortune formed the cavalry. They were armed with shields and

javelins. The cavalry was terrifyingly powerful, if we judge by
the panic that the clashing of its weapons caused in the
Moroccan ranks during the war against Morocco (June
1609).

What frightened the Moroccans most in this encounter was
the noise of the shields pounding aginst the legs of the horses
when they were galloping. The entire Moroccan army, chiefs
and soldiers, fled as far as Lake Debi, where the men were
thigh-deep in water. But having recognized the cause of their
terror, they left the water after having experienced the greatest
terror and the most extreme fear.[50]

Foot Soldiers

Foot soldiers were armed mainly with bows and arrows.
The infantry included a special élite corps, which was distinguished by the wearing of gold bracelets. Whatever the
fortunes of war, the members of this élite corps could not turn
their backs on the enemy: which is what happened at the end
of the first battle that Djuder, under orders of the Sultan of
Morocco, fought against Askia Daud on the left bank of the
Niger River. The army of Songhai was defeated because it had
no firearms. The whole élite corps allowed itself to be decapi-
tated rather than run away.

There also perished that day a large number of important
people among the foot soldiers. When the army was defeated,
they threw their shields on the ground and squatted on these
sorts of seats, awaiting the arrival of Djuder's troops, who
massacred them in this position without any resistance on their
part; this because they were not to flee in case of rout. The
Moroccan soldiers took the gold bracelets from their arms.[51]

The army had a band consisting of drums, trumpets
(*kakaki*, cf. *Tarikh el Fettach*, p. 136), and cymbals. When El
Hadj revolted, he marched on Kaoga to the sound of such
trumpets. "He had put on a breastplate and let the trum-
peters, drummers, and so on, march ahead of him."[52]

The war drum of the Damel of Cayor was called Djung-Djung. It was used to beat out the *bur dakha djap rendi*, a march signifying: "The king follows [the enemy], catches him, kills him." The auxilliary corps of the Tuareg vassals were composed essentially of camel-drivers; there must also have been an infantry armed with long javelins, marching ahead of the camels and fighting according to the Berber technique, as described by Bakri. The Tuaregs wore puffed trousers, a tunic, a turban, and a litham.

Flotilla

There existed on the Niger an entire flotilla no doubt composed of small boats equipped with outrigging—hence uncapsizable—like those found today on Lake Chad, Lake Victoria, and other large lakes of Central Africa. In case of war, this fleet was used for military purposes; the director of the port of Timbuktu or some other place where the battle took place then played a leading role. At the time of the war against Morocco, he was to hide the boats so Moroccan soldiers could not cross the river.

Mahmud [leader of the Moroccan army] then decided to march against Askia Ishâq. First of all he set about procuring boats, since the director of the port, Mondzo-El-Fa-uld-Zerka, had taken them all with him at the time of his flight toward Binka, when Askia Ishâq had demanded the evacuation of the city of Timbuktu.[53]

Those were the different corps that made up the African army of Songhai. They lacked one essential weapon, firearms; they did not have the time to acquire any because the very people who might have sold them to them, either manufacturers (Europeans) or intermediaries (Arabs), took advantage of this major weakness to try to conquer Black Africa. The first firearms sold to the Africans exploded in their hands.

Royal Guard

The king was surrounded by a very large body of guards in which the sons of vassal princes served side by side with other members of the nobility. Within this army, in which a lordly, aristocratic mentality reigned, the role of the griot assumed all its sociological significance. Through his songs, which were living accounts of the history of the country in general and the families whose members he addressed, he helped, he even forced the indecisive, fearful warrior to act bravely, and the brave to act like heroes, to perform miracles. His contribution to victory was very important: his bravery and often temerity were beyond question, for he too was as exposed to danger as the warriors whose exploits he celebrated; even at the height of battle, they needed to hear his exhortations which boosted their morale. The griots, then, were not superfluous beings; their usefulness was obvious: they had a "Homeric" social function to fulfill. The division of labor was thus valid at all levels of society. European conquest dimmed the interest to be found in the character of the griot, but it is impossible to give an historical account of the mentality of precolonial African armies without assessing his part in it. To a certain extent, he even held the fate of the princes in his hands. After having been lectured by his mother, Otsman had given up all idea of revolt and was once again determined to obey his brother who had become Askia Daud; he even loaded some boats with food, to go and do him homage at the head of his troops. But the feelings of pride awakened by the song of his griot as he was setting forth were stronger than his sense of discipline: he no longer deemed it necessary to rub dust on his head as a sign of obeisance to anyone:

> But almost immediately, as his griot began to sing, he went into such a fury that he almost burst with rage, and addressed his entourage, crying out, "Unload everything on the boats. Upon my life, the one speaking to you will no longer put any dust on his head for anyone."[54]

Strategy and Tactics

Strategy and tactics were quite different from one country to another; there were different ways of combining the attacks of cavalry and infantry. The use of scouts and encampments with tents was common.

Friday, the eighteenth of the month of Djomada First [April 15, 1588], Balama Mohammed es-Sâdeq camped with his troups at Konbo-Koraî. After his tent was put up, the Balama went inside and the first person who came to attack them was Mârenfa-El-Hâdj.[55]

The Askia Daud also camped before the walls of Timbuktu. "On his return, Askia Daud passed through Timbuktu and camped in this city in the square behind the mosque."[56]

They carried on long sieges, lasting for years, with consummate technique, in no way less expert than that of Agamemnon before Troy. This was the case in the siege of the city of Djenné by Sonni Ali. The cities were fortified by a system of ramparts, with a variable number of guarded gates. A fortified city was called a *tata*. "Djenné is surrounded by a rampart with eleven gates. Three of them were later sealed, so that only eight remain today."[57]

To conquer a city thus fortified, which never before had been subjugated, if we are to believe the *Tarikh es Sudan,* Sonni Ali laid a siege which lasted seven years and some months. His camp was set up at Zoboro, former site of the city; he left there each day to fight before the walls until evening. These battle scenes took place daily throughout the entire low-water season. When the water rose, surrounding the walls of the city, making it unapproachable, he withdrew with his troops to the place which today bears his name: Nibkatu-Sonni, or Sonni's Hill. While waiting for the water to recede, the troops cultivated the soil to produce their own food. Things continued in this way until, at the end of seven years, Djenné surrendered, chiefly for lack of supplies. During that time, the king had died and his young son had replaced him.

Sonni Ali treated the latter benevolently and married his mother.[58] After his death, the city of Djenné was to keep his horse's trappings in a kind of museum as relics. According to Kâti, however, the siege lasted only about six months, with some battles at night. Djenné was blocked, he reports, by four hundred warships. Since Sonni Ali reigned for only twenty-seven years, the duration of the siege indicated by Sâdi does appear excessive. Perhaps the truth lies somewhere between these two extremes (six months and seven years). Further research will enable us to come closer to the historical truth.[59]

The effects of surprise and secret missions were in common use. On August 21, 1563, Askia Daud ordered the fari-mondzo Bokar to go and fight Bani, a rebel chief in Barka land. Bani was very clever and had in the past given much trouble to the central power. The Askia resolved to keep secret the mission with which he had entrusted the fari-mondzo. The most unfavorable time of year for such a maneuver was chosen so as to overcome the vigilance of Bani, who could never have suspected that so many obstacles would be faced in order to reach him. The direction of the march also was unlikely: troops would go up into the mountains, from which they would then pour down, to the great surprise of the enemy who at most might have expected to see them lining up on the usual horizon. The fari's troops were kept completely ignorant of the goal and destination of the operation. Even the Askia's son, who was along on the expedition, was unable to learn the secret known only to the general, the fari-mondzo. Thus, Bani was defeated.[60]

Military demonstrations were also used. Askia Daud, for one, deployed his forces as far as Mossi and Lulami country without engaging in battle or pillaging, for the sole purpose of impressing his neighbors and taking away any desire they might have to venture into the interior of his lands.[61]

The *Tarikh el Fettach* also stresses the development of military science in Songhai. Its author underlines the difficulties of the kurmina-fari's expedition against Tenidda (Tengella, Tia-N'Della), king of Futa. Tendirma, the point of departure, was two months' march away; even so, the expedition was victoriously completed with a large army. The defeated enemy was put to death and the troops returned with a great deal of booty (March 8, 1513).[62]

Although the Cayorians were formidable warriors, their military tactics, until the accession of Lat Dior, seem not to have been so well regulated as in Songhai.

The knights charged in total anarchy, each one whenever he felt like it, after having gotten carefully "plastered" far in the rear; they felt that their noble station was incompatible with the idea of an organized command, especially when it was headed by a slave generalissimo, the *diaraff bunt ker*. The fact was, that they often arranged to let the foot soldiers take the first rounds of fire, the only ones that usually were fatal. The firearms the Cayorians had at the end of the Damel period were loaded with powder, pottery shards, and other small fragments of cast iron. It is easy to imagine that during a battle, the soldiers did not often have time to replace such loads. So, after the first rounds, what followed was nothing but fireworks, causing, at most, slight superficial burns. More than one brave knight chose such a moment to enter the fray, seeking out among the enemy knights a single personal adversary he might defeat; he fired his gun only when in sight of this enemy. He had sworn to do so on the eve of battle at the time of the "Khas": this was a ritual, often held at night, in which all the valiant warriors, plunging their lances repeatedly into a pile of sand they had surrounded, proclaimed their intended exploits for the next day.

It was Lat Dior who probably introduced mobile war into Cayor. Before the technical superiority of Faidherbe's armies, the Damel, who had accepted the teachings of the French school, knew how to adapt to the situation. Instead of putting forward the bulk of his army, he divided it into small corps, posted at strategic points; so it was a war of harassment, a guerrilla war he waged against Faidherbe. His men even dug individual holes in the ground, fully covered, with just one opening through which to aim a weapon: a surprise salvo thus greeted the arrival of the enemy on the scene; this was the tactic called *guedjo* (individual hole). This period of mobile war was called the "Time of the Werwerlo" (whirling). Lat Dior stalked Faidherbe's troops who were stalking his: so people wondered, with a touch of mockery, who was chasing whom.

JUDICIAL ORGANIZATION

In the traditional empire, justice was inseparable from religion. It was a compensatory punishment ritually administered to one who offended against social order.

With Islamization, the situation became more complex: it became more and more secular, although its foundation remained religious, to the extent that the Koran was everywhere adopted as the civil code: Ghana, Mali, Songhai.

However, there had always been throughout history two types of justice: royal justice and the justice of the cadi. The cadi was the Muslim judge appointed by the king; he handled mainly common-law misdemeanors, disputes between citizens, or between citizens and foreigners. These were the sorts of cases under the jurisdiction of the cadi of Ghana or Timbuktu. A tribunal was built for rendering justice. In Ghana, the procedures employed to make the accused confess were quite rudimentary; in cases of murder, or other crimes, or debts, the provost used the ordeal by water: the accused was brought before him rather than the king. A tribunal was built for the rendering of justice. The ordeal by water[63] consisted of steeping a piece of special wood in a given quantity of water which the accused was then made to drink: if he vomited this bitter brew, he was innocent. The ordeal by water was only a variant of the ordeal by fire practiced until present times in Black Africa, although prohibited by French law; the most recent case I know of occurred around 1936: it was at Djurbel, in Senegal, in the Baol. It consisted of heating till it was white hot a thin metal blade, usually a sort of old spike polished in earth, which each of the accused in turn had to lick: the guilty ones were those who had swollen or split tongues the following day; truly a barbarous method, in every way comparable to those employed in the Middle Ages, mainly in the Germanic judicial system. The guilty, of course, sometimes confessed in time; but how many of the innocent must have been victims! The most extraordinary fact about it is that several defendants undeniably underwent this ordeal with success. This can be explained only by a large dose of self-suggestion, due to the mystical religious conviction widespread among the common people, according to which the innocent "could not" be burned. One can imagine the terrible result that might occur when an innocent defendant of skeptical temperament was involved.

With the influx of merchants to Timbuktu and the development of the city's international character, it was eventually found necessary to name another judge, besides the cadi, of a clearly more profane character, qualified exclusively to settle disputes between foreigners or between foreigners and locals. One of them temporarily appointed, was Mohammed Baghoyô, a man of Wankoré origin, under Askia El Hadj.[64]

The cadis' intellectual level was very high, their sense of duty very acute. One fact concerning the reign of Askia Ishâq proves this. The Askia twice in vain offered the position of cadi to the jurist Abu-Hafs Omar, who refused it. Another jurist, Takonni, advised the Askia to threaten Abu-Hafs that he would appoint an ignorant man to the position, in which case, having so obstinately refused this office, Abu-Hafs would be responsible before God for the incompetence of all the judicial acts rendered. Only when reduced to this extreme did he accept and take office on February 1, 1585.[65]

A judge's house and a mosque were inviolable sanctuaries. The cadi could with impunity admonish the king; to the princes, he was the respected intercessor whose words were heeded. When Saïd Mâra was banished from society by Askia El Hadj, he got as far as the mosque, where he took refuge, implored and obtained the intercession of the cadi with the sovereign, and was granted a pardon.

A public crier announced the decisions of the cadi or the king when they affected the population at large. Common punishments were incarceration (there were prisons at Kanato, at Kabara near Timbuktu, and elsewhere), confiscation of goods, and bastinado, which might accidentally prove fatal. El Hadj's maternal uncle, who had organized a revolt against the Askia in favor of his nephew, died in this manner.

Crimes of lèse-majesté and high treason were under the jurisdiction of the king. Thus, Askia El Hadj insisted on himself judging all those who had participated in the conspiracy aimed at toppling him from the throne; the punishments he inflicted on the guilty, as he himself pointed out, were based on the degree of their involvement in the revolt and the rank of their social positions. The same was true under Askia Ishâq II, who condemned the Hombori-koî to be sewn alive into a bull's hide and buried in this way.[66]

With Askia El Hadj, we see how royal justice banned a person from society. Saîd Mara was to be led throughout the city, while a crier announced his outlawry: this meant that anyone could henceforth kill him with impunity, since no law any longer protected his life. It was while he was being turned over to the mob that he took refuge in the mosque, under the protection of the imam.[67]

In Mossi land, the Nakomsé (nobles) could be judged only by their peers, so to speak: the Moro Naba alone was qualified to do this.

When the king was on his throne to render justice, in any part of Africa, he was the only one allowed to wear headgear, the symbol of dignity and wisdom. The Pharoah of Egypt in the same position was referred to as the *Atef,* although Egyptologists have been unable to find an exact term to translate this word. If *Até* was a revised Egyptian verb, *Atef* would signify in Egyptian "he judges," assuming that this root meant "to judge." It is interesting to note that *Atef* in Wolof means "let one judge." Despite their very great importance, the cadis were dependent on the king. Whereas the *Tarikh es Sudan* gives us to understand that the one of Timbuktu was the most important of all, that all others were subordinate to him and he could remove them, the *Tarik el Fettach* is more categorical: it was Askia Mohammed who appointed all the cadis of his kingdom: "Thus it was that he appointed a cadi at Timbuktu, a cadi in the city of Djenné, and a cadi in each city of his territory which had one, from the Kanta to the Sibiridugu."[68]

The use of notarized documents was widespread. The author of the *Tarikh es Sudan,* for example, was asked to draw up a notarized inventory of the goods belonging to a convict, one Salti, when he went to prison, during the war with Morocco:

> Tuesday, when we entered the prison, we found the unfortunate Salti in a pitiful state. I read him the register of the inventory, and as he declared that this was indeed his entire fortune, we attested to it in writing on the register to vouch for its authenticity.[69]

The author was accompanied by another notary.

Ibn Battuta described the spirit of immanent justice in the people and the security which covered foreigners and their goods, two facts worthy of a society already open to international affairs.

> Acts of injustice are rare among them; of all the peoples, they are the one least inclined to commit any, and the Sultan (Black king) never pardons anyone who is found guilty of them. Over the whole of the country, there reigns perfect security; one can live and travel there without fear of theft or rapine. They do

not confiscate the goods of white men who die in their country; even though they may be of immense value, they do not touch them. On the contrary, they find trustees for the legacy among white men and leave it in their hands until the rightful benficiaries come to claim it.[70]

So wrote Battuta in 1352–53, at the time of the Hundred Years War, relating the good he found in the behavior of the Blacks.

In certain holy cities dominated by the clergy, such as Timbuktu, Diaba in Mali, Kundiûro in Diâra, the cadi had the right of pardon or punishment (life and death) over the accused. If Kâti is to be believed, the Mansa of Mali could not enter the sacred city of Diaba even if the murderer of his son had taken refuge there, because it was the city of God, where salvation was guaranteed to all fugitives.[71] Such must have been the case of N'Diaré, the holy city of the N'Diayé in Senegal.

Judges must often have been unpopular for quite human reasons; that explains the numerous refusals of appointments related by Kâti and Sâdi.

NOTES

1. Leroi-Gourhan, *op. cit.*, p. 100.
2. Al Bakri, *op.cit.*, "Route de Gahana á Ghîarou," pp. 34–36.
3. *Idem.*, "Description de Ghana et moeurs de ses habitants," pp. 327–328.
4. *Idem.*, "Route du Dera au pays des Noirs," pp. 309–318.
5. Ibn Khaldun, *op. cit.*, p. 112.
6. Al Bakri, *op. cit.*, "Route de Tademekka à Gahdamès," p. 341.
7. Ibn Khaldun, *op. cit.*, p. 111.
8. Delafosse, *Les Noirs de l'Afrique* (Paris: Ed. Payot, 1922), p. 62.
9. Ibn Khaldun, *op. cit.*, pp. 114–115.
10. Ibn Battuta, *op. cit.*, p. 10.
11. *Présence Africaine* magazine, No. XVIII–XIX, Feb.-May 1958, pp. 176–177.
12. Ibn Khaldun, *op. cit.*, p. 113.

13. Sâdi, *T.S.*, ch. XIII, p. 121.   14. *Idem.*, III, 14.
15. He was the first to assume the title of Dali, which, in African tradition, is the equivalent of Caesar.
16. Sâdi, *T.S.*, XII, 104.   17. *Idem.*,XVII, 178.   18. *Idem.*, XVI, 164.
19. *Idem.*, XVII, 174.   20. *Idem.*, V, 24.   21. *Idem.*, XIII, 121.
22. Ibn Khaldun, *op. cit.*, p. 107.   23. Sâdi, *T.S.*, VII, 40.
24. *Idem.*, XVI, 164.
25. Al Bakri, *op.cit.*, "Description de Ghana et moeurs de ses habitants," p. 330.
26. *Idem.*, p. 330.   27. Ibn Khaldun, *op. cit.*, p. 115.
28. Could Kaarta derive from Carthago? (See map p. 000.)
29. Al Bakri, *op. cit.*, p. 334.   30. Sâdi, *T.S.*, XIII, 129–130.
31. *Idem.*, XVIII, 193.   32. *Idem.*, XXVII, 298.   33. *Idem.*, II, 10–11.
34. *Idem.*, XVII, 171–172.   35. *Idem.*, XIII, 116–117.
36. *Idem.*, II, 12.   37. Delafosse, *Haut-Sénégal–Niger, op. cit.*
38. Sâdi, *T.S.*, XIV, 134–135.   39. *Idem.*, XXI, 216.
40. *Idem.*, VII, 40.   41. *Idem.*, XVIII, 185.   42. *Idem.*, IV, 20.
43. *Idem.*, V, 25.   44. *Idem.*, XIII, 118.   45. *Idem.*, XVIII, 190–192.
46. *Idem.*, XIX, 199.   47. *Idem.*, XX, 204.   48. *Idem.*, XXI, 216–217.
49. This also happened to the Crusaders on the roads of Palestine.
50. Sâdi, *T.S.*, XXVII, 301–302.   51. *Idem.*, XXI, 219–220.
52. *Idem.*, XVII, 191.   53. *Idem.*, XXI, 226.   54. *Idem.*, XIV, 136.
55. *Idem.*, XX, 203.   56. *Idem.*, XVII, 178.   57. *Idem.*, V, 23.
58. *Idem.*, V, 26–27.   59. Cf. Kâti, *T.F.*, ch. V, pp. 94–100.
60. Sâdi, *T.S.*, XVII, 175.   61. *Idem.*, XVII, 179.   62. Kâti, *T.F.*, III, 74.
63. Al Bakri, *op. cit.*, "Route de Ghana à Ghîarou," p. 335–336.
64. Sâdi, *T.S.*, XVIII, 190.   65. *Idem.*, *loc. cit.*   66. *Idem.*, XX, 205.
67. *Idem.*, XX, 207–208.   68. Kâti, *T.F.*, VI, 115.
69. Sâdi, *T.S.*, XXXIII, 360–361.   70. Ibn Battuta, *op. cit.*, pp. 19–20.
71. Kâti, *T.F.*, XVI, 314.

Chapter Six

ECONOMIC ORGANIZATION

Africa, in the eyes of the specialists, is depicted as a land which prior to colonization was only at the level of a subsistence economy: the individual, virtually crushed by the force of nature, was able to produce only what he absolutely needed to survive. No creation, no activity reflecting a society freed from material constraints might be found there. Exchange relationships were governed by barter. Notions of money, credit, stock market, thrift, or accumulation of wealth by individuals belong to a type of commerce connected with a higher economic organization: they could not have been found at the alleged level of African economy.

Seldom has an opinion been so little founded on fact. This one arose from a preconceived idea of African societies: they had to be specifically primitive, therefore endowed in every respect with systems characteristic of such a condition.

BARTER

Undeniably, at the periphery of the African kingdoms, some backward tribes, such as the Lem-Lem in Southwest Ghana, perhaps on the banks of the present-day Falémé River, had been carrying on barter trade since the Carthaginian period.[1] Herodotus attests to this. That situation remained inflexibly unaltered until the twelfth century, as corroborated by the accounts of Arab travelers, e.g., Ibn Yakut. For these peoples, in every way comparable to the still-unassimilated barbarians who roamed on the outskirts of the Roman Empire, the notion of merchandise in the modern sense was probably unknown: barter was the foundation of all their commercial activity. After crossing the desert separating Ghana from Upper Senegal, the Arabs reached the banks of the Falémé, unloaded their goods in small bunches (varied products from the Orient), gave a signal, and then retreated; the Africans then came out and in front of each bundle placed the quantity of gold dust they judged it to be worth, then withdrew. The Arabs came back and collected the gold if they found the amounts satisfactory; if not, the cycle was repeated, still without any direct contact. Sociologists and ethnologists agree that commerce conducted under such conditions excludes any awareness of merchandise: the gold in this instance is not even money, but a local product which is traded for goods or other materials not native to the country.

These tribes living in a virtually closed society had much less need for the glittering Oriental baubles to improve their living conditions than did the Carthaginian and Arab traders for the gold they "harvested." One may assume, therefore, from the very fact that they were in a less developed state, that the honesty governing these exchanges came from them; they imposed it, from the start. If they were swindled, they could, without loss to the essentials of their life, suspend relations with any given group of traders so identified.

This was the nature of commerce along the borders of the kingdom. Only by applying it, in a misguided generalization, to all the rest of the continent, could one reach the abovementioned theories.

MODERN-TYPE COMMERCE

In actuality, there was another form of commercial activity, already modern in type, that was much more extensive, covering all of the kingdoms. It was carried on by the best organized and most dynamic elements of society, by those, in a word, who were already detribalized. There were already entire merchant classes in the empire of Ghana and Songhai. The *Tarikh es Sudan* alludes to their activities in the already-international centers of Timbuktu and Djenné.[2]

The density of Niger River traffic between these two cities at that period could never be suspected today. Kabara was the true military and commercial port through which all goods were exported from Timbuktu, to Djenné, Mali, and the Upper Niger in general, or Tirekka, Gao, and Tademekka, Kukia and the Dendi country, that is, present-day Upper Dahomey (Benin). According to the *Tarikh el Fettach*, entire groups were devoted to commerce:

> If you ask what difference there is between the Malinke and the Uangara, know that the Uangaras and Malinkes share the same origin, but that Malinke is used to designate the warriors, whereas Uangara serves to indicate the merchants who carry on trading from one country to another.[3]

Bakri likewise informs us that the Nunghamarta were a group of traders who exported gold from Iresni, on the Upper Senegal, to all countries. This city is very close to the gold-bearing stronghold of Ghiaru, previously mentioned.[4] After the destruction of Carthage by Scipio Africanus Minor, the Roman expedition which pursued the fleeing Carthaginians to discover where they got their gold, reached this point, the source of the Bambuk (the name given by the Romans to the Senegal River).

The existence of whole groups devoted to commerce (the ancestors of the present-day Djula and Sarakolle) being confirmed, there remains to be defined the type of exchange they practiced. The characteristics of modern economic activity could already be detected in it: the existence of money, a well-defined tariff system, and cosmopolitan commerce centers throughout each country. In addition to the two previously mentioned cities, Timbuktu and Djenné, known as far as Asia and Europe, there were Biru, Soo, Ndôb, Pékès,[5] and so on. In all these centers foreign nationals had their own quarters in which they could live in the utmost security with their goods, while pursuing their business.[6] For the most part these were Arabs from North Africa, Egypt, and Yemen, and Europeans, especially Spaniards. Some of them were even students in Timbuktu, as will be seen later. Black Africa was hospitable to foreigners. We already know that the king of Djenné wished for there to be more foreigners than natives in his capital, but his last wish—the last of three—was "that God might weary all those who had come only to peddle their wares, so that, bored with staying in this place, they might sell their shoddy goods at bargain prices, to the benefit of the inhabitants."[7]

CURRENCY

Economic concerns existed on all levels. The sale of goods was strictly regulated: there were fixed market days. The economic officer of the city then levied taxes in the name of the king; they might be paid in either goods or cash, especially in Timbuktu. As earlier observed, an appropriate duty was placed at the border on all goods imported or exported.[8]

The currency used consisted of salt, cowries, or gold in either dust or pieces (of foreign or local mintage). It at first glance might appear astonishing that blocks or pieces of salt of different sizes should constitute a currency. It must be remembered in this regard that certain substances such as salt and copper were as rare in Africa at that time as gold was abundant; indeed in certain regions copper jewelry was more highly prized than that of gold; in ancient times, gold was less expensive than copper in Nubia, that is, the Sudan, of which Khartoum is the present capital. According to Bakri, salt was worth its weight in gold among the people he calls El Feruin, who were said to be in Northern Senegal in the vicinity of the Lake of Guiers.[9] The value assigned to any substance is always in terms of its rarity. Thus, cowries which came from the Indian Ocean via Persia, according to Leo Africanus, could serve as currency. It was, therefore, not a matter of backward peoples unable to conceive and produce coins of gold or other metals, for, as we shall see, such coinage was very widespread in Black Africa at the time.

As for gold dust, a conventional quantity of approximately 4.6 grams (probably more often measured than weighed) constituted what was called the *mitkâl* of gold dust; this was the gold standard, in the strictest modern sense of the term, on the basis of which minted coins (whose composition might be adulterated with nonprecious metals), as well as cowries, were exchanged. The *mitkâl*, depending on the rates of exchange, was worth anywhere from 500 to 3,000 cowries, available documents inform us.[10]

Obviously, all this was relative to prevailing conditions. A gold-dust standard was used because in this form the metal was more difficult to adulterate.

Identical weights of gold or heavier ones were effectively turned into coins with embossed designs at mints, for commercial exchange purposes, as evidenced by this passage from Idrisi, about gold collection among the Lem-Lem:

> When the river returns to its bed, everyone sells his gold. The bulk of it is bought by the inhabitants of Wardjelan [in present-day Libya] and by those from the tip of West Africa, whither this gold is transported to the mints, coined into dinars, and traded commercially for goods. This is how it happens each year. This is the principal product of the land of the Blacks; great and small, they make it their livelihood. In the country of the Uangara there are flourishing cities and renowned fortresses, its inhabitants are wealthy; they possess gold in abundance, and receive the products brought to them from the other remotest portions of the earth. They attire them-

selves in robes and other kinds of raiment; they are altogether black.[11]

One remark made by Bakri about the Berbers of Tademekka indicates that coins without markings must have been rather rare in Africa. After having described the kind of prostitution customary among them (the women grabbing hold of strangers), he gets around to mention of the sort of money they used: "The dinars they used were of pure gold and were called *sola* [bald] because they bore no imprints."[12] Thus these documents allow us to be sure of the use in Black Africa of imprinted gold coins, without, however, being able to know whether such imprints were effigies of local emperors or kings, or to know whether there was any generalized imperial currency minted apart from the *mitkâl* standard. The situation must have been comparable to that of the Greco-Latin city-kingdoms after the invention of money by the Lydians in the sixth century B.C.; among other peculiarities, each of these cities had its own system of measures and, as a result, its own urban coinage stamped with the city's coat of arms; there existed no accepted relation of the exchange value of these currencies. According to the *Tarikh el Fettach*, Askia Daud "was the first to build financial depositories and even libraries."[13]

So there existed in West Africa a whole gamut of currencies usable according to the value of the goods purchased. There was even a curious sort of currency in the form of squares of fabric (four spans to each side) manufactured in the textile center of Terenka, on the Upper Senegal, according to Bakri; these squares, called *chigguiya*, were in use at Silla, also on the Senegal, along with other currencies such as salt, copper rings, and *dora*, a cereal.[14]

The *Tarikh es Sudan* mentions, in describing the poverty resulting from the Moroccan occupation of Timbuktu, the existence of a "stock exchange" in that city: "The exchange rate fell to 500 cowries . . ."[15]

A remark by Ibn Haukal attests to the use of acknowledgment of debts in writing and at the same time gives an idea of the enormous wealth of the country: he saw a text in which an inhabitant of Sijilmasa acknowledged his indebtedness to a citizen of Aoudaghast in the sum of 40,000 dinars. To the author of *The Book of Roads and Kingdoms,* such an occurrence was unique in the trading world of the tenth century. Even in Baghdad, the capital of the Orient, one could find nothing like it.[16] So Africa was distinguished in the world for its legendary wealth which led the Arabs to say: "Against the camel's mange use tar, and against poverty make a trip to the Sudan."

IMPORT-EXPORT

The exported materials were gold, iron, tin, etc. Domestically, commerce in cola nuts, cereals such as *dora,* and millet from which a kind of beer was fermented, was active; the same was true for weaponry: spears, javelins, arrows, bows, etc. As for manufacture, one might mention the glass industry which had made extraordinary strides in Benin. Commerce between East Africa and India and China was no less active in the tenth and eleventh centuries. In that region, contrary to common opinion, the tribal stage was outgrown: the land was united into one great monarchy under the Monomotapa. Metals, gold, tin, copper were exploited largely for his own personal gain, according to well-established procedures. Organization of the work was very advanced. Experts have estimated the quantity of tin mined at Rockpoort as approximately thirty thousand tons. The experts went to the East and the Chinese Far East through the port of Sofala. There was a whole merchant class; its conflicts with the Arab immigrants are described in a book by Burueg Bin Shariya entitled *Of the National Pride of Negroes and Their Disputes with White*

Men. All of these facts concerning East Africa are taken from a study by M. A. Jaspan.[17]

In West Africa, the products imported were wheat, raisins, figs, Saharan salt, cowries, copper, dates, henna, olives, tanned hides, silk, cloth, brocade, Venetian pearls and mirrors, and so on. Tobacco was probably introduced into Muslim West Africa at this time.[18] Other products such as gum, gummiferous mimosa, cucurbitaceae, and euphorbiae added to the trade. Bakri tells of a strange plant that existed at the time: it yielded a kind of fireproof wool that was woven into clothing; it was called *turzi.* But among the Berbers there was a stone possessing the same properties when softened. So we may well conclude that this strange product was asbestos, rather than a plant. The Berbers from the region of Tademakka and the Blacks of Bornu locally mined a kind of agate that was sold as far away as Ghana: in the Sudan it is made, up to the present day, into necklaces and pendants of impressive size. Along the Senegal River, according to Bakri, whips of worldwide reputation were made of hippopotamus hides.[19]

MEANS OF TRANSPORTATION, ROADS

The usual method of transportation in the interior of Black Africa was on a donkey, ox, camel, or "mongrel" horse, where there were no navigable waterways. Connection to the Mediterranean and Egypt, across the Sahara, was made by camel caravans. It is important to stress that this commercial initiative was taken by Arabs and not by Africans, who traded only at the domestic markets of Djenné, Timbuktu, Waleta, Aoudaghast, Gao, and so on. It seems that the wealth of the continent always made it unnecessary for its inhabitants to risk the dangers of the high seas or the great international routes for commercial purposes. Likewise, in ancient times, Ethiopians and Egyptians virtually never left their homelands.

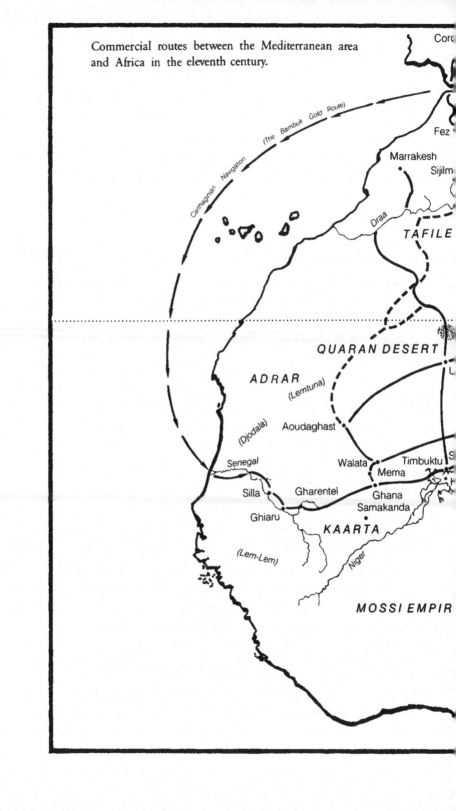

Commercial routes between the Mediterranean area and Africa in the eleventh century.

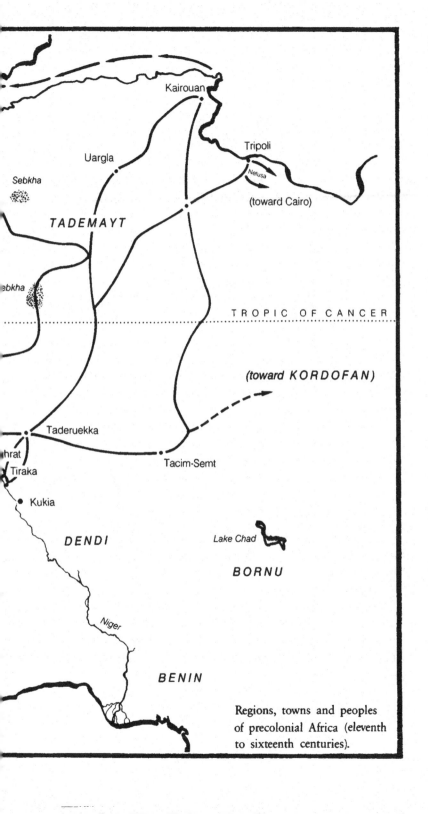

Kairouan

Tripoli

Uargla

Sebkha

Nefusa

(toward Cairo)

TADEMAYT

ebkha

TROPIC OF CANCER

(toward KORDOFAN)

Taderuekka

hrat

Tiraka

Tacim-Semt

Kukia

DENDI

Lake Chad

BORNU

Niger

BENIN

Regions, towns and peoples
of precolonial Africa (eleventh
to sixteenth centuries).

Egypt possessed all the technical means and material resources to assure her mastery of the seas; but throughout the course of her history she left it to her cousin, Phoenecia. Except for a few solitary navigators, mentioned in tales and legends, not until the Eighteenth Dynasty did she build a fleet on the Red Sea. Egypt was born and remained an essentially continental power. Neither she nor Nubia ever became trading nations.

One might suppose that, during the precolonial period, West Africa was not technologically capable of taking to sea, and attempt to explain in this way the absence of African maritime commerce created by local initiative. Some documents which we will quote below prove that this point of view is not acceptable. Even if it were, there was nothing in any case to prevent the peoples of the African empires from establishing camel caravans, as the Arabs did, and transporting their wares to the shores of the Mediterranean. All the technological conditions required for the Africans to develop caravans and become international traders by crossing the Sahara were at hand. But they never did so, because economic abundance and their own social structure obviated this necessity. So the dromedary has remained to this day in the use of Arab traders alone; it is the ideal animal for crossing the desert. This is why: not only can it endure thirst, but it is able to store in its body hundreds of liters of water which if need be can be restored to a more or less drinkable condition by slaughtering the beast. In this way, camel-drivers have with them a ready supply of meat and water.

According to Ibn Battuta, the roads in the interior of Africa were absolutely safe: "Having decided to visit the latter city [Mali], I hired but one Messufite to serve as my guide since there is no need to travel by caravan, for the roads are that secure."[20]

From the documents left by Bakri, we can describe the network of routes that connected Black Africa with the Mediterranean and the Orient, its complexities, and the traveling conditions of the caravans. Along most of the routes there were few wells of drinking water: it took several days' travel to reach one. One can see on the map that two principal routes connected the South Sahara with Black Africa: one of them went from Wadi Draa to Aoudaghast; the other started out from Sijilmasa and went to Tamedelt and Uanu, which was a crossroads for all the routes leading to Black Africa. It took fifty-one days from Sijilmasa to Aoudaghast. The wells along them were, for the former, Tezamet, Bîr el Djemmalîn, and Nalili; and for the latter, Camel-drivers' Well or Bîr el Djemmelîn . . . The trip took two weeks from Aoudaghast to the imperial capital of Ghana; from Ghana to Silla, along the Upper Senegal, the caravans took twenty days; from Ghana to Gao, two weeks; from Ghana to Augham, probably five days; from there to Ras Elma, four days; from this center to Tiraka, on the Niger, six days; from Gao to Tademekka, nine days were required; from there to Ghadamès across the desert, forty days; from this crossroads to Tripoli, eleven days; and, finally, from Ghadamès one went to Kairouan.[21]

ECONOMIC WEALTH

From the economic point of view, Africa is characterized by abundance. Travelers of the precolonial era encountered no poverty there; according to the *Tarikh el Fettach*, the emperor of Ghana, seated upon a "platform of red gold," daily treated the people of his capital to ten thousand meals.[22] Such material comfort resulted in an increase in demographic density scarcely imaginable today: in the region of Djenné alone there were 7,077 villages.

The following fact is enough to give us an idea of the proximity of these villages one to another. If the sultan, for example, wishes to summon a person inhabiting a village situated in the neighborhood of Lake Debo, his chosen messenger betakes himself to one of the gateways of the ramparts and, from there, cries out the message he has been charged to convey. The people, from village to village, repeat this call and the message immediately reaches the intended party who goes to the convocation sent to him. No need for further demonstration to show how densely this territory is populated.[23]

Under the Askia El Hadj a census taken by a group of students which lasted three days established that Gao consisted of 7,626 blocks of houses of solid construction (clay?), not counting straw huts.[24]

It has been estimated that the slave trade swallowed up one hundred to three hundred million individuals, dead or shipped to America. So, had it not been for slavery, the total figure of Black population on the continent would probably have been four times what it now is: it would have been in the vicinity of four hundred million. The *Tarikh es Sudan* stresses how exceptional poverty was in Black Africa when describing that caused by the Moroccan occupation of Timbuktu:

> The high cost of food in Timbuktu was excessive; a great number of people died of hunger and the famine was such that people ate the corpses of draft animals and of human beings. The exchange rate fell to 500 cowries. Then the plague came in turn to decimate the population and killed many that the famine had spared. This high cost of food, which lasted two years, ruined the inhabitants, who were reduced to selling their furniture and utensils. All the elders were unanimous in saying that they had never seen such a calamity and that not one of the elders before them had ever told them of anything like it.[25]

COMPARISON OF SOCIO-ECONOMIC STRUCTURES IN AFRICA AND EUROPE

The time has now come to examine the passage from feudal production to capitalist production in Europe, to see whether such a development, such a transformation occurred in the African economy of the corresponding period. And if not, why not?

Karl Marx showed in *Das Kapital* that the feudal organization in the countryside and the corporations in the cities for a long time kept the money-capital, resulting from usury and commerce in the Middle Ages, from being transformed into industrial capital. The upheaval which was to give birth to modern capitalism, according to the same author, began at the end of the fifteenth century and developed with increasing intensity during the sixteenth, especially in England. Royalty and parliament went to war against the feudal lords to try to win back central authority. In increasingly difficult circumstances, the lords successively got rid of everything superfluous in their lives; that meant liquidation of the "lordly entourages," and the abandonment of pomp in court life. Then came the first exodus of country folk to the cities. Overnight, there was thus created a proletariat without either hearth or home, whose numbers would go on increasing even more for other reasons. Against the violent repression of king and parliament, the lords reacted by progressively confiscating the lands of all the peasants who were tilling the soil under "feudal tenure": serfdom was no more. Those formerly bound to the soil were now independent peasants, at most paying some fixed tribute to the lord. Then these peasants in turn were driven into the cities. The movement of expropriation spread to the ecclesiastical communal domains by a system of "enclosure," which consisted purely and simply of annexing the lands adjoining the lord's domain by putting a fence around them. The lords had in fact found that, due to the prodigious development of the manufacture of woolens in Flanders, it was henceforth more profitable to turn all the arable lands into pastures for raising wool-bearing sheep.

Later, some domains of the Scottish highlands would be turned into hunting forests, for profit. "Of cities and townes

... pulled downe for sheepe-walks, and no more but the lordships now standing in them ... I could saie somewhat."[26] Conditions suitable for the birth of capitalism had been created. For this system to appear, as Marx says, there must be a separation between work and working conditions, making a true class of wage-earners, in the modern sense of the term. Before expropriation, the peasant family tilling the soil at the same time carried on a whole range of artisanal activities, constituting cottage industry: they wove their clothes from the flax they harvested, and manufactured most of the things they needed. In becoming a wage-earner, the peasant no longer had anything but the strength of his labor to sell to urban manufacturers or country farmers: he could no longer produce at home the things he needed for domestic use, but had to buy them as manufactured products on the home market which the capitalist circuit had established between countryside and city.

A man who, to begin with, inherited or could borrow enough money, might go the country and sublet from the lord a part of his land: he became a farmer to whom the land was "leased." His capital was all he had to work with. In a second phase, he might hire hands to work his land: he became the rural capitalist supplying raw materials to feed the industries of the cities. From him, the manufacturer would get the flax for his weaving; the one and the other found it to their interest to pay the lowest possible wages for the greatest amount of work: no matter that working conditions might be inhumane, that workers might become "alienated." This form of economic activity would constantly be dominated by the goal of profit and superprofit. It would not take long for the importance of manpower to be minimized by the introduction of the machine. The capitalist system thus appears better suited to the development of applied science than had been the one based on domestic economy which it had just destroyed. The use of machinery was limited and unnecessary in the latter, because there was no concern with profit and productivity in the capitalistic sense of the term. So it would seem to be more judicious to explain the development of mechanization by the needs of capitalist production, rather than to justify the system as being a consequence of the use of machinery. The needs of the new home market thus created, with its peculiar structure, and those of the world market, resulting from the great voyages of discovery, would constantly stimulate the economic activity of the European countries: the modern type of trading country had thus been created, the very type whose wealth excludes that of the people.

Of course, the newly created proletariat was not entirely and automatically absorbed by industry; but it was subject to the law of supply and demand. The unemployment which resulted turned a great many individuals into vagabonds, thieves, or vagrants, as they were called. This ever-increasing flood of unemployed hands finally frightened the masters of industry, although they had at first seen it as a happy divine intervention intended to make the economy prosper. The parliaments of the different European countries soon began to consider it the germ of future revolutionary troubles. There was, as yet, no experience of modern revolutions: it had not yet been sufficiently realized that in order to be revolutionary, it was not enough to be numerous and malcontented, but that organization and education were required. So a panic, as widespread as it was unadmitted, took hold of the parliamentary legislators and led them to pass laws so terrible, so coercive that it is hard for us to imagine them today. In 1530, in England, under the reign of Henry VIII, a vagrant picked up for the second time was whipped and had half an ear cut off; taken for a third time, he was "to be executed as a hardened criminal and enemy of the common weal."[27] Seventy-two thousand vagrants were thus executed during that reign. In the time of Edward VI (1547), "if anyone refuses to work, he shall be condemned as a slave to the person who denounced him as an idler."[28] The owner of such a slave might whip him, chain him, and brand him on cheek and forehead with a letter S (for

Slave), if he disappeared for two weeks. If he ran away a third time he was executed.

The master can sell him, bequeath him, let him out on hire as a slave, just as any other personal chattel or cattle. If the slaves attempt anything against the masters, they are also to be executed. Justices of the peace, on information, are to hunt the rascals down.[29]

An idler caught on the highway was branded on the chest with a V (for Vagrant) and returned to his native city, whose slave he became, doing municipal work without pay, held in irons. If he gave the name of a false city, he was nonetheless made its slave, marked with an S. Inhabitants of the said city were allowed to take possession of his offspring, present and future, and keep them as apprentices until the age of twenty-four for boys and twenty for girls. If the latter tried prematurely to take their freedom, they automatically became the slaves of their employers, who whipped and chained them. They had the right to weld on the neck, arm, or leg of the slave an iron ring, as a distinctive mark to keep him from escaping. Slaves of towns or parishes subsisted into the nineteenth century, under the name of roundsmen, as Marx points out.

The same laws remained in force under the reign of Elizabeth (1572). An eighteen-year-old vagrant, arrested for the second time, was to be executed "unless some one will take them into service for two years . . ." Under the reign of Queen Bess "rogues were trussed up apace, and in one year commonly . . . three or four hundred were . . . devoured and eaten up by the gallowes."[30] The situation was exactly the same under James I: idlers were branded with the letter R (for Rogue) on their left shoulders. Only in 1715 was this legislation abolished in England. Similar laws existed in France. Until the beginning of the reign of Louis XVI,

> every man in good health from 16 to 60 years of age, if without means of subsistence but not practising a trade, is to be sent to the galleys. Of the same nature are the statute of Charles V for the Netherlands (October, 1537), the first edict of the States

and Towns of Holland (March 10, 1614), the "Plakaat" of the United Provinces (June 26, 1649), etc.[31]

Because of all these European-originated deportations, it can be asserted without exaggeration that present-day America is populated in part by citizens of slave (or indentured) origin, whether they be white or black.

To conclude, we must recall the terrible conditions under which child labor was exploited, the one-sided legislation on wages that was constantly intended to favor the employer.

Thus the capitalistic ownership of the social means of production by the few was the negation and superseding of the "dwarf property" of the earlier domestic economy. According to Marx, in the latter, because of the excessive spreading of the means of production among an infinite number of individuals, there was no possibility of cooperation in production on any large scale, nor of the

. . . division of labour within each separate process of production, the control over, and the productive application of the forces of Nature by society, and the free development of the social productive forces. It is compatible only with a system of production, and a society, moving within narrow or more or less primitive bounds. To perpetuate it would be, as Pecqueur rightly says, "to decree universal mediocrity."[32]

The accidents of European history which led to the systematic expropriation of the peasants are not general laws. But without this phenomenon of expropriation, capitalism would not have come to be. One would therefore like to know the immutable sociological laws which explain the necessary passage from the stage of domestic economy to capitalism, in all societies; to know why India, China remained for millennia in relative stagnation, despite the terrible poverty which existed in those countries; why the industrious population of Japan, with its great density which necessitated microcultivation, did not undergo an identical evolution; why the politico-social balance of Africa was broken only at contact with an external influence. To what degree does the ideological superstructure constitute, for some social structures, an iron collar equivalent to an immense weight holding down the society for some unpredictable period, thus outweighing for a long time such material factors as poverty?

Modern capitalism, wherever it may be found, is a European export and not the result of natural local evolution. We may therefore regret that there is no precise answer to these questions to be found in *Das Kapital*. The latter indicates only that when this industrial regime of small independent producers reaches a certain stage of development,

> it brings forth the material agencies for its own dissolution. From that moment new forces and new passions spring up in the bosom of society . . . It must be annihilated; it is annihilated. Its annihilation, the transformation of the individualised and scattered means of production into socially concentrated ones, of the pigmy property of the many into the huge property of the few . . . this fearful and painful expropriation of the mass of the people forms the prelude to the history of capital.[33]

No writer until this date has ever attempted to evaluate correctly the "stage" after which the material agencies of dissolution are engendered so that the necessary historical transformation can take place. Domestic industry is the thesis, capitalism is the antithesis, but the dialectical link, the path inexorably leading from the one to the other, has not been recognized and described in satisfactory fashion for all societies. At any rate, it goes without saying, some societies today can be spared the capitalist phase.

Precolonial Africa, was, then, at the stage of "pigmy property." The peasant family wove its own clothing; Bakri tells us that each house had its own spinner. Obviously, the division of labor reflected by the caste system did not allow the manufacture of everything that was needed: all one could do was work in the craft allowed for his caste. For everything else, they had to turn to the open market, sometimes by barter, but in general by actual purchase for money. This system which precluded competition with others in their professions constituted a true monopoly: each caste monopolized an economic activity, sanctified by tradition. The same frame of mind was to be found in the European corporations or guilds of the Middle Ages. However, it seems that they had not gone so far as to form professional associations for the defense of group interests: the living tradition was amply sufficient to guarantee that. Therefore, no separation between domestic industry and agriculture, a separation prerequisite for the appearance of capitalism.

We have seen that the term "property" implied different realities from Europe to Africa, where appropriation of the land was concerned. In Africa, it would be more precise to speak of use of the land, even in the so-called royal domains. The accent was placed rather upon the "human domain" of the king working these lands; enumeration of the different families of captives was what expressed the wealth of a personage. The African king, however powerful, was easily persuaded that the soil did not belong to him; this is especially applicable to emigrant kings: they easily accepted the sacred authority of the original occupants, even if the latter were presently without any material power. This explains the deference of the powerful king of the Mâcina to one of the local princes of the Mima region, the Tukifiri-sôma.

> Before him, the king of the Mâcina had to remain standing, cover himself with dust while swearing fidelity to him, and remove his boubou to drape himself in it; . . . The title of this prince has survived to this day, but the one who now bears it has fallen from power and can only walk, having no steed; his authority has vanished, but his title remains . . . The king of the Mâcina still goes to visit this personage, asserting that this brings him good luck; he consults him and asks him to pray for him; he dismounts to salute him and visits him at the place where his ruined capital used to be.[34]

This singular personage so described is the former sovereign, still the master of the soil, in the ritual sense of that term; he is the one who allots lands to newcomers, without first consulting the king. He has received the land in trust; he never sells it—he would not dare to do so for religious reasons—he allots only the use of it. The sale of land, properly speaking, seems to have been unknown in traditional precolonial Africa. To grasp the historical peculiarities of the country, one would have to imagine a victorious Julius Caesar showing similar deference to Vercingetorix, the vanquished autochthonous prince, the original occupant of the land. We might go even further and observe that, in truth, the problem of land ownership appears never to have existed in Africa. Instead of land having constituted a wealth beyond the reach of certain social categories, it was within everyone's grasp, with no need to forfeit one's freedom, like the serf bound to the soil, in order to make use of it, to "possess" it. The slave had his own patch of ground; the stranger who just this morning came to the village would also get his. Expropriation of the sort seen in sixteenth-century Europe was unthinkable in the history of precolonial Africa. Perhaps, it was the vast expanse of arable lands that shielded Africa from this social problem. So Africa never had the rural capitalist who was the farmowner acting as intermediary between the true owner of the soil and the expropriated agricultural wage-earner.

NAVETANISM

The category of peasants called *navetânes* in Wolof do not constitute a class: its members do not know one another, are not bound by any traditional group solidarity; they are mobile because, in the main, they are young bachelors who go away to look for work so as to accumulate a dowry with which they can return to marry in their villages and settle down permanently. Navetanism is thus a transitional stage in the life of a young man: he goes away with the permanent intention of one day returning home. He is no man's slave, no contract could permanently bind him to the land of any lord. The root of the word in Wolof means, literally, "to spend the winter," i.e., the "rainy season"; contracts automatically end with that season and are renewable only by agreement.

Drought and progressive exhaustion of the soil are the principal reasons impelling young men of a particular village to spend the rainy season in a region with more water, not yet exhausted by cultivation, in a word, better endowed by nature. Since the desert is creeping into Black Africa from north to south above the Equator, these peregrinations follow the same direction. It was drought which brought about the dispersion of the inhabitants of the former capital of Ghana and the entire region of the Ouagadou. It also caused the successive retreats on the left bank of the Senegal River. Many of the people of the Djambur and Cayor regions, today half desert, withdrew toward the Baol, while the inhabitants of that area, especially the peasants, went off in the direction of Sine Salum, the British Gambia, and Casamance, all regions located farther south and decidedly more humid. Only the powerful attraction of Dakar's economic pole was able to swing this tide westward, insofar as Senegal is concerned. The peasants who thus escaped the hard and monotonous seasonal rhythm of local economic life, ended up by settling in the suburbs of that city, although that was not their original intention: they had come with the idea of returning home as usual. Once settled there, under the changed living conditions, they gradually lost their peasant attitudes as they found work at the docks or in various urban industries, and this finally made them aware of the fact that they were workers. Thus, a phenomenon of growing proletarianization.

THE TAALIBÉ

The set of mind of the *taalibé* (the believer) in the Murid, Tidjane, and other communities carried no seed of social upheaval, for the believer was not bound to the marabout against his will. He had voluntarily submitted himself so as to enter Paradise in which he believed; he could at any time break the spiritual bond tying him to the marabout. This relatively rare act of disaffiliation was called, in Wolof, *vudet*. The body of such believers were grouped in the community *(Dara)*, in which all the means of production were concentrated. The believer shunned possessions. He felt that his own power to work (apparently the only thing left to him) did not belong to him: it was in the service of the marabout with whom he had made a metaphysical contract assuring him a place in Paradise after death. Thus, even the precolonial marabout system could not lead to social revolutions, because the believer was unaware that he was expropriated and exploited.

SLAVE MANPOWER: CONCENTRATION

The end of the Middle Ages and the whole of the Renaissance in Europe were characterized by a degree of slavery as intense as and more detestable than what Africa had known. This will become clearer by what is to follow. It is customary to consider slavery as a specifically African phenomenon, but we have just seen that until the end of the aforementioned period white men were in the habit of reducing their own fellows to slavery. The serf of the Middle Ages was as totally in thrall as the African slave (Fustel de Coulanges referred to him as the rustic slave). So, this institution was characteristic of all mankind, regardless of color. It is erroneous to believe that European slavery, especially in modern times, was but an exceptional and fragmentary social phenomenon. After its contact with Africa, sixteenth-century Europe progressively lost the custom of internal slavery and, taking advantage of its superiority in arms, substituted Black slavery. After the contact with Europe, the lot of Africa's slaves suddenly got worse, since it then became possible for them to be sold to persons who would export them, with the whole chain of well-known evils entailed in these forced crossings.

Slavery is certainly the great chink in African social organization; but the documents available prove that the African slaves who were not deported in general enjoyed living conditions incomparably superior to those of white slaves in Europe. Slaves of the kings of Mali and the Askias of Gao enjoyed complete liberty of movement. Thus, an ordinary slave of the Askia Daud, a native of Kanta, was able to carry out a pilgrimage to Mecca without his master's knowledge; on his return, instead of listening to the hypocritical words of his *uandu* (herald), who tried to incite him against the slave, the king pardoned him along with a hundred members of his tribe.[35] The Diam-Uali, Diam-Téné, and Sorobanna tribes, while being slaves of the Askia, occupied a whole territory whose soil they cultivated for their own account, giving only a predetermined share of their crops to the sovereign. When the latter made a present of them to an erudite Muslim named Mohammed Tulé, they remained on their lands unhindered: their life in no way changed and their new master, according to tradition, merely went on getting the same share of the crops from them.[36]

When Askia Mohammed defeated Sonni Baro Dau, the son of Sonni Ali, he took over some twenty-four slave tribes that belonged to him. The *Tarikh el Fettach* gives details about the social life of these tribes and, in particular, the system of shares which was applicable to them. Before belonging to the Songhai, they too had first been the property of the king of Mali; starting only with Sonni Mâdogo did they change imperial masters. The first three tribes were of Bambara origin and had most likely not yet been converted to Islam, if Kâti is to be believed; in other words, the slave might be of a religion other than that of his master. The king of Mali selected his domestic servants from among them. When one of

the men wished to marry, the king would furnish a dowry of
forty thousand cowries

> to the parents-in-law of the groom, so as to prevent the wife or
> children from claiming their freedom, and in order to make sure
> that they and their progeny would always remain the property
> of the *Malli-koï* . . . In the days of the *Malli-koïs,* and ever since
> these tribes first belonged to them, they had been obligated to
> pay an annual tribute of forty cubits [of cultivated land] per
> couple, man and wife; thus it was until the time these tribes
> were handed over to the chîs.[37]

With these crops the king fed his army; if they were insuffi-
cient or of poor quality, a new compensatory tax was levied
upon the tribes for having been responsible for bad agricultural management. Under Askia Mohammed, however, the
shares taken became more reasonable, more humane; they
were collected in the following manner: a graduated tax, in
kind, was levied on each couple at harvest time. After having
appraised the holdings of each family, the king's tax-collector
would take ten measures of flour from any who could supply
only that much, twenty from those who could supply no
more, and thirty from all others, even if they were capable of
providing a thousand. This limit, indeed, was never to be
exceeded, however much individual wealth the slave might
have. A dark shadow clouds this almost too beautiful picture:
the Askia bartered some of the tribe's children for horses.

The fourth tribe, the Tyindiketas, were dispersed from
Gao as far as Sibiridugu. No one tried to stop the peregrinations of these people; when the Askia met one of them along
his way, at a strongpoint or in a village, he could tell only by
the individual's ethnic name that he was one of his slaves. He
might then do with him whatever he wished. From the period
of Mali until that of Gao, the only kind of tax imposed on this
tribe was to supply the feed necessary for the king's horses;
the hostlers were furnished by it as well, and the adults built
the boats needed to transport the hay, at least during the reign

of the Askias. The tax thus assumed an increasingly functional character: one's occupation or economic status was the basis for the tax imposed on him.

The Zendji (the fifth tribe, extending from Kanta to Sibiridugu), who lived by fishing, paid their tax in dried fish when the water was low: it ranged from one to ten parcels of dried fish, according to the means. The ten-packet maximum was never to be exceeded. This tribe also supplied the boats and crews needed for certain types of transportation. The sixth tribe, the Arbis, were exempt from the levy since, under the Askias, it was from them that all the domestic servants and confidential special emissaries came. The women served the king's wives, while the youth escorted the king on his peaceable or warring outings. The seventh, eighth, ninth, tenth, and eleventh tribes were blacksmiths of foreign extraction. Their male ancestor had been the blacksmith slave of a Christian master living somewhere on an island in the Atlantic: one of the Canaries or Cape Verde Islands? We do not know. At any rate, this slave was said to have escaped and taken refuge in Kukiya, under the reign of Sonni Mohammed Fari. We have noted that, in general, men of the castes could not be taken as slaves. If that rule was broken, it was perhaps because the individual in question was of foreign extraction. He had come into the country already a slave. However that may be, his descendants, instead of being concentrated in one place, were dispersed so as to avoid any coalition among them. Kâti observes that these aliens followed filiation through the paternal line, contrary to African customs. The taxes imposed from time immemorial on these five tribes amounted to "one hundred spears and one hundred arrows per family each year."

The twelfth tribe occupied the territory betwen Gao and Fâni.

According to Kâti, the Askia Daud had plantations throughout the land, from the Erei, the Dendi, the Kulane, etc. He estimates the total annual crop at four thousand sacks of grain, which by present-day calculations does not seem a great deal. The work on these plantations was carefully organized, and done by slaves. Each plantation was managed by a *fanfa*, who might have under him one hundred, sixty, fifty, forty, or twenty slaves; the name means both slave-master and ship's master.

The plantation of Abdâ, in the Dendi territory, employed two hundred slaves with four *fanfas*, all under another head named, Missakulallah; it yielded one thousand *sunus* of rice: *sunus* were leather sacks holding about 250 liters. Seed and sacks were supplied by the Askia. Ten boats were used to transport the cereals. At harvest time, the agent sent to collect it brought from the Askia to the head *fanfa*, according to custom, one whole block of salt, a thousand kola nuts, and a black boubou and a black loincloth for his wife. The personal wealth of this head *fanfa*, who was nonetheless a slave, could easily exceed in cereals alone a thousand *sunus*. His situation was thus in no way comparable to that of a member of the plebs of antiquity or a serf of the Middle Ages bound to the soil.

Such agricultural wealth was stored in clay granaries used for purposes of silage. It sometimes happened that such a plantation, with all those working on it, was given as a present to a Sherif, a scholar, or any other friend of the king. This is how the plantation of Djangadja was given to the alfa Kati, a native scholar: the crops then went to a new master, but the social situation of the workers remained unchanged.

One institution of Askia Daud's seems to indicate that the soldiers must have been mostly of slave origin:

> It was he who inaugurated the system under which the king was heir to all his soldiers' goods, because, he said, they were his slaves; before that, it had not been so, and the king inherited only the soldier's horse, shield, and javelins, nothing else. As for the custom the kings had of taking the daughters of their soldiers and using them for their own pleasure, it was a deplorable custom which existed before his reign.[38]

A freed slave was entitled to a deed of manumission drawn up in proper legal form. This was the case of an old woman who was part of the legacy of the *diango* Mussa Sagansâro, who, according to Kâti, was freed by Askia Daud.[39] The facts mentioned in this chapter constitute additional information on the organization of civil administration and labor; one can see in general how taxes must have been levied. The social condition of the slaves has been clearly shown: their treatment was not inhumane, for the period, as long as they remained within the area; they were, more and more, sort of "subjects" of the king. Their misfortune lay in the awful and hateful fact that they might at any moment be sold. From that viewpoint, their situation was identical with that of the white European slave of the same period. Beyond that, they were better off, as we have just shown.

RETRIBALIZATION

We can see at work here the characteristically African phenomenon of apparent retribalization. Kâti tells us the ethnic family names of the first slaves who were the originators of the twenty-four tribes belonging to the emperors of Mali and Gao; they were ordinary individuals whom the sovereign allowed to found a house which would proliferate in geometric progression through the generations. These large families, which numbered thousands of members after a short while, had all the external appearances of a clan or tribe, as to number, identity of name, and collateral relationships. Yet they totally lacked the social structure and organization of the clan. Their members were merely a juxtaposition of individuals integrated into an already highly developed monarchic society who were at most only conscious of their degree of kinship through the ethnic names appearing in the census.

PRIMITIVE ACCUMULATION

We now have a general idea of the productive forces, the means of production, accumulation, and disposal, and whom they belonged to. There was not, on the one hand, a social minority possessing these means and accumulating them in a few shops and, on the other hand, a mass of expropriated persons forced to sell their labor power to this minority in order to live. According to the later analyses of Marx and Engels, Africa was thus at the stage of "natural economy," characterized by the production of only what is barely necessary for existence. Such an economy is an obstacle to the appearance of capitalism. However, on examining things more closely, we see that it was not exactly that way; in the marketplaces of Timbuktu, Djenné, and elsewhere, there were people producing with the sole purpose of resale; and, as Rosa Luxembourg points out, this is the main condition for the appearance of capitalism. Nevertheless, if one considers the duration of this period of "natural economy" in Africa, one must realize that the process of "primitive accumulation," that is, the separation of labor and the conditions of labor, took place there at the slow pace of a secondary chemical reaction thoroughly negligible when compared to the principal reaction. It seems that it was the African collectivism described in the preceding chapter, the moral and material security it assured every individual, which made useless, if not superfluous, the accumulation of excessive wealth; even the riches of the king do not seem huge by modern standards. Hoarding, usury, and all forms of excessive concentration of individual wealth are only the reflection of social anxiety, uncertainty about tomorrow, a sort of shield for oneself and one's kin against a cruel fate. It is in an individualistic society that we see the great growth of such a phenomenon: this was true of the West throughout its history. Indo-Aryan individualism, dating from earliest antiquity, and the feeling of social insecurity inherent in it, developed the spirit of struggle for life more than anywhere else. When the history of societies is written, it will be seen that, from the Aegean period to our own day, that of the Europeans was the hardest, roughest, least clement for the individual who was forced, condemned to a constant struggle, lest he disappear. Of course, the struggle for life is a law of nature, but it applies there more than anywhere else. Without any margin of safety, one whose means give out sinks before the indifferent eyes of others. This social coldness extends far beyond the period of modern capitalism to cover the history of Europe from the time of Athens until today. No politico-social education has so far radically changed the Occidental mind in this respect. The technical and intellectual progress due to constant and necessary busyness, the energy with which one must imperturably amass ever more wealth, the peculiar forms that these activities assume and their repercussion upon the social order, the development of mercantilism—all these seem to flow, in large part, from one same initial principle. Even a certain love of risk results from this necessity: in order to escape from slavery in Europe, as we have seen, one had to have a remunerative means of support; the same social reason accounted for the search for an inheritance or credit so as to set up as a farmer-employer in the country or commission a ship and try one's luck on the high seas. The rise and development of maritime commerce remained, for a very long time, a private business, before being taken over by the various European countries.

From Homer's day to our own, through Athens, Rome, and the Middle Ages, it would be difficult to find a period with a properly "natural" economy. The mercantilism inherited from the Cretans and Phoenicians has gone on and grown stronger, except for a few moments of decline. Two factors appear to have stimulated commerce: the small size and, especially, the comparative poverty of the mother country, on one hand, and on the other, a certain numerical weakness of the population which eliminated all hope of achieving fortune by force of arms, by the conquest of other countries. Commercial activity often seems the form of economic adaptation of minorities. Such was the case with the Phoenicians, beside the powerful Egyptian nation; such was also the case for Genoa and Venice until the destruction of Constantinople by Mohammed II; and the Lebano-Syrians and Israelites in our times; such would seem to have been the case for certain Black African groups, such as the Djula, among others. The commercial activity of Athens must have been stimulated by the geographic context and the poverty of Greece. Numerous and powerful peoples living in underendowed regions, such as the Germanic, throughout history have been conquerors. In modern times, with such universal and pacifistic minds as Goethe, the Germanic drive from north to south took on a literary turn: *"Kennst du das Land wo die Zitronen bluehn?"* (Do you know he land where the lemon-trees bloom?)[40] To the extent that African collectivism and European individualism grow out of the material conditions of existence, the preceding considerations are founded upon a objective basis.

NOTES

1. See position of Kaarta on map, pp. 138–139.
2. Sâdi, *T.S.*, XXXV, 387.
3. Kati, *T.F.*, II, 65.
4. Al Bakri, *op. cit.*
5. The last two of these were in Senegal (Cayor).
6. See quotations from Ibn Battuta.
7. Sâdi, *T.S.*, V, 24.   8. See p. 85 above.   9. Al Bakri, *op. cit.*
10. Kâti, *T.F.*, XVI, 319, and Sâdi, *T.S.*, XXXI, 338.
11. *Idrissi géographe, op. cit.*, vol. I, p. 18.
12. Al Bakri, *op. cit.*, p. 340.   13. Kâti, *T.F.*, XI, 177.
14. Al Bakri, *op. cit.*, pp. 324–326.   15. Sâdi, *T.S.*, XXXI, 338.
16. Ibn Haukal, *Of Roads and Kingdoms.*
17. M.A. Jaspan, "Negro Culture in Southern Africa Before European Conquest," *Science and Society*, vol. XIX, no. 3, Summer 1955, pp. 193–218, translated by Thomas Diop as "La Culture Noire en Afrique du Sud avant la conquête européenne," *Présence Africaine*, no. XVIII–XIX, February–May 1958, pp. 143–165.

18. Kâti, *T.F.*, XVI, 320.   19. Al Bakri, *op. cit.*, pp. 324–327.
20. Ibn Battuta, *op. cit.*, p. 14.   21. See map, p.
22. Kâti, *T.F.*, IV, 77.   23. Sâdi, *T.S.*, V, 24–25.   24. Kâti, *T.F.*, XIV, 262.
25. Sâdi, *T.S.*, XXXI, 338.
26. Karl Marx, *Capital: A Critique of Political Economy*, trans. by Samuel Moore and Edward Aveling, ed. by Frederick Engels, reviewed and amplified according to the Fourth German Edition by Ernest Untermann (Chicago: Kerr, 1915), Vol. I, Part VIII, ch. XXVIII, p. 790, quoting William Harrison's "Description of England, prefixed to Holinshed's Chronicle" (1577).
27. *Idem.*, p. 806.   28. *Ibid.*   29. *Idem.*, pp. 806–807.
30. *Ibid.*, fn. p. 808, quoting *Styne's Annals of the Reformation and Establishment of Religion, and other Various Occurrences in the Church of England during Queen Elizabeth's Happy Reign*, Second ed., 1725, vol. 2.
31. Marx, *op. cit.*, p. 808.   32. *Idem.*, XXXII, 835.   33. *Idem., loc. cit.*
34. Kâti, *T.F.*, V, 81.   35. *Idem.*, XI, 204–207.   36. *Idem.*, I, 52–53.
37. *Idem.*, V, 108.   38. *Idem.*, XI, 211.   39. *Idem.*, XI, 192–193.
40. Goethe, *Wilhelm Meisters Lehrjahre*, III, 1.

Chapter Seven

IDEOLOGICAL SUPERSTRUCTURE: ISLAM IN BLACK AFRICA

Analysis of the conditions in which Islam succeeded in Africa will lead us to see the part it also played in civilizing the country.

Only during the Almoravide movement of the first half of the eleventh century did some white people, Berbers, attempt to impose Islam on Black Africa by force of arms. Yahia ben Ibrahim, head of the Lemtuna and Djoddala tribes, which respectively occupy the regions of Mauritanian Tagant and Adrar, was the originator of that movement. On his return from Mecca, around 1035, he brought a preacher, Abdallah ben Yasin, to convert the members of the tribes under his jurisdiction. The first result was total failure. The preacher was on the point of leaving, when Yahia succeeded in convincing him it was a good idea for the two of them to take a retreat in a fortified monastery, on an island at the mouth of the Senegal River, and lead an ascetic life, which through their example might attract some disciples. This was the beginning of the Marabout movement in West Africa ("marabout," from the Arabic *el Morabbatin,* meaning "living in a monastery"): "Almoravide" in turn derives, by alteration, from *el Morabbatin.* According to Ibn Khaldun, when the number of disciples had reached one thousand, Yassin said to them:

> A thousand men cannot easily be beaten; therefore must we now work at remaining steadfast in holding to the truth and forcing, if need be, everyone to recognize it. Let us leave this place and fulfill the task imposed upon us.[1]

PEACEFUL PENETRATION

The Almoravides besieged Aoudaghast and Ghana. This was the only time white troops attempted to impose Islam through violence. One of Yasin's disciples, King Uardiabi, converted part of the Tuculor on the Senegal River: they became zealous allies of the Arabo-Berbers in the holy wars, from the eleventh century on. The Almoravide thrust pushed northward across the desert, through Sijilmasa and the Maghreb, to reach part of Spain. It did not spread, in West Africa, to the east and south: conversion of these regions was to be the work of autochthonous marabouts.

The primary reason for the success of Islam in Black Africa, with one exception, consequently stems from the fact that it was propagated peacefully at first by solitary Arabo-Berber travelers to certain Black kings and notables, who then spread it about them to those under their jurisdiction. This was the case, according to Bakri, with the king of Mali, whom he calls El Mussulmani, and who must have been none other than the Mandingo king Baramendana Keita (1050) of whom Khaldun speaks. A Mohammedan traveler abided for a long time with him when drought swept the land; legend has it that he caused it to rain by his prayers. The king, who took this to be a miracle, then converted to the new religion. What is to be emphasized here is the peaceful nature of this conversion, regardless of the legend surrounding it.

THE ROLE OF AUTOCHTHONOUS CHIEFS

The second period of Islamization was marked by the conversion of the people, whether through automatic imitation of their chiefs, or through some violent action of these chiefs, sometimes going beyond their borders and becoming veritable holy wars: all such holy wars were conducted by Black chiefs. The king of the town of Silla, in the eleventh century, was already waging holy war against the inhabitants of Kalenfu,[2] as had Askia Mohammed against the Mossi emperor Naséré, Amadu Sheiku against the Damel of Cayor, and Lat Dior Diop against Koki in 1875.

Ousman Dan Fodio (1801), El Hadj-Omar (1850), and Ahmadu Ahmadu (1884) were the great religious conquerors of the Sudan in the nineteenth century.

With the Sultan of Djenné, Konboro, we witness the phenomenon of automatic imitation of the sovereign by the people; they adopted the faith of Islam immediately following the conversion of the king. The *Tarikh es Sudan* places this event in the sixth century of the Hegira (twelfth century).[3] Sâdi fails to mention the name of the Muslim scholar who must have exerted a religious influence on the king of Djenné: but the fact seems undeniable; when he decided to change his religion, he summoned all the Ulemas living in the country, and renounced the traditional faith in their presence. This instance substantiates the ideas already expressed. These Ulemas, these solitary marabouts, not only were unable to undertake any military action to convert their sovereigns, but absolutely needed their protection and the good will of politico-social circles, to live safely in the land during the transitional period before the conversion of the king.

Such royal conversions were, moreover, taken amiss by the people and all of the sovereign's prestige was needed for them to be accepted. It occasionally happened that a converted king concealed his new religious convictions from his people as long as possible. This was the case with Kan-Mer, the son of Bessi, who ruled the town of Aluken, near Gao, in Bakri's day.[4]

The special character of conversions effected by national chiefs is that the latter, however ruthless their methods, could never have been considered, in the eyes of the people, as foreign oppressors or as being in league with such. Impossible as it was for the people to see El Hadj-Omar and the others as agents of a colonizing power, just so inevitably did the missionaries see them in this light.

METAPHYSICAL REASONS

A third cause for the success of Islam in Africa seems to reside in a certain metaphysical relationship between African beliefs and the "Muslim tradition." In the latter there is to be found an invisible world, a doppelganger of the visible one; it is indeed an exact replica of it, but the initiate alone can see it. Askia Mohammed, in carrying out his pilgrimage to Mecca, having come back by way of Egypt, pitched camp not far from Cairo for the night. He was accompanied at that time, among other scholars, by one Salih Diawara; the latter was able to "see" and shake hands with the Muslim genie, Chamharuch. According to the "Islamic tradition" related to Kâti, this was a beneficent genie whose followers were like marabouts and made pilgrimages like them. Around him, there were some freed genies, for in that spirit world there are also slaves, some good and some evil. The malevolent, pagan genies, just like their counterparts in our visible world, go to Hell when they die: they spend their time in tormenting us.[5] In 1928, following the death of Amadu Bamba, originator of the Mohammedan sect of the Murides, a great wind swept the region of his capital, Djurdel, for an entire day. It was blowing toward the sea, and it was spontaneously concluded that this was the genie who had accompanied the holy man during his exile in Gabon, now returning to the ocean. Everyone was convinced that, during his life, this genie never left his side, acting in a way as his rampart against all evil. This metaphysical being is not to be confused with a guardian angel.

It goes without saying that this conception of a dual

world is to be found, in various forms, in the beliefs of
Africans to such a point they they feel completely comfortable
in Islam. Some of them do not even feel they have changed
their metaphysical horizon. That is what led Dan Fodio to
criticize severely all those who, though calling themselves
Muslims, continue such practices as libations, offerings, divination, the Kabbala, etc., and even write verses from the
Koran in the blood of sacrificial animals.[6] Dan Fodio's text,
although rather recent (nineteenth century), reflects a tendency already imperative in the days of the Askias (fifteenth–
seventeenth centuries). African religions, more or less forgotten, were in the process of atrophying and being emptied of
their spiritual content, their former deep metaphysics. The
jumble of empty forms they had left behind could not compete
with Islam on the moral or rational level. And it was on that
latter level of rationality that the victory of Islam was most
striking. That was the fourth cause of its success.

The imperative need for rationality reflected in the writings of Dan Fodio was henceforth better satisfied by Islam
than by the dying traditional faiths. Nevertheless, it must be
noted that, in the domain of artistic creativity, the Islamized
African underwent, for a long time, a throttling, a kind of
cultural impoverishment. During the initial years of Moham-
medanism strict formalism was needed, so as to check any
return to idolatry through the devices of artistic representation. It will be recalled under what conditions Islam tri-
umphed over Sabaism. Therefore, it was necessary to
proscribe for centuries any representation in animal form, and
even more so, in human form. The notion of God, especially,
was one which might not be concretized by means of art.
Exegetes of Islam may realize today that this phase of fears is
considered historically outgrown within the framework of the
evolution of Muslim consciousness. It is unthinkable that the
renaissance of sculptural and pictorial art (featuring the
human form) might entail an offensive return to idolatry in
any Muslim country.

POWER OF RELIGIOUS BELIEFS

What was the strength of religious belief in precolonial Islamic Africa, its political and social role, the imprint it left? In the Sudan, the reign of Askia Mohammed was a watershed. Before him it seems, to a certain degree at least, the Islamism of the emperors of Gao was rather fragile: with the last two of these, if we are to believe Kâti, there was undisguised hostility. Askia Mohammed was only the lieutenant of Sonni Ali, whose faith was very lukewarm; his son, Bâro, who replaced him, refused to embrace Islam. Mohammed became a dissident and insistently urged Bâro to convert. Following negotiations which lasted fifty-two days, and were conducted in large part by the scholar Sâlih Diawara, already allied with the future Askia, the two went into battle. Bâro stood firm: there was no question of his embracing Islam; in this, he went farther than his father who had apparently been converted. The battle ended with his defeat. Kâti considers that God thus assured the Askia's victory over the infidel, which is quite reminiscent of the episode mentioned in *La Chanson de Roland:* Charlemagne, the Christian emperior, emerged victorious over the "Saracens" at Roncesvalles because the swords of his men, especially that of Roland, were guided by the Angel Gabriel. From the Christian viewpoint, this was a victory of Light over Darkness.[7]

Islam was, and remains in large part, a living religion in Black Africa, in contrast to the Christianity of the West, which tends to become among Europeans a mere religious custom. The Askias included the Ulemas in all their imperial decisions:

> After Sâlih Diawara had informed the Askia of what he witnessed at his interview with *chî* Bâro, the prince called together his council, made up of the Ulemas, the notables, and the chiefs of his army, and consulted them as to the course of action he should pursue.[8]

Islam practically ran the government under Askia Mohammed. Cadi Mahmud did not hesitate to dismiss the envoys of the Askia and purely and simply refuse to obey his orders. Not only did this do him no harm, but he was able to address the Askia as follows (using the familiar "thou" form):

> Have you forgotten, or do you pretend to have forgotten, the day you came to see me at my home, and you seized my foot and my clothing, saying: "I have come to place myself under your protection and entrust to you my person, so that you may save me from the flames of Hell; help me and hold me by the hand so that I may not to fall into Hell; I entrust myself to you"? That is the reason why I dismissed your envoys and disobeyed your orders.[9]

This action by which one entrusts his metaphysical lot, his fate in the hereafter, to a living saint, is characteristic of the marabout phase of Islam in West Africa. The marabouts are the living intermediaries between laymen and the Prophet, who is in direct communication with God. After death, the marabouts raise their disciples up to Paradise, carrying them on their shoulders past Purgatory (in Wolof: *djegi jirat*). It is while the saint is asleep that his soul, his double, leaves his body to go and carry out such missions of rescue. One can see the reason why even a king, like Askia Mohammed, would feel it imperative to entrust himself to such a savior. So, in Black Africa to this very day, despite the formal doctrines of the Koran, there are no believers who dedicate themselves only to God and his Prophet; a third personage, the one known as his marabout, is needed by all laymen, from the masses up to the sovereign.

The power of Islam was such that it might have eliminated or attenuated slavery in the Middle Ages if it had decreed that the enslavement of one man by another was a mortal sin. But the Koran's point of view on this question is shaded. One may have a slave under the following conditions: to begin with, if he is a prisoner of a holy war—but then he must be educated, cared for, and converted; but, on the other hand, it is forbidden to take as a slave a Muslim as well educated as oneself; so a slave must be freed as soon as he reaches the intellectual level of his master. Be that as it may, during the period under consideration, it is quite clear that it was the fear of Hell which kept the faithful within the moral discipline of religion.

MYSTICAL UNDERPINNING OF NATIONALISM

Islam has often been the mystical underpinning of African nationalism. This explains the fantastic epics of the Mahdi (1881), the national hero and liberator of the former Anglo-Egyptian Sudan, Rabah (1878), and the conquering Tuculors of the Senegal River and western Sudan. The wars of the Mahdi, with their unusual character, deserve a little more attention. The Mahdi, according to Muslim tradition, is the Messiah, the Saviour who, before the end of the world, will bring the entire earth to Islam. Proclaiming himself such, one Mohammed-Ahmed, a Sudanese by origin, galvanized his men, and succeeded in defeating Rashid-Bey, the governor of Fashoda. In 1882, he defeated an Egyptian column and occupied all the Kordofan: he completely massacred an army of ten thousand men commanded by Hicks Pasha. In 1883, Slatin Pasha, the British governor of Darfur, and Lupton-Bey (the British governor of Bahr-el-Ghazal, who affected Arab aliases as did the former) were also beaten by him. They capitulated in 1884. He conquered the Berber country as well as the Sennar. On January 26, 1885, he entered the citadel of Khartoum and there slew Gordon Pasha (Chinese Gordon). Eight-tenths of the Sudanese territory had been reconquered from the Anglo-Egyptian coalition opposing the Sudanese Blacks, when he died.[10] His victory was the more valiant in that the victorious Sudanese had only bows and arrows while the Anglo-Egyptians were equipped with the most modern firearms available. The West was stupefied by the event, which brought a shout of admiration from Friedrich Engels.

The victory of Amadu Sheiku over Lat Dior, cited earlier, was due to just such causes: the Damel of Cayor owed his salvation to the help of General Faidherbe whom he was abie to get as an ally in this circumstance. The Tuculors, accompanied by women, fought while singing hymns that had a profound effect on both the soldiers and their enemies, according to accounts I received from my maternal grandmother: the Tuculors were fanaticized, the Cayorians terrified. The secular pseudo-nationalism of the latter, their mundane *tieddo* spirit, very quickly fell before the unshakable faith of the Tuculors, who, of course, were convinced they would go directly to Paradise when they died on the battlefield of this holy war. African nationalism among them had found an efficacious mystical underpinning.

The difference between the extraordinary epic of Samory and that of the Mahdi consists in the fact that Samory, although a Muslim, acted without any mystical underpinning to his nationalism, as if he had weighed the consequences of it. He was able to crystallize the national resistance of almost all the territories of West Africa on a strictly secular basis without the assistance of any belief, idea, or foreign power to galvanize his troops. He did not wage holy wars as had Askia Mohammed or the religious leaders of the nineteenth century. He waged a national resistance of the very best "Vercingetorix type."

In his childhood, Samory lived in the circumstances of the masses as an African chieftain rarely had. This was what the originality of his political action and his glory were perhaps due to.

Although of lesser magnitude, the resistance of Behanzin, the last king of Dahomey (end of the nineteenth century), and that of Lat Dior (Senegal) were of the same type. As for Chaka, the Zulu chief, it will be necessary to make further studies to ascertain whether the English succeeded in channeling his "turbulence" inward, toward the other African clans and tribes, or whether he was consciously making ready so that, when the time came, he might deal them a decisive blow.

The fact was that due to the modus vivendi which was always respected, Chaka never waged war against the English in South Africa. On the other hand, the military and social organization with which he endowed his army and his people was the most technical and efficient of all those in Black Africa in modern times. It contributed mightily to the rapid and systematic fusion of the Zulu clans and tribes and the birth of the present-day nationalities in South Africa.

Chaka's internal conquests were as rapid as they were extraordinarily farreaching. It is for all these reasons that he is sometimes referred to as the Napoleon of Black Africa or at least of South Africa.

Chaka never followed European examples.

RENUNCIATION OF THE PRE-ISLAMIC PAST

Islam, in contrast to (present-day) Christianity, takes no account of the traditional past. The Christian West of today proudly recognizes its classical, pagan heritage, and does its utmost to preserve the works of that period. One discovers nothing of the sort in Islamized countries. The equivalent of the Western pagan past must be hushed up, renounced, permanently forgotten. A museum in Mecca filled with relics from the Sabaean period would be pure idolatry, an unthinkable initiative from the Muslim viewpoint. Reasons such as these explain why today the Blacks of Khartoum have a sense of shame at acknowledging their relationship to the ancient past of Meroë. The ruins from that period, the eighty-four pyramids still standing in the ancient capital, the temple of

Semna, Meroitic writing, the remains of the astronomical observatories, the vestiges of the metal industry which made the Sudan the Birmingham of antiquity, all this is of no interest because it is tainted with a pagan tradition no good Muslim would think of recalling. How could they, in all decency, hark back to these people who knew nothing of the Koran, and who did not pray as we now do, to a time before religious wisdom?

"SHERIFISM"

One might term as "Sherifism" the irresistible impulse on the part of most Muslim chiefs of Black Africa to link themselves, by whatever sort of acrobatics, to the family tree of Mahomet. One of my uncles, Mahtar Lô, maintained until his dying day that twenty ancestors, whose names he would quote, linked him to the Prophet; anyone who disagreed with him was a heretic. This tendency spread throughout Africa after the introduction of Islam in the eighth century. All the royal families, without distinction, after Islamization invented Sherifian origins for themselves, often retroactively adjusting local history. This was the case of the royal branch of the Dias of Kukia, the former capital of Songhai, before Gao, until the eleventh century. An oral post-Islamic etymology has it that *Dia* derives from *Dja Men el Yemen* ("he came from Yemen"). It seems there were two brothers, natives of Southern Arabia, who arrived in that region in "the most piteous state," barely able to conceal their nakedness under "bits of animal hide." Whenever they were asked where they came from, one of them would answer in Arabic with the aforementioned expression. Henceforth, that was the name of the elder of the two. After he defeated the fish known as Demon of the River, which was king of the region and periodically emerged from the water to dictate its laws, he supplanted it at the head of the nation and founded the Dia dynasty.

Such legends have proliferated in Black Africa since Islam came in and have contributed to altering the authentic history of the continent.[11] We find variants of them for the genesis of the first dynasties of Ghana, Bornu, Wadaï, all of the Kordofan, and so on. On the other hand, a migration starting from the Nile Valley seems beyond doubt to the extent that, even today, it can be substantiated by the ethnic names of the various clans.[12] This migration, however, is mentioned nowhere except in pre-Islamic legends that gradually grow vaguer and vaguer, according to which, as noted by Delafosse, the Blacks of West Africa relate their ancestors came from the east, from around the "Great Water." We will see that very probably this "Great Water" is the Nile rather than the Indian Ocean.

Consciousness of the continuity of the people's historical past has been progressively weakened by religious influences. Even within our own families, we know that our parents prefer to forget systematically and keep their children unaware of a certain "pagan" past, which it has become indiscreet to mention, except for a few nostalgic reminiscences. In the search for ancestors as far away as Yemen, they might have been better off to stop at the Nile Basin, but this happens less and less often because, beginning with the seventh century, the history of that region appeared as if polluted by the image of the Pharaoh, the Biblical curse on whom is perpetuated in Islam.

However that may be, Mohammedan Black Africa in the Middle Ages was no less original than Christian Europe at the close of antiquity. Both continents were invaded in the same way by alien monotheistic religions which ended up being at the foundation of the entire sociopolitical organization, ruling philosophical thought, and carrying forward intellectual and moral values during this whole period.

A hierarchy as powerful, old, and permanent as that of the Christian Church is nonexistent in Islam; it is the replica, on the religious level, of the old Roman administrative organization. Immediately after the wars of the times of the first caliphates, there was coexistence and reciprocal tolerance among the different sects. None prevailed sufficiently to be able to anathematize the others and consider them schismatic, so as to erect a durable hierarchy upon its own concepts and its own interpretation of the religious texts. This situation gave rise in Black Africa to the possibility of a multiplicity of sects. Thus, alongisde the old Tidjane sect, native to North Africa and propagated by El Hadj Malick Sy in Senegal, there appeared at the beginning of the twentieth century, the new Muride sect created by Amadu Bamba. The French authorities very quickly interpreted this as the integrating of Islam into local nationalism. Instead of expressly recommending a pilgrimage to Mecca, considering the material obligations one would have to fulfill vis-à-vis his family so as to be in a position to make such a journey, Muridism created shrines on the local level: Djurbel, the residence of Amadu Bamba, with its mosque, was the substitute for Mecca during the marabout's life. After his death, it was shifted to Touba, where he is buried. Thus, from 1900 to 1935, no Muride made a pilgrimage to Mecca; the idea of making one occurred to no one, not even the creator of the sect. Cheikh Anta, the most independent of all the young brothers of Amadu Bamba, thought of making it only after Amadu Bamba's death.

To recapitulate, then, in the Middle Ages the religious superstructure played an equally important role in Europe and in Africa. Christianity gave the West politico-administrative organization, and ensured the continuity of historical consciousness. Islam, in Black Africa, merely superimposed itself on the politico-administrative organization: even when, in consequence of the cosmopolitanism of the period, a foreigner (Arab or otherwise) was invested with a position by the sovereign, he bore the indigenous title. The sense of an ancient past was weakening but the Arab chroniclers noted the events of African history with praiseworthy objectivity: their writings today constitute a precious source of documentation. In Europe, as in Islamized Black Africa, the notion of the seven arts, that is, the trivium and the quadrivium, was carried forward, as we shall see in the following chapter.

NOTES

1. Ibn Khaldun, *op. cit.*, II, p. 69.
2. Al Bakri, *op. cit.*, pp. 324–333.
3. Sâdi, *T.S.*, ch. V, p. 23.
4. Al Bakri, *op. cit.*, p. 334.
5. Kâti, *T.F.*, ch. VI, pp. 123–126.
6. Cheikh Otmane Dan Fodio, *Nour-el-Eulbab* (Algiers, 1898), p. 7 (quoted in Leroi-Gourhan and Poirier, *Ethnologie de l'Union française*, p. 359).
7. Kâti, *T.F.*, ch. V, pp. 104–106.
8. *Idem.*, ch. V, p. 104.
9. *Idem.*, ch. VI, p. 117.
10. Delafosse, *op. cit.*, p. 113.
11. Sâdi, *T.S.*, ch. I, pp. 4–8.
12. Cf. Chapter X below.

Chapter Eight

INTELLECTUAL LEVEL: TEACHING AND EDUCATION

THE UNIVERSITY

As in the Western Middle Ages, teaching was in the hands of the clergy which, in the case of West Africa, was Mohammedan. Documents now at our disposal permit us to describe in detail the intellectual life of the university, particularly that of Sankoré, in Timbuktu. The student body was made up of all those who, regardless of age, were possessed of an insatiable thirst for knowledge. Today, it is difficult for us to picture the extent of this need among Africans of that period. The mosque was at one and the same time also the place of learning, the university. It was not an official building, but the religious undertaking of a devout cadi, apparently helped, in the beginning at least, by the people. Thus, Cadi El Aquib restored the mosque built by Mohammed Naddi, the work being finished between July 16 and August 14, 1569. The Great Mosque of Timbuktu long remained unfinished, until the Askia Daud, passing through the town, undertook to assist the cadi, saying to him: "What remains to be done, I shall take upon myself; it will be my share in this pious endeavor."[1]

The schedule of courses lasted all day, interrupted only at the times of prayers. Some scholars even taught for part of the night. Immediately following prayers, the students gathered around the professor, who imparted his teaching, commented upon the texts, and discussed them with the students. These professors were not officially paid: they taught for the love of teaching; in return, they enjoyed immense respect and gratitude from their pupils (learning the Koran) and their more advanced students who, after mastering the Koran, went on to the various branches of Higher Education. On Wednesday, the day off from school, pupils and students each brought him some honorarium, for him to live on. According to Kâti, in Timbuktu, there were 150 to 180 Koran schools, and a professor such as one Ali Takaria each Wednesday received approximately 1725 cowries; each of his students brought him from five to ten cowries.[2] The pupils of the Koran were also obliged to bring the wood for the fire around which the class met in the evening and at dawn.

TEACHING METHOD

The current teaching method was scholastic. The discussions carried on in those days about the texts might appear to us today as useless quibbling; such was not the case. The grammar method then in use, which consisted in making clear the grammatical significance of the text, was so revolutionary that for a long time it was considered suspect in Europe. The attempt to grasp the exact sense of a text and to stick to it, whether one realized it or not, meant ridding it of its mystical, revealed aspect, and reducing it to the dimensions of a profane vocabulary. Therefore, for a long time, many exegetists avoided applying such a method to the Bible. In Africa, the language of Higher Education was Arabic, as was Latin for Europe of the same period. The Koran was the equivalent of the Bible; it was the principal text to be studied, the one from which all others derived. It contained the sum of all that existed: past, present, future, the whole Universe. It was thus necessarily laconic and dense; so short a text to cover so many things. The commentary, the learned explanation was thus imperative in the very first place. The place given to explication of the Koran within the educational programs is thus easily understood.

THE PROGRAM

But what actually was the program? Recollection of the Seven Arts never altogether vanished in Europe, but it was the Arabs who introduced the Aristotelian texts to it, well before the Crusaders' contact with Byzantium. They introduced the same texts into Black Africa in the same period. The trivium, i.e., the study of grammar, Aristotelian logic (formal logic, grammatical logic), and rhetoric, was on the list of subjects taught, as shown in the *Tarikh es Sudan*. Chapter X of that work gives the biographies of seventeen scholars of Timbuktu, indicating all the subjects they had mastered. Almost all of them were dialecticians, rhetoricians, jurists, etc., who, in addition, had written works mentioned by title but for the most part not yet recovered. One of them, the famous Ahmed Baba, is said to have left more than seven hundred works. Each one of them had an immense library, also lost to us today. The intellectual tradition was already well established at the time of Sâdi (sixteenth century). About Mohammed Ben Mahmud, he writes: "He made a commentary of El Moghili's poem in Redjez on logic. My father studied rhetoric and logic under him. He died in the month of Safar in 973 [September 1565]."[3]

Sâdi himself studied all these subjects, and commented on several texts; he was the pupil of an inhabitant of Timbuktu, a scholar of Uankori origin, by the name of Mohammed Ben Mahmud Ben Abu Bekr.

In a word, he was my professor, my master, and no one was more useful to me, whether directly or through his writings . . .

He awarded me graduate diplomas written in his own hand, covering the subjects he had taught according to his own or someone else's methods. I sent him a certain number of my works; he wrote on them annotations quite flattering to me; he even reproduced the results of some of my research and I heard him quote some of them in his lectures, thus displaying his impartiality, his modesty, and his respect for the truth in all circumstances. He was with us at the time of our misfortune.[4]

AWARDING OF DIPLOMAS

That text informs us of the existence of diplomas, the manner in which they were awarded (the same as that of Europe of the period), their individual character. A diploma was for a long time nothing more than a certificate of conscientiously completed study. We can see here an aspect of the intellectual practices, with the mention of the works used as documentation, the existence of research activity. Thinking, thus, was a conscious activity; as such, it was becoming scientific.

INTELLECTUAL DEVELOPMENT

In the Middle Ages, four centuries before Lévy-Bruhl wrote his *Primitive Mentality,* Muslim Black Africa was already commenting upon Aristotle's "formal logic" and practicing dialectics. Sâdi mentions by name the dialectician El-Qalqachandi.[5] Students came from all directions, all regions: "At this time, the city was full of Sudanese students, Westerners, in ardent pursuit of science and virtue."[6]

The quadrivium had also been introduced into Black Africa by the same means at the same time. It did not develop there as well as the trivium. The four disciplines constituting it (arithmetic, geometry, astronomy, music) belong to the domain of science, of knowledge, which Muslims were led to neglect through a certain interpretation of the Koranic text. Since the latter covers everything, including the future, true science consisted in plumbing its depths; religion was the center of everything; all knowledge was merely secondary for the mind, whatever its practical value; such considerations held true for the entire Muslim world, Asian as well as African. In the seventh century, the Arabs, having inherited the learning of antiquity, were more advanced than the West in the exact sciences, which they, in large part, introduced into Europe. But whereas the West developed these sciences, the Arabo-African world merely remained where it was and even retrogressed in some areas. Islam made systematic development of the quadrivium superfluous: the "race" of Arab mathematicians, isolated researchers, progressively disappeared instead of fanning out. Europeans, on the other hand, were *ahlul kitâb*, "those who believe in books, those of the books," those who believe that solutions to all profane problems are to be found in nature and systematically devote themselves to this relatively vain pursuit.

This situation has continued to our own day. My previously mentioned uncle boasted of being one of the few to have some knowledge of astronomy, to be interested in this realm of knowledge, considered vain because not leading directly to God. Yet, a certain kind of scholasticism sees everything deriving from the Divine Unity and should thus have led to the justification and revalorization of science. In the Muride community, the school at Guédé, a village in the Baol, under professor M'Backé Busso taught mathematics, applied mechanics, some aspects of thermodynamics (steam engines), and especially the precise measurement of time, whatever the condition of the sky, this last activity being connected with the need to pray exactly on time. This school, in the 1930s, was well on the way to launching scientific research of the same quality as that which existed during the Renaissance, based exclusively on Arabic sources, without any direct influence from Europe. None of its members could either read or write French. Its astronomic knowledge was rather well developed because of the need to find the direction of Mecca by celestial observation, even beyond the familiar horizons. Yet, it would be erroneous to suppose that its general level reached that of a class in elementary mathematics. Only the scientific character, the quality of thinking at the Guédé school deserves our attention. Bachiru M'Backé is today, in all probability, the marabout best versed in modern scientific movements. From our conversation in the summer of 1950, I learned that atomic physics is not beyond his ken. Cheik M'Backé is by far the one among all of them most extraordinarily open to philosophical thought; his double access to both French and Arabic has even permitted him to become acquainted with Marxism.

Among the Tidjanes, with whom I am less familiar, I believe Abdul Aziz, Ahmadu Sy, Mustafa Sy, Malik Sy, and the young Cheikh Tidjane Sy are best developed in the areas of knowledge. The structure of marabout society, its present-day customs and concerns are exactly the same as four hundred years ago, as the *Tarikh es Sudan* allows us to see.

The Sudanese scholars of the African "Middle Ages" were of the same intellectual quality as their Arab colleagues; at times, they were even better. Thus, Abderrahman-El-Temini, a native of the Hedjaz brought to Mali by Kankan Mussa, was able to discover:

> He settled in Timbuktu and found this city full of Sudanese legal experts. As soon as he realized that they knew more than he in legal matters, he left for Fez, devoted himself to the study of the law there, then returned again to Timbuktu to settle here.[7]

The books by Kâti and Sâdi prove that historical consciousness existed in a very definite way, with a feeling for dating events very precisely. Kâti went even further and expressed his fear of passing errors on to posterity. The *Tarikh es*

Sudan gives not only the year, month, and day, but even the hour whenever possible. Upon verification these dates turned out to be exact in almost all cases. It was customary to work from documents, to quote earlier or contemporary authors, to build oneself immense libraries at the cost of sacrificing all other needs, and to write books oneself. Kâti commented at length on a mutilated safe-conduct, considered to be a document.[8]

The writings of Khalima Diakhaté (a scholar at the court of Lat Dior, circa 1858), Amadu Bamba, El-Hadji Malik Sy, Mussa Ka, *et al.,* are merely the continuation in our own age of this powerful intellectual movement of earlier centuries. Writing was done on paper and calligraphy became an art, as in Europe in the Middle Ages.

> He [Askia Daud] was the first to order the building . . . of libraries; he employed scribes to copy manuscripts and he often made presents of these copies to the Ulemas.[9]

Askia Kati's son tells of the beneficence of Askia Daud toward his father: "Then he purchased for him this copy of the Qâmûs [dictionary] at a price of eighty *mitkâls.*"[10]

The author of the *Tarikh es Sudan* and other scholars of the period wrote, as we can see from the above, several other works, of which all traces have been lost. Also lost were the judicial and administrative archives: assistants of cadis kept minutes of the sessions. But tons of documents have disappeared. It may be that those manuscripts, of which students of the time made several copies, now lie dormant among the remains of forgotten hereditary libraries in the Sudan. It was in just such circumstances that the *Tarikh es Sudan* and the *Tarikh el Fettach* were discovered. So it is worthwhile to keep looking for such documents in the archives and libraries of North Africa, Spain, Portugal, Egypt, Baghdad, and perhaps even in Chinese annals. Our Arab scholars have their work cut out for them. They can already work on the manuscripts discovered by M. Gérincourt concerning the history of Black Africa.

These are three hundred items lying dormant at the Institute since 1900, for want of a translator. If Sâdi is to be believed, the intellectual tradition covered an enormous period, the extent of which we do not know today. After having shown that the ancients were in the habit of writing down historical events and transmitting them to future generations, he even stresses a kind of retrogression of learning in his own time (sixteenth–seventeenth centuries).

The generation which followed did not have the same concerns; none of its members attempted to follow the example of the past generation. There was no longer anyone with the noble determination to get to know the great men of the world or, if there were some individuals consumed with this curiosity, they were very few in number. From then on, there remained only vulgar minds given over to hatred, envy, and discord, who took an interest only in things which did not concern them, gossip, slander, calumny of one's neighbors, all those things which are the source of the worst of our troubles.[11]

The author then takes up the analysis of the collapse of historical science in the Sudan:

I was witness to the ruination of [historical] science and its collapse and I observed that its gold pieces and its small change were both disappearing. And then, as this science is rich in gems and fertile in lessons since it gives man knowledge of his own country, his ancestors, his annals, the names of heroes and their biographies, I beseeched divine assistance and undertook to record myself all that I had been able to glean about the Sudanese princes of the Songhai race, recounting their adventures, history, exploits, and battles.[12]

These texts, written by a Black scholar in the seventeenth century, permit us to form an exact picture of the intellectual level of the African élite of the period and their scientific and ethical aspirations. They reveal, among other things, the historical consciousness of the author and the importance he already accorded to history in the life of a people. Since Sâdi was subsequently named Imam of the mosque of Sankoré, we may gather some idea of the general level required to fill that office.

His work methods, like those of Kâti,[13] which we will examine later, reveal a highly rational and deductive mind. We should not be misled by the occasional supernatural events related in these writings: according to Islam—as well as other religions—the divine world does not conform to earthly logic. This same supernaturalness is found in other Arab scholars, such as Bakri, who reports, on the basis of witnesses' accounts which he seems completely to believe, the coupling of goats with plant life. This is in the description of the impregnating of small goats in the city of Iserni on the upper Senegal.[14]

Kâti devotes a paragraph to the etymology of Soni (Chî), gives the names of the authors who are his authorities, such as Bâba Gûro, discourses on the date of the introduction of the titles of askia and hi-koï, quotes various documents and discusses them in deep detail. He had carried out an extensive inquiry into the common origin of the Sonis, the Askia Mohammed, and all those with the surname of Moï.

> Meanwhile, I questioned all the people I met coming from Kanâga, Bîtu, Mali, Diâfurnu, etc., inquiring of them whether in their respective countries there was a tribe called Moï-Kâ or Moï-Nanko, and they all answered: "We have never seen nor heard of anything like that."[15]

The author was very conscious of his duty as a researcher:

> The building of [the kanfari's] capital was then begun. From our research concerning the chronological history of this period, it appears that the time was the year 902 [September 2, 1496 to August 29, 1497]. The number of masons employed at the start was exactly one hundred. They were under the direction of one Uahab Bari.[16]

Long before colonization, then, Black Africa had acceded to civilization. It might be argued that these centers of civilization were, for the most part, influenced by Islam, and that there was nothing original, nothing specifically African about them. All that has gone before allows us to evaluate that. Moreover, we have already stressed that Christian Europe at the time was no more original than Mohammedan Black Africa; Latin, until the nineteenth century, had remained the language of science. Gauss, "the prince of mathematicians," wrote his memoirs in Latin. Forgetfulness of our past now becomes a tangible fact. Just as much as the documents allow, as we have done, the resuscitation, the defossilization of African history for the last two thousand years or so, just that much has the memory of it had been driven from our consciousnesses during the colonial period.

Alongside Islamized Sudan, in the region of Benin, another, strictly traditional center of civilization shone with incomparable brilliance: one can say, without exaggeration, that the "realistic" art of Ifé and the Benin, with its harmonious proportions, its balance, its serenity that makes one think of certain Greek works of the sixth century, represents African sculptural "classicism." The Yoruba had been civilized just as well as the Islamized Africans: entire studies should be devoted to that civilization.

Black Africa developed its own scripts. In the Cameroon there is a hieroglyphic script, the systematic development of which (by the Ndyuya) may be of recent date, but not so its origin. The syllabic script of the Vaï in Sierra Leone and the cursive of the Bassa have been studied by Dr. Jeffreys. The Nsibidi system is alphabetical. In Sierra Leone, these scripts have even been used for the writing of some modern texts. Five years ago, an assembly was held to discuss both the means of defense against the invasion by Occidental characters, and the introduction of foreign phonemes. Thus, it is a script which still has a certain vitality.

It was customary to give to science a character of revelation: this made it more prestigious. Kâti does not hesitate to attribute a goodly portion of the results of his inquiries to the benevolent genie Shamharush: he is the true revealor of knowledge. He was the one who permitted the origin of the Songhai and other tribes to be traced.[17]

By such thought processes, the Koran gradually was turned into a kind of Book of Thoth. The Egyptians believed that this book contained all the magic formulae the incantation of which, according to prescribed ritual, allowed for controlling the universe in all its forms. This frame of mind, which is found everywhere in Black Africa, reminiscent of the beliefs of the Middle Ages, had an influence on the Koran: recitation of a given verse would allow one to find lost objects, another verse would protect one from his enemies, or from bad luck, and so forth, because the Prophet was supposed to have uttered them in identical circumstances.

IMPORTANCE OF THE SHERIF

Along the same lines, one cannot exaggerate the importance of the Sherif, i.e., the descendant of the Prophet, in the social life of the time. When Askia Mohammed made his pilgrimage, he begged the Abasside caliph Mulay Abbas to convince one of these holy personages to go and live with him in the Sudan. It was thought, indeed, that such a person radiated blessedness all around him; the ground he walked on, his clothing, everything he touched, all assured salvation; his look, his handshake were salvatory. The inhabitants of a whole country could thus accede to paradise by associating with a Sherif living in their land. This belief explains all the consideration which Black Africa until our day has shown the Sherifs. Not only were they exempt from all the duties of citizenship (taxes, etc.), but they received gifts of impressive value. It was with a gift of one hundred thousand dinars, five hundred slaves, and a hundred camels, if we are to believe Kâti, that Askia Mohammed greeted the Sherif sent from Mecca by Mulay Abbas. The latter did not hesitate to decree in a letter all sorts of administrative exemptions for the Sherif, as preconditions for his journey. Immediately upon receipt of this message, the Askia complied by having his secretary, Ali ben Abdallah, draw up on the spot an edict granting all these privileges throughout the whole country, which he gave to his distinguished guest. These advantages due to being descendants of the Prophet (especially in Black Africa) are the reason that most Arabs, even Muslim Berbers of Mauritania, invent out of whole cloth Sherifian family trees in Black lands where checking on their authenticity is virtually impossible. The offspring they leave here and there in large measure explain the claims of certain Africans, of more or less mixed ancestry, that they are of Sherifian origin. From four hundred years ago (the time of Kâti and Sâdi) to this day, the situation has remained unchanged.[18]

The Sherifs, in order to hold and increase their prestige, make consummate use of drugs (opium and hashish) which they discreetly mix with tobacco for smoking or give to their followers (the *tâlebs*) to chew. This gives rise to wonderful visions. The believer who comes back to his senses when the effects of the drug wear off is thus convinced that the gates of heaven were opened to him for a moment, and that he was thus miraculously, divinely transported to paradise. Such practices, in those days, were in common use throughout the religious Orient. Askia Mohammed fell victim to them as soon as the holy personage he had so loudly called for arrived. All others were excluded so that the two men might meet tête-à-tête, after which the Askia reported: "I saw the entire world as if transformed into a mass of water, the stars seemed to come from this water and rise toward the heavens, and birds appeared to converge around me and kill one another off . . ."[19]

Some characters of written *vaï* (from Baumann and Westermann *Les peuples et les Civilisations de l'Afrique*).

Nsibidi symbols.

Bassa words.

Written characters common to *mende* and Egyptian.

Written characters common to *moum* and Egyptian.

moum word	meaning	1907 1º	1911 2º	1916 3º	1918 4º	phonetic value
'pwô	arm					pwô p
mi	visage					mi m
na	to cook					na n

Several examples of the evolution of *moum* writing between 1907 and 1918.

SURVIVAL OF THE BLACK TRADITION IN EDUCATION

It is now time to examine what parts of traditional education survived the experience of Islam. The African has an apparently paradoxical conception of the formation of the individual and character-building. He believes that it is during earliest childhood, before the setting-in of noxious habits, that body and mind must be trained for both physical and mental endurance. The Koranic school in Mohammedan Africa became the place for such training: attendance begins between the ages of four and five. Outside of such large cities as Dakar, Saint-Louis, Bamako, etc., children are separated from their parents for months and even years. It is the exception for one to choose a teacher from the same village; in that case, the child would not be in the condition of material and moral isolation considered indispensable to the formation of his personality. He would be the victim of an excess of maternal affection. I was thus sent for four years to Koki, returned to Djurbel-Plateau[20] and then again to Ker-Cheikh (Ibra Fall).

On average, one can recite the Koran at age eleven, without being able to translate a single passage of it. One is even at that time able to write out the entire text from memory, including proper punctuation. This first cycle of study, which ends at age eleven, constitutes the primary level; next, one enters upon what may be called secondary and higher education, having as its program the study of grammar, Mohammedan law, and history—especially that of Islamized Asia—as well as the theoretically prohibited subject of the Kabbala (which is useful for making talismans). Koranic verses are also used for this purpose.

Before Islam, children were marked by the period spent with other members of their generation at the time of circumcision: this lasted approximately one month, the time it took for the operation to heal. Ordinarily one was circumcised at age twenty. This custom was altered in Muslim Africa, where the child was circumcised as early as possible, between six and ten years of age, during the time of his Koranic schooling. However that may be, all the groups of circumcised form classes by age and are initiated into the secrets of the universe on the same day, at the completion of this ordeal. A bond of solidarity is thus established that lasts throughout life: it implies mutual support in time of misfortune, loyalty, open camaraderie, and wholesome familiarity. This bond is stronger than that uniting soldiers having served in the same outfit, for one feels a kind of religious or moral fear of breaking it, or not respecting the obligations inherent in it: one is, according to a Wolof expression, a *mbok lel,* that is, a member of the same "local." The "local" is the fortuitous establishment set up by the circumcised individuals themselves, outside the village, far from any other habitation and, especially, far from women.

An older, already-circumcised individual, having had the experience, directs all the local's activities for the whole period. Being already initiated, along with some of his coevals, he works for a month at initiating the younger group. During the day they go hunting, armed with two sticks (called *lengué*), used to bring down poultry when they break into a village to grab supplies by main force. Tradition tolerates this kind of plunder in the circumstances. The marauders' faces are covered with ashes, making them unrecognizable; they paint their "boubous," their "Phrygian" liberty caps, sometimes even their faces. At night, they gather around the fire at the local to sing and solve the riddles of the *sélbé* (the second in command of the local). These songs are the purest variety of lay folk poetry in Black Africa: they deserve to be collected from one end of the continent to the other. They contain practically all the riddles the circumcised youth is expected to solve; he must understand and explain the significance of the allusions made in them, the true meaning of their special vocabulary. By the training the circumcised lad is given, the discipline to which he is subjected, the local is, in more than one way, reminiscent of the army barracks; it puts the final touches to his education, is his rite of passage to maturity, and his entry into "the city," in the sense of that term in antiquity. There is a tendency in Muslim Africa to neglect physical education, especially among the clergy. This is not a new situation: Sâdi had emphasized its drawbacks. When the scholars of Timbuktu, fleeing Sonni Ali, wanted to go on camelback to Biro (Ualata), they had the greatest difficulty in remaining on their mounts, for they were so weak and emaciated, so unaccustomed to physical exertion:

> On the day of departure, one could see mature men, with full beards, trembling with fear when they were to mount the camels, then tumbling back to the ground as soon as the animals rose to their feet. It was simply that our virtuous ancestors kept their young tied to them, so that they grew up knowing nothing of the things of this life, because when young they had never played. But playing at that age shapes a man and teaches him a great many things. The parents then regretted having acted as they had and, when they returned to Timbuktu, they gave their children time to play, and relaxed the constraints they had imposed upon them.[21]

HISTORICAL REMINDER: THE MOROCCAN INVASION

We may conclude this chapter by a brief reminder of the Sudanese—Moroccan War of 1593. The Moroccan troops sent by Mulay Ahmed were under the command of Djuder. Thanks to the firearms they had, they were easily victorious over the troops of Askia Ishâq II, and seized Timbuktu. The Moroccan occupation was as short as it was violent and limited. Limited, because the actual authority of the pashas, who represented the king of Morocco, in fact never went beyond Timbuktu. Since the reign of Ishâq I, Morocco had been interested in the salt mines of Teghezza, the area which formed the northern border of Songhai, on the Tropic of Cancer. A Sudanese governor, the Teghezza-mondzo, traditionally administered this frontier borderland, in the same way as the *farbas* of Ualata and Aoudaghast. The Tropic of Cancer, by and large, was the limit of Black Africa; beyond it lay a no-man's land extending as far as the south of Morocco and Algeria. According to Sâdi, the sultan of Morocco, after having secretly gathered all useful intelligence regarding the forces of Gao at that time, deliberately launched his troops into the country. The first commander of these troops, Djuder, was quickly replaced by Pasha Mahmud ben Zergun, because he had not been ruthless enough. The latter immediately undertook inside Timbuktu a series of roundups, massacres, and extortions of all sorts, the cruel character of which beggars the imagination—particularly when one considers that the victims were not only brothers in religion, but mainly scholars and jurists. The entire Sudanese intelligentsia were tricked into congregating in the Sankoré mosque and captured; all doors were sealed, then all those present were let out "with the exception of the jurists, their friends, and their followers." They were thus arrested by Zergun, on October 20, 1593, without their having conspired, without any pretext whatsoever. They were divided into two columns, in order to be led away to their new forced residence. One of these columns was completely massacred en route as a result of an incident. Sâdi supplies the long list of the victims' names, all scholars and learned men, who were afterward buried in a potter's field:

> Among the victims of this massacre there were nine persons belonging to the great families of Sankoré: the very learned jurist, Ahmed-Moyâ, the devout jurist, Mohammed-El-Amin, and so on, and so on . . .[22]

An order was issued to Amrâdocho, under whom the massacre had taken place, to bury the corpses within his own house. The residences of these notables were completely emptied of all their belongings:

> The pasha's people carried off all they could lay their hands on, forcing both men and women to strip naked so they could search them. They then abused the women and led them as well as the men away to the casbah where they were held captive for six months.[23]

At the end of this period the prisoners were deported to Marrakesh: the famous Ahmed Baba, the highly educated scholar of Timbuktu, was among them: "They thus left in a great body, made up pell-mell of fathers, children, grandchildren, men and women all together. The caravan set out on Saturday . . . March 18, 1594."[24]

Zergun was later to be disgraced for having given the Sultan only one hundred thousand *mitkâls* out of the immense booty he had extorted from the Sudanese. Meanwhile, national resistance began to organize around Askia Nuh, who had not accepted Moroccan domination. All the inhabitants of the Gao region followed him south, to the land of Dendi. For two years, he harassed the Moroccan troops, at times inflicting bloody defeats on them, despite the inequality of arms between them. During one encounter Pasha Zergun was killed, his head cut off and sent to Askia Nuh. The Moroccans attempted to set up as Askia an individual favorable to them (Seliman), but he was never accepted by the people. Shah-Makaï studied the military tactics of the Arabs, which at the time were copied from those of the Turks. He then joined the resistance movement, harassed the Moroccan troops, and caused them great losses.[25]

It is impossible to describe all the dramatic turns of this atrocious war waged by Morocco against Black Africa. Our quotation on page 195 gives an idea of the extent of the desolation, poverty, and ruin into which the country had fallen; people were even reduced to eating human flesh, as had occurred during the Hundred Years' War in Europe. Plague ravaged the land, as a result of a breakdown of hygiene. Kâti and Sâdi agree in situating at this time the corruption of morals and, especially, the introduction of sodomy into Black Africa.

One could not completely enumerate all the evils and losses suffered by Timbuktu through the installation of the Moroccans within its walls; one could never exhaust the list of atrocities and excesses they committed there. In order to build boats they ripped the doors off houses and chopped down the city's trees.[26]

Moroccan authority rapidly waned; the pashas, who were obeyed less and less even in Timbuktu, tried to distance themselves from the sultan and became local pseudo-chiefs. The Moroccan army, some of whose members were Spanish mercenaries, left in Sudan what were called "armas": these were the halfbreeds of Timbuktu, born of the occupation; the last of the pashas were chosen from among them.

It is out of concern for historical truth that we today recall these painful events.

NOTES

1. Sâdi, *T.S.*, XVII, pp. 177–178.   2. Kâti, *T.F.*, XVI, p. 316.
3. Sâdi, *T.S.*, X, p. 66.   4. *Idem.*, pp. 76–77.   5. *Idem.*, X, p. 65.
6. *Idem.*, X, p. 78.   7. *Idem.*, X, pp. 83–84.   8. Kâti, *T.F.*, VI, p. 141.
9. *Idem.*, XI, p. 177.   10. *Idem.*, XI, p. 201.
11. Sâdi, *T.S.*, Introduction, pp. 2–3.   12. *Idem.*, p. 3.
13. Kâti began writing his book in 1519.
14. Al Bakri, *op. cit.*, pp. 331–338.
15. Kâti, *T.F.*, V, p. 94 (see also pp. 67, 80, 82, 83, 88, 100, 101).
16. *Idem.*, VI, p. 123.   17. *Idem.*, I, p. 48.   18. *Idem.*, I, pp. 23–30.
19. *Idem.*, I, p. 39.
20. To Ker Gumag (the Great House, that of Ahmadu Bamba, the founder of Muridism).
21. Sâdi, *T.S.*, XII, p. 106.   22. *Idem.*, XXIV, p. 259.
23. *Idem.*, p. 261.   24. *Idem.*, p. 264.   25. *Idem.*, p. 276.
26. Kâti, *T.F.*, XV, p. 282.

Chapter Nine

TECHNICAL LEVEL

This chapter deals with the creation and development of techniques in precolonial Africa. From this viewpoint, architecture assumes special importance, judging from the remains of it found on the continent.

ARCHITECTURE IN NILOTIC SUDAN

According to all the documents currently available to us, the Sudan was one of the earliest civilizations in Black Africa: it was the Ethiopia of antiquity. Present-day Ethiopia was merely an eastern province which was not separated from it until well after the Ptolemaic era in Egypt.

The discovery of the ancient capital of Meroë by Cailliaud, following the information given by Herodotus and Diodorus Siculus, has allowed unearthing of the sub-foundations of several ancient structures. Lepsius later discovered the foundation of an astronomical observatory there: on the walls of this edifice was found a scene representing persons operating an instrument which it might not be inappropriate to call an astrolabe (see illustrations pp. 197 and 198). There was also found a series of numerical equations relating to astronomic events which occurred two centuries B.C.

Still standing around the capital are eighty-four pyramids which, like those in Egypt, were royal sepulchers; also some temples, such as the one at Semna.

ARCHITECTURE IN ZIMBABWE

In the Zambezi River basin of Zimbabwe (formerly Rhodesia), monumental ruins, today fallen into disuse, cover a surface practically as large as France; they are almost cyclopean structures, with walls several meters thick: five at the base, three at the top, and nine meters in height. Edifices of all types are to be found there from the royal palace, the temple, and the military fortification to the private villa of a notable. The walls are of granite masonry. De Pédrals, quoting Miss Caton Thompson, cites an opinion according to which these remains might be attributed to the present-day Ba-Venda tribe of South Africa, for the following reasons:

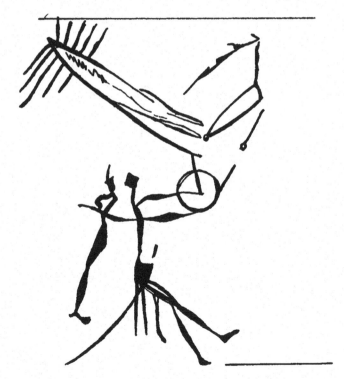

A scene representing persons operating an astronomical instrument (redrawn by Lepsius: see *La Science mystérieuse des pharaons*).

the peoples proved that they knew the uses of stone, as evidenced by the Dzata ruins left by them in Zimbabwe; moreover, the instruments of divination found in Zimbabwe are those of the Venda cult.[1]

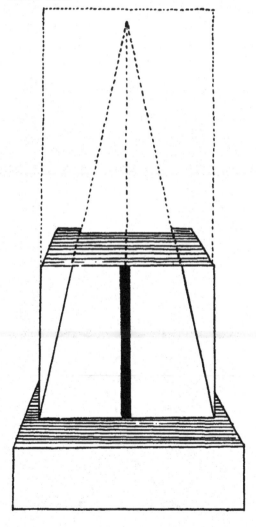

This instrument was used to make observations of the position of the sun on the meridian at Meroë (from *La Science mystérieuse des pharaons*).

In any case, the notion of attributing these ruins to a non-African, non-Black people (Persians, Arabs, Phoenicians, or Israelites: King Solomon's Mines) is once and for all invalidated. All of the digs carried out so far at the site have indeed yielded only Bantu-type skeletons.

It may be that these peoples found it necessary to build systems of defense against Oriental enemies coming from Asia via the Indian Ocean:

> MacIver's conclusions on the "Niekerk" ruins are that "they were inhabited by a people who must have lived in perpetual·apprehension of attack and therefore protected themselves behind one of the vastest series of entrenchment lines to be found anywhere in the world."[2]

ARCHITECTURE IN GHANA AND THE NIGER BEND

It will be remembered that, according to Idrisi, the emperor of Ghana lived in a stone-fortified castle equipped with glass windows and adorned inside with sculptures and paintings. It is said to have been built in 1116. The other houses in the capital were of stone, with beams of acacia; they were, according to all appearances, the homes of the notables; those of the common people were clay huts covered with straw roofs. On these last points, Bakri's testimony is confirmed by that of Idrisi. The digs made in this region by Bonnel de Mézières early in this century (1911–1913) support in large measure the statements of the Arab chroniclers and geographers of the eleventh and twelfth centuries. A city was discovered which is presumed to be the old capital, with vestiges of houses of several stories, nearly inhabitable but for some missing fixtures, with walls thirty centimeters thick, some metallurgical workshops, and so on. But at the height of the Ghanaian empire, there were in this region several large cities with houses and other buildings made of stone (Nema, Ualata,

Aoudaghast, and Kumbi, which was probably the autochthonous name of Ghana).

So we must conclude that in truth we are not absolutely certain that Bonnel de Mézières discovered the old capital, rather than only the location of some one of these old cities, other, however, than Aoudaghast, which was situated much farther west; it was Delafosse who identified one of the four ruined centers as Ghana.[3]

What was the style of this architecture? In the present state of research, that is hard to say. We can, on the other hand, infer what it might have been by comparison to the apparently more recent style known as that of Djenné and Timbuktu. European manuals ordinarily attribute this style to some North African Arab origin, introduced, it is claimed, by Es Sakali (the builder), who was brought back from the Maghreb by Kankan Mussa on his return from his pilgrimage, so that this Spanish Arab architect-poet might build him a mosque. Among the accounts which might allow for such a belief, that of Ibn Khaldun, drawn from his *Prolegomena,* is one of the most decisive: he relates as follows what was told him by one of the Arab companions of Kankan Mussa.

> We accompanied him as far as the capital of his kingdom; and, as he wished to have a new reception hall built, he determined that it would be solidly constructed and overlaid with plaster, for such buildings were as yet unknown in his country. Abu-Ishac-el-Tuedjen [Es Sakali], a man skilled in several arts, undertook to fulfill the king's wish and built a square-shaped hall surmounted by a cupola. He employed all the resources of his genius in this construction, and having overlaid it in plaster and adorned it with arabesques in brilliant colors he made of it an admirable monument.[4]

On rereading this text attentively, we realize that the authors went greatly beyond what it allows us to affirm. In the first place, it deals with a reception hall and not a mosque;

while they have it that Es Sakali built a mosque, the ruins of which can still be seen at Gao. But the architectural details as revealed in the text are even more interesting when contrasted with those of the style alleged to have been imported. Khaldun is categorical: a square hall, surmounted by a cupola and decorated with arabesques. Now, these three architectural features which characterize the style allegedly introduced by Es Sakali, are absolutely not to be found in the Sudanese style. The buildings there are never square, but rather oblong: there are never any arabesques. Its soberness of line, its massive rather than frail appearance, and the absence of arabesques would seem to make it the lone Arabic art form not authentically Arabic. There are never any cupolas: in the whole area of West Africa, from the Sudan to the Ivory Coast, it is impossible to find the slightest cupola atop any one of the mosques built in this style. This is significant, in the extent to which ecclesiastical Arabic architecture has remained unchanged from that time to our own day.

By contrast, the pyramidal columns enjambed into the wall and the pointed sides that characterize Sudanese style have no parallel in either Arabic or European architecture. There is lacking any explanation of the devices by which a people might export what it does not have. It would indeed be paradoxical for a makeshift architect, an amateur (as Es Sakali was), to be able to import into a foreign country a style which did not exist in the architectural traditions of his own country. This elementary condition would have to be fulfilled for the supposition made in the manuals to become acceptable. It is more judicious to abandon this erroneous interpretation of the texts, which consists of making them say what simply is not in them out of the desire to defend one's cherished notion.

There is as much difference between the Arabic style of whatever period (including Spain) and that of the Sudan, as there is between a Gothic cathedral and a Romanesque basilica. It must also be pointed out that it is in the construction of mosques that Arabic architecture is most immutable. Almost all of them are built on the same plan, growing out of the same style (cupola, minaret, etc.). So we are asked to believe that in Black Africa alone this style is not followed. On the contrary, the originality of this Sudanese art is readily apparent: a glance at a single example suffices to show that the pyramidal motif was exploited throughout. This whole architectural style is based on this principle. The general shape of the edifice clearly grows out of a truncated pyramid; all the massive columns which adorn the facade are more or less discreet recalls of the same motif. Even the architecture of the tombs of this region (called tumuli) reveals the same kinship: they are pyramids truncated through erosion, built of brick-red terra cotta, often arranged in a semicircle on an East-West axis. Their average dimensions range from 15 to 18 meters high, with 150 to 200 square meters base surface, according to Desplagnes:

> These tumuli are particularly numerous in the lake region comprised between the cheerless dunes surrounding Timbuktu to the East and the great grazing plains fertilized by Lake Debo to the West.[5]

Thus, under the same latitude, from Nubia to the Sudan, interment was done under the same conditions, all the tombs having the same pyramidal shape. It would rather be to the Temple of Edfu (Egypt) with its symmetrical pyramidal pylons that one might if need be compare the Sudanese style. At the time of Kankan Mussa, Black Africa already had her own masons, organized into bodies, each with a foreman. Kâti tells of a tradition according to which, whenever Kankan Mussa passed through a village on a Friday, he had a mosque built there. Which is said to be why he built the mosques of Timbuktu, Dukurey, Gundam, Direy, Uanko, and Bako.[6] It is hardly necessary to mention that Kâti, who relates this opinion, considers it groundless, as representing a material impossibility. It belongs to that category of legends developed after the fact which often enjoy wide currency in Black Africa.

When the Askia Mohammed seized Djâga in 1495, he captured five hundred masons, with their foreman Karamogho; of these he kept four hundred, sending the other hundred to his brother the viceroy, the prime dignitary of the kingdom, the Kanfari, Amar Komdjago, to build his capital city of Tendirma, on the right bank of the Niger, not far from Timbuktu.[7]

The notion that Black Africa had no architecture of its own before the arrival of Sakali is contrary to the facts: the testimony of Arab authors themselves mentioned above, Bakri and Idrisi (for Ghana) and Battuta (for Mali), prove this point. The digs carried out by Bonnel de Mézières and Desplagnes in the Ghana region and on the Nigerian plateau confirm it. The existence of fortified cities called *tatas* (the equivalent of fortified castle or stronghold) dates back well before this time.

When Ibn Battuta visited the capital of Mali, it was already customary to lay out wide, very straight thoroughfares, flanked by trees on both sides.

At Tamberma, Northern Togo, some veritable fortified castles with peripheral towers and lookouts have been found. This architecture is all the more interesting in that its style is an extension by artful exploitation of the lines of the customary hut.[8]

In former times, the palace of the Oni of Ifé "was a structure built of authentic enameled bricks, decorated with artistic porcelain tiles and all sorts of ornaments."[9]

The houses of the Habés (the Dogons studied by Marcel Griaule) are built of stone, with several stories, cut into cliffs. Some of these buildings are partially below ground level, and thus have subterranean cellars.

The tiered attics in the shape of parallelepipedal towers are of a style directly related to that of the crenellated walls of the *tatas* and Sudanese mosques.[10]

Finally, despite the hiatus in jumping from recorded history to prehistory, the Saharan period before the last great drought (7000 B.C.) seems to be part of the cultural cycles of Black Africa, if we are to judge by the cave paintings brought out by Henri Lhote.

METALLURGY

From Nubia to Senegal, still along the same latitude which seems to belong to the same area of civilization, active blast furnaces produced the iron required for technological and economic activity. It is almost certain that wood was the fuel used. The use of metallurgy in Black Africa dates back to time immemorial. Mining of ore, smelting of metal, and working with it were not taught to Africans by any foreigner. In 1956, M. Leclant, director of the Center for Egyptian Studies at the University of Strasbourg, during a lecture at the École des Hautes Études, alluding to the British metal industry, strongly pointed out that, in classical times, Nubia (Meroë) was comparable to Birmingham in metallurgical production and distribution.

Today the blast furnaces of the Baya, Durru, Namchi, Tchamba, Wuté, Marghi, Batta, Dama, etc., are still in operation.[11]

The appearance in bronzes of the Benin of knights arrayed in all manner of cuirasses, armored from head to toe, seems to prove that metallurgy was put to all kinds of uses, for all of this armor was, without doubt, of local manufacture. Beginning at an early period, in view of the climate, every effort was made to manufacture these items in a material other than iron, while retaining the same shape, provided, of course, that they would be sufficiently protective. That is why this armor ended up, in the final period of Benin history, appearing to be purely decorative items. Here we must recall the many knights of medieval Europe who succumbed beneath their cuirasses on the road of the Holy Land, during the Crusades, due to the rigors and heat of the climate.

The technique of casting bronze by the lost wax process, which accounts for the beautiful realistic artworks of the Benin, was shared between this Gulf of Guinea region on the Atlantic and ancient Meroë. Goldsmithery, the making of gold filigree, which is a specialty of Black Africa, the working of copper, tin, and alloys, all had already become widespread in precolonial Africa. It will be recalled that Samory, during his resistance against France, had had European rifles duplicated by local blacksmiths. Admittedly, their efficiency was not the same, since the metal was not of the same quality. Locksmithing was also known in Africa at the time.

The repeated victories of Nubia over the Roman army (Cornelius Gallus) in 29 B.C. may perhaps give us some idea of the technological level of Nubia in this period.

GLASSMAKING

It is glassmaking, however, especially in the Benin region, which deserves our attention. On the one hand, because it is least expected, and on the other, because it had already at that time attained a semi-industrial stage, the workers having organized into veritable guilds (with community workshops, refectories, and dormitories). This industry has survived to this day, and the Nigerians often utilize as raw material, no longer sand, but shards of bottles and glasses which they blow or mold into various objects (beads, bracelets, etc.). Thus, besides beads of Egyptian, Phoenician, or Venetian origin, there are those of properly local creation.

MEDICINE AND HYGIENE

Empirical medicine was quite developed in Africa. Here, as in ancient Egypt, a family practiced a single branch of medicine on an hereditary basis. One was specialized in the eyes, the stomach, and so on. Sâdi's brother underwent a successful cataract operation at the hands of the physician Ibrahim es Sussi in the port city of Kabara. "The doctor carried out the operation and God willed that my brother be delivered from his malady and brought from the darkness into the light."[12]

In Senegal especially, war wounds were treated by extracting the bullets or shrapnel, then cauterizing the wound with a mixture of boiling oil and clean sand, before sewing it up. It thus happened that some soldiers still had, after recovery, lumps of matter (sand) which had remained under the skin. It seems no one ever thought of removing them. That peculiar process is called *rukâb* in Wolof.

Empirical toxicology was highly developed, whence the efficacity of the poisoned arrows used in warfare. They were covered with snake venom or the sap of poisonous plants.

The use of soap, connected with the rise of urbanism, created a level of hygiene quite remarkable for the period. The soap was of local manufacture: a female slave freed by the Askia guaranteed him, as a sign of appreciation, ten cakes of soap each year.[13]

WEAVING

The treadle loom, a local invention, was known to Africa, as well as the Yoruban vertical loom; with them may be woven fairly narrow strips of fabric, variously decorated, which can then be assembled into loincloths or other articles of clothing. Cotton was the raw material, as well as a kind of wool in Sudan. Linen, silk, and broadcloth, from the time of Askia Bunkan on, were imported from Europe. But the native velvet of the Balubas was famous.

Dressmaking, an ancillary trade, assumed capital importance especially in Timbuktu where, according to Kâti, there were master tailors who employed, in establishments known as *tindi*, fifty, seventy, or as many as a hundred apprentices.[14] This would seem to suggest that there was a certain concentration of the means of production, of which presently available documents do not allow us to measure the full scope.

AGRICULTURE

Cultivation of the soil was done either with the *daramba* (hoe) or with the *hilaire* (hand plow) in Senegal. The latter tool allowed one to till the soil while standing up, whereas with the *daramba* one had to bend over. Its use, therefore, was a great improvement in places where it was impractical to use a plow. It should be pointed out that the Egyptian plow and the African hoe are identical. All the Egyptians had to do was to attach a wooden crossbar perpendicularly to the shaft to accommodate a harness: the Egyptian plow is just an African hoe harnessed to an animal.

In Black Africa, crop rotation, irrigation, and manuring of fields were all practiced.

CRAFTS

Basket-weaving, ceramics, and dyeing were highly developed crafts. The same was true of shoemaking, thanks to plants such as the *neneb*, which could be used in tanning skins, particularly goatskins.

These techniques having been abundantly studied and described in manuals, we need not enlarge upon them here.

HUNTING

The hunting of the hippopotamus, on the Senegal River, deserves to be described. We can do so, thanks to the testimony of Bakri. The hunters, bunched along the bank, were armed with short javelins having rings through which passed a long lanyard the other end of which was attached to the hunter's wrist. They would patiently lie in wait for the animal; when its back came into view, all the converging javelins struck different parts of its body. It was dragged out of the water by the lanyards, after it had many convulsions which left the animal exhausted. This was how the natives of Kalenfu hunted the *kafu* (or hippopotamus).[15]

NAUTICAL EXPERIENCE

It is clear from the preceding that the navigable watercourses of Africa were studded with wharves and landing docks, which were at one and the same time commercial ports and, when necessary, military ones. The largest craft *(kanta)* could carry a crew of up to eighty men.[16] On the Niger, in place of the inverted sails characteristic of Black Africa, the boats were covered by a mat that formed a kind of roofing against the elements. The Askia alone owned over a thousand pirogues. Each of his daughters had one for transportation or pleasure cruises on the river: just as the Pharaoh's daughters had on the Nile.

The question has often been asked whether the Africans ever left the continent by sea, whether to the West the Atlantic Ocean had allowed them, before the arrival of Europeans, to establish relations with any other country. Considering the enormous obstacles to overcome (all rivers have a bar), specialists have tended to answer in the negative: this is the point of view of Professor Théodore Monod. Yet, it seems that the Arabic documents allow us to shed some light on the matter. Muhammad Hamidullah, quoting Ibn Fadallâh Al Umarîy, shows that the Emperor of Mali, Kankan Mussa's predecessor, made two attempts at exploring the Atlantic. In the first he equipped two hundred ships for a two-years' stay at sea:

only one of the captains was able to return with his vessel. The recital of the catastrophe he gave the king, instead of discouraging him, prompted him to undertake a second expedition. He is then said to have equipped two thousand ships, turned his throne over to Sultan Mussa, and embarked with the fleet himself. This time nobody returned. The author of this study puts forward several arguments to demonstrate that this fleet, or perhaps another earlier one, must surely have reached America before Columbus. In the first place, not only did Columbus's crew say they had found Blacks already there before them, but they even gave details of their lives: they stressed that the Blacks often fought with the "Redskin" Indians. The same author reminds us:

> Christopher Columbus speaks of pirogues allegedly leaving from the coast of Guinea laden with merchandise and heading west. He also recounts the arrival of such vessels in the Americas. Jane (the translator of the journal of Columbus's third voyage) writes: ". . . and that he considered checking the veracity of what the Indians of Hispaniola [Haiti] said that they had come to their island from the south while the Blacks had come from the southeast, and that they had javelins with tips made of a metal they called *guanin* . . ."[17]

The pirogues actually seen by Christopher Columbus prove that the bars of the rivers had been crossed, that there were indeed precolonial maritime ports, and that the Atlantic was no wall to the Blacks of West Africa. The author of the article goes further and attempts to establish that relations between Africa and pre-Columbian America were relatively constant:

> Such navigators, taking to sea again from the Americas for the return voyage to Africa, would have loaded provisions of new World origin, and of these items the two that would keep the longest were sweet corn and tapioca. We thus have an explanation of the presence in Africa of two American foodstuffs before Columbus had ever made a voyage there.[18]

We might mention, without however being able to determine how early it began, that the Blacks of the Petite Côte in Senegal travel from Dakar to M'Bour by coastal navigation on masted cutters of their own construction. One might also recall that it was on longboats very similar to these pirogues that the Vikings skimmed the seas for centuries. With just such vessels, they journeyed up the Seine as far as Paris, and went as far as North America, before Christopher Columbus. The African vessels, equipped with outriggers and therefore impossible to capsize, were perfectly capable of venturing onto the high seas.

Of course, there still remain many gaps to fill, but the above allows us a glimpse of the actual technical level of precolonial Black Africa. But even now, what we do know may prove quite surprising, and we may close this chapter by meditating upon the following idea of M. Leroi-Gourhan, which reads almost like a maxim:

"If there be a goal for humanism, it lies in a humanism which would not only reach the limits of mankind everywhere on the entire Earth, but also integrate the reality of material man with the reality of religious or social man."[19]

NOTES

1. D. P. de Pédrals, *Archéologie de l'Afrique Noire* (Paris: Payot, 1950), p. 59.
2. M. A. Jaspan, *op. cit.*, p. 207 (*Présence Africaine*, p. 151), quoting from D. R. MacIver, *Mediaeval Rhodesia* (London, 1906).
3. Leroi-Gourhan and Poirier, *op. cit.*, p. 225.
4. Ibn Khaldun, *op. cit.*, p. 113.
5. Louis Desplagnes, *Le Plateau Central Nigérien* (Paris: Larose, 1907), p. 57.
6. Kâti, *T. F.*, ch. II, pp. 56–58.
7. *Idem.*, VI, pp. 118–119.
8. Cf. Baumann, *op. cit.*, p. 411.
9. Leo Frobenius, *Mythologie de l'Atlantide* (trans. from the German by Gidon) (Paris: Payot, 1947), pp. 154–156.

10. Cf. Baumann, *op. cit.*, p. 411.
11. *Idem.*, pp. 319–320.
12. Sâdi, *T. S.*, XXXV, p. 445.
13. Kâti, *T. F.*, XI, p. 196.
14. *Idem.*, XVI, p. 315.
15. Al Bakri, *op. cit.*, "Notes sur le pays des Noirs," pp. 324–325.
16. *T. F.*, XV, p. 270.
17. *Présence Africaine* magazine, No. XVIII–XIX, February–May 1958, p. 180.
18. *Idem.*, p. 182. Since these lines were originally written, an American Black researcher, Ivan Van Sertima, has published a masterful book on the subject, which leaves no doubt about these pre-Columbian navigations: *They Came Before Columbus: The African Presence in Ancient America* (New York: Random House, 1977).
19. Leroi-Gourhan and Poirier, *op. cit.*, p. 43.

Chapter X

MIGRATIONS AND FORMATION OF PRESENT-DAY AFRICAN PEOPLES

In West Africa, one can be certain only that Neolithic remains are attributable to tall Blacks. The Paleolithic are, generally speaking, of uncertain age: some are found at Pita, in Upper Guinea. The testimony of Herodotus about the expedition of the Nasamonians, who left from Cyrenaica, and of Hanno and Satapses converges to prove that in the fifteenth century B.C., on the whole, tall Blacks had not yet peopled West Africa, despite the more or less enigmatic mention made by Hanno of "Lixist interpreters."[1] The whole continent at that time was partially peopled by Pygmies, with the exception of a few places such as the Nile basin; that is why archeologists generally consider Pygmies responsible for all Paleolithic traces found in West Africa, especially since they are usually just on the surface. Consequently, it is important to stress the fact that West African archaeology is rather special; one would be hard put to find in it any stratification of civilizations at a given spot, since most of the peoples migrated at relatively recent dates. It is therefore understandable that one should be able to hear in this region legends according to which the Blacks came from the East, from over near the "Great Water," without the latter being identifiable as the Indian Ocean. Two reasons, indeed, contradict that: when South African populations are questioned, they say they came from the North; those of the Gulf of Benin say they came from the Northeast. In antiquity, the Ethiopians called themselves *autochthons*, those who had sprung from the ground. Egyptians considered themselves to have come from the South, from Nubia (Sudan, Khartoum, locations of their ancestors: the country of Punt). Nubia is the Ethiopia of antiquity. Even if mankind did not originate in Africa, even if the tall Blacks came from elsewhere, say, from the Indian Ocean as in the Lemuric thesis, it could only have been hundreds of thousands of years before. But we have just seen that in the fifth century B.C., a very recent date, tall Blacks had not yet expanded toward the West, while we know for certain that they existed on the continent. The idea of a center of dispersal located approximately in the Nile valley is worth consideration. In all likelihood, after the drying of the Sahara (7000 B.C.), Black mankind first lived in bunches in the Nile basin, before swarming out in successive spurts toward the interior of the continent.

By an investigative method using linguistic, ethnological, and toponymic data, we will try to bring out, in a practically certain manner, the origins of the Laobé, Tukulor, Peul, Yoruba, Agni, Serer, and other peoples.

First, however, we must recall that D.P. de Pédrals mentions[2] the Burum who are found on the Upper Nile and in the region of the Benue in Nigeria, the Ga (Gan, Gang) who are found in the region of the Great Lakes and present-day Ghana, Upper Volta, and in the Ivory Coast, the Gula (Gule, Gulaye) on the Upper Nile and the Chari. The Kara are a nucleus living at the borders of Sudan (Khartoum) and Upper Ubangi. The Karé are near Logone; the Karé-Karé in the northeast of Nigeria, their name being nothing more than the doubling of Karé, which is made up of Ka + Ré or Ka + Ra, two Egyptian ontological notions which we will analyze below. The Kipsighi (Kapsighi) are in the region of the Great Lakes and North Cameroon; the Kissi northeast of Lake Nyasa and in the forest of Upper Guinea; the Kundu in the former Belgian Congo (Lake Leopold) and the Southern

The queen subdues a group of vanquished enemies. Méroé, Sudan, bas-relief (redrawn by Lepsius in *Histoire ancienne de l'Egypte* by Lenormant).

Cameroon, at the estuary of the Wouri; the Laka live among
the Nuer of the Upper Nile and the Sara of the Logone and
Northern Cameroon; the Maka (Makua) on the Zambezi and
in the Cameroon; the Sango northeast of the Nyasa and on
the banks of the Ubangi; the Somba (Sumbwa) in the region of
the Great Lakes and Northern Dahomey.

One could extend this list and thus localize in the Nile
Valley, coming from the Great Lakes, the primitive cradle of all
the Black peoples today living dispersed at the various points
of the continent.

It must be recalled that Kandaka (Candace), the name, or
rather the title, of the queens of the Sudan, beginning with the
time of Augustus Caesar, was also borne by the first kings of
Kau (Gao), according to Al Bakri; they were called Kanda.
The women of this region, according to the same author, in
the tenth century wore wigs such as those worn in Egypt and
Nubia. In antiquity there was a Nubian nome called Kau, the
exact location of which has not yet been identified, according
to Budge.[3] The inhabitants of Upper Egypt were called Kau-
Kau in the Egyptian tongue. We know that Gao is both an
abbreviation and a deformation of the real name of that city:
Kau-Kau.[4] Inhabitants of the interior of Senegal even today
have the name of Kau-Kau (Cayor, Baol), which those of the
coast, as in ancient Libya, are called Lebou: they are the
fishermen of the whole region of the Niaye (coastal palm
forests).

In old Egyptian, as today in Wolof, *Kau* has the same
meaning: high; and in both languages, *Kau-Kau* means inhabitants of high places, or high plateaus. It can then be
presumed that, if present-day inhabitants of Cayor and Baol,
living on an absolutely flat plain, still bear this name, it might
be due to a geographical reminiscence explainable by migration, especially since between them and the coast, then and
now, there were the Lebou. It is likely that the populations
who were forced to emigrate did not have time on the way to

shed their habits: the inlanders (Kau-Kau) would have settled in the interior, and the coasters (Lebou) on the coast. It may be recalled that, until the eleventh century, the capital of Songhai was Kukia, some one hundred kilometers from Kauga (Gao); in all of northern Senegal, the various villages one finds name Koki seem to be replicas of that ancient historical city on the Niger, the more likely since the phoneme o does not exist in Arabic, but must be translated u, barring some arbitrary convention. Yet the documents that today permit us to refer to the historical city of Kukia are all written in Arabic. Bakri says that Kau-Kau (Gao-Gao) is the sound emitted by the royal tom-tom of that capital city. The Cayorians of Senegal also say that the *diung-diung* of the Damel (the royal drum) goes *gau-gau*. It would seem that we must conclude that we are dealing here with an oral etymology which does not exactly fit in with historical reality, to the extent that we find roots of the same word, beyond any possible doubt, right up into the valley of the Nile.

Having made this recall, let us look at the origins of the principal peoples of West Africa.

ORIGIN OF THE YORUBA

According to J. Olumide Lucas,[5] the Yoruba during antiquity lived in ancient Egypt, before migrating to the Atlantic coast. He uses as demonstration the similarity or identity of languages, religious beliefs, customs, and names of persons, places, and things.

> Abundant proof of intimate connection between the ancient Egyptians and the Yoruba may be produced under this head. Most of the principal gods were well known, at one time, to the Yoruba. Among these gods are Osiris, Isis, Horus, Shu, Sut, Thoth, Khepera, Amon, Anu, Khonsu, Khnum, Khopri, Hathor, Sokaris, Ra, Seb, the four elemental deities, and others. Most of the gods survive in name or in attributes or in both (p. 21).

I-Ra-Wo in Yoruba means the star that accompanies the Sun (*wo:* to rise), Khonsu has turned into Osu (the Moon). The linguistic variations are explained by the author on the basis of the phonetics of Yoruba. He reminds us that the ontological notions of ancient Egyptian, such as Ka, Akhu, Ku, Saku, and Ba, are to be found in Yoruba. He also points to the existence of hieroglyphics and expounds all these ideas at length over four hundred pages.

It may be pointed out that the "pope" of the Yoruba, the Oni, has the same title as Osiris, the Egyptian God, that there is a hill called Kuse, near Ilé-Ifé, and another of the same name in Nubia, near ancient Meroë, to the west of the Nile, in the very heart of the country of Kush.[6] The name Kuso is repeated in Abyssinia.

ORIGIN OF THE LAOBÉ

They would seem to be survivors of the legendary Sao people. As a matter of fact, what do we learn about the Sao from the Bornu manuscripts and the excavations of M. Lebeuf and my late professor Marcel Griaule?

These references tell us of the Sao that (1) their name was Sao, Sow, or Si; (2) they were giants; (3) they spent entire nights dancing; (4) they left innumerable terra cotta figurines; and (5) these statuettes reveal an ethnic type with pear-shaped head.

All five of these traits are found in the Laobé. Their sole totemic name is Sow, which has been mistaken for a Peul name. The only sacred object left them, the instrument with which they carve, is called a *sao-ta*. They are all giants, the women averaging six feet in height, and the men six feet six or more, very easily. They have extraordinarily handsome limbs and are always built like athletes.

Their skulls are pear-shaped, identical with those of the ethnic type seen on Sao statuettes.

Map of migrations of the peoples of black Africa
(from *La région du Haut-Nil et des Grands Lacs*).

The Laobés' only occupation is carving wooden kitchen utensils from tree-trunks, for all other castes of African society, and not only the Peul. Laobé women make terra cotta figurines for the children of other castes. The Laobé, especially the women, love to dance; they take part in all fêtes and other local events. Their main dance, in Senegal, is the *kumba laobé gâs*.

The Laobé were wrongly considered a caste of Peul and Tuculor sculptors. This mistake comes in part from the fact that they speak the language of these two peoples. It has been overlooked that the Laobé are always bilingual, at least in Senegal. They speak Wolof as fluently as Peul; but their accent in Wolof is not that of a Peul or Tuculor, which would not be explicable if they belonged to the same ethnic group as the latter, differing from them only in caste. The Laobé seem to be a people who have lost their culture and whose dispersed elements adapt, according to circumstances, by learning the languages of the regions in which they reside. The totemic names other than Sow which they bear reflect their mixture with the Peul, Tuculor, and other groups. The reverse is also true; and that explains why some Peul have the name of Sow, alongside Ba and Ka.

The Laobé live scattered over different villages in Senegal and elsewhere. They have no fixed dwellings; it is inaccurate to say that they inhabit the Futa Toro (in Senegal) or the Futa Jallon (in Guinea), territories of the Tuculor and Peul. They form sporadic groupings within larger ethnic groups. The Laobé of Senegal can no longer pinpoint their original habitat; their social organization has completely dissolved; they no longer have traditional chiefs. The most respected member of the group rides a mule, while donkeys are reserved for others. Thus, the case of Med Sow Wediam, a very influential Laobé, but who could not properly be called a king; moreover, he owed his influence mainly to his conversion to the Muridism of Amadu Bamba. The Laobé swear on the *sao-ta*, which is used not only to carve, but also to circumcise the young, a custom they seem to have borrowed from neighboring peoples.

ORIGIN OF THE PEUL

At first sight, one might believe that the Peul branch originally came from that part of West Africa where Semitic Moors and Blacks long remained in contact.[7] Though the hypothesis of this crossbreeding must be accepted, the initial site where it took place must be sought elsewhere, despite appearances.

Like other West African populations, the Peul probably came from the East, only later. This theory can be supported by perhaps the most important fact to date: the identity of two typical totemic proper names of the Peul with two equally typical notions of Egyptian metaphysical beliefs, the Ka and the Ba.

According to Moret, the Ka is the essential Being, the ontological part of the individual which exists in the sky. Thus, in the texts of the Old Empire, there is the expression "to go to one's Ka," meaning to die. The Ka, united with the Zet, forms the Ba, the complete being reaching perfection and living in the sky.[8]

Zet was the part of the being that was purified in the "Jackal's Basin," according to the Egyptian religion. *Set* (there is no *z* in Wolof and it automatically becomes *s* when used in a foreign word) means clean, in Wolof. Obviously, it is not identifiable with the third totemic name of Sow, borne by some Peul.

On the other hand, Ka and Ba, these two Egyptian ontological notions, are authentically Peul proper names, the only ones they must have had in the beginning.

Ka, or *Kao,* in old Egyptian, means high, above, great,

husband, standard, height—whence the description of the word by a hieroglyph made up of two arms extended toward the sky. It has the same meaning in Wolof, and one should make the connection with Kau-Kau mentioned above.

Ba, in Egyptian, is represented by a bird with a human head, living in the sky; it also is the name of a long-necked earthly bird. *Ba* in Wolof means ostrich. So it can be seen that these elements of Egyptian metaphysics underwent different changes depending on who transmitted them; whereas in Wolof the Egyptian meaning is retained, in Peul the words have become proper names. It is a known fact that, until the Sixth Dynasty, the time of the Osirian revolution (2100 B.C.), the Pharaoh alone was entitled to immortality and, consequently, fully enjoyed his Ka and his Ba; it is also known that several Pharaohs bore this name, among them King Ka, of the protodynastic era, whose tomb was discovered at Abydos by Amélineau. The name of the Peul branch of the Kara or Karé would then come from Ka + Ra or Ka + Ré.

The other Peul names, such as Diallo, would have been acquired later, despite appearances. As for their language, it has a natural unity with the other Black African languages, especially Wolof and Serer, as shall be shown.

The relative hatred which existed, in olden times, between the seminomadic Peul and sedentary Africans can be explained by their different life styles: the Peul frequently took advantage of unguarded fields to let their flocks graze in them: whence perhaps the origin of the evil, for this fact is far from accidental and its importance cannot be exaggerated. But the idea of a Peul hegemony in West Africa is just a legend; it does not conform to the documents. According to Kâti and Sâdi, Sonni Ali made several expeditions against the Peul; he practically destroyed the clan of the Sangaré (San-Ka-Ré), the survivors being so few they could gather within the shade of one tree.[9]

Following one of these expeditions, Sonni Ali distributed

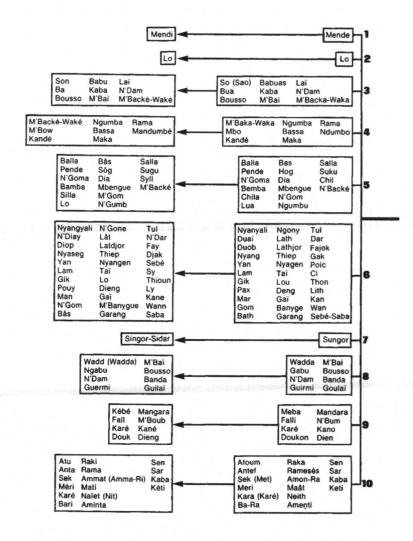

Groups of Wolof peoples, by their ethnic names. Prevalent names in various regions have been grouped by origin (1–10) in the right column. The left column shows the corresponding Wolof names.

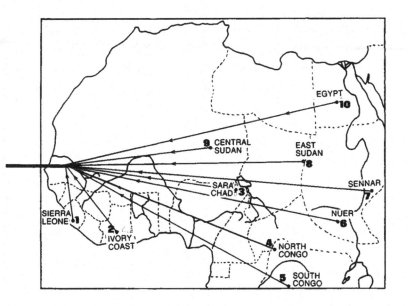

several captive Peul women as concubines to those Timbuktu scholars who were his friends; Sâdi says that one of them was his own grandmother.[10]

The idea that the nomadic Peul people was feared in precolonial Black Africa is also unfounded. It grows out of a preconceived notion which tries come what may to exalt the pastoral life, for reasons peculiar to the authors. On the contrary, Sâdi stresses the lack of material or social strength of the nomads who, by the fact that they were constantly on the move, never had the chance or possibility to acquire any power that might threaten the sedentary.

ORIGIN OF THE TUCULOR

Today, among the Nuer of the Sudan (Khartoum) on the Upper Nile, one finds unaltered the totemic names of the Tuculor who live on the banks of the Senegal River, thousands of kilometers away. It must be recalled that totemic and ethnic names are identical, being the names of the clans.

Sudan (Khartoum)	Senegal (Futa-Toro)
Kan	Kan
Wan	Wan
Ci	Sy (Ci)
Lith	Ly
Kao	Ka (Peul)[11]

In the same region, at a place called Nuba Hills (Nubia Hills), we find tribes of the Nyoro and Toro. These two names in a way mark out the route followed by the Tuculor migration from the Upper Nile. The region between the Senegal and Niger rivers, in which the Tuculor would remain for a certain length of time, was to be known as the Nyoro; when they arrived on the two banks of the Senegal, the region would be known as the Futa-Toro. When one fraction of them went down into the Gambia, under Maba Diakhu, at the time of General Faidherbe (1865), the region would assume the name of Nyoro-du-Rip, the latter word being the old name of the region, before the Tuculor arrived.

ORIGIN OF THE SERER

They also probably came from the Upper Nile. According to Pierret's dictionary, Serer in Egyptian would mean "he who traces the temple." That would be consistent with their present religious position: they are one of the rare Senegalese populations who still reject Islam. Their route is marked by the upright stones found at about the same latitude from Ethiopia all the way to Siné-Salum, their present habitat. This seems to be substantiated by an analysis of the article by Dr. Maes on the upright stones of the French Sudanese village of Tundi-Doro, previously discovered by Desplagnes.

Dr. Maes attributes the origin of these stones, on the basis of pure hypothesis, to Carthaginians or Egyptians. He analyzes the name of the village as follows: *Tundi* would come from the Songhai meaning stone, *Daro* from the Arabic *dar* meaning house. So Tundi-Daro would be "stone house." This analysis would be valid and acceptable only if these stones represented houses, or if one could find that, in one way or another, they suggested houses. But this is not the case; they are described as follows:

> They are monoliths cut in the shape of a phallus, usually with the head (glans) well delineated, the grooves follow the lines of the glans, and the pouch is depicted by rounded bulges whose longitudinal folds resemble those of the scrotum. Other smaller stones are not phallus-shaped. Deprived of rounded protuberances, with the triangle outlined in the form of a pubis, by the union of the lower two-thirds with the upper third they seem instead an attempt to represent the female organ.[12]

The author thinks this might have been a cemetery. That would seem likely if any bones were found beneath the stones; but there are none. The author himself recognizes this problem.

The stones might rather be linked to an agrarian cult; they symbolize the ritual union of Sky and Earth to give birth to their daughter, Vegetation. According to archaic beliefs, rain was the water impregnating the Earth (Mother-Goddess) sent down by the Sky (Father-God, a celestial God who became atmospheric with the discovery of agriculture, according to Mircea Eliade). The vegetation that grew out of this union was a divine product; whence the idea of a Cosmic Trinity, which, through a series of successive incarnations, would evolve into the Christian Trinity of Father, Son, and Virgin Mary (later replaced by the Holy Spirit), by way of the Triad Osiris-Isis-Horus. Same must produce same; therefore, they carved in stone the two sexual organs so as to invite the divinities to couple and bring about the growth of the vegetation that supported the life of the people. Thus, it was the need to insure his material existence which drove man to such practices. The vital impulse, in archaic materialism, could be expressed only in this transposed form, disguised as metaphysics.

The present inhabitants of the Tundi-Daro region are not responsible for the erection of these stones, nor are their ancestors, according to the author's research. We can therefore assume that the Serer-Wolofs, before Islamization, went through such a stage. The Serer still have the same cult of the upright stones. In Bakri's time, the inhabitants of the upper Senegal River planted pestles which were used as altars for libations and were called in the vocabulary of the times *dekkur* (*dek* in Wolof meaning anvil, and *kur*, pestle), but *dek* could also be taken to mean altar, in the sense of a receptacle, which is indeed its basic meaning. But the analysis of Tundi-Daro in Wolof is even more interesting: *tund* = hill, *daro* = sexual union, in the ritual sense. This was euphemistic. The vowel *i* makes it plural. Tundi-Daro, in present-day Wolof, means precisely hills of union. That is so, because these rites took place on high places, mountains, or hills, considered sacred because they represented the point at which sky and earth seemed to touch; the idea of the center of the world, as in Jerusalem, the Kaaba of Mecca, the Sacred Mountain of the Mongol shaman.

This idea is corroborated by the fact that the village of Tundi-Daro does indeed stand against hills of reddish sandstone. The excavations so far done in the area confirm the idea to the extent that the tombs (tumuli) studied are not of too recent date in relation to the Serer migration. The latter's funeral materials and burial rites were the same as those of the ancient Egyptians and the emperors of Ghana: the deceased was buried, more or less luxuriously depending on the wealth of the family, and laid on a bed; around him were disposed all the usual domestic objects he used in daily life, and even a rooster to wake him in the morning. He was probably even mummified in the beginning, for apart from Angola, where mummification is still practiced, we know from Sâdi that Sonni Ali, the Songhay sovereign who was closest to the old pre-Islamic traditions, was mummified.[13]

It should then be possible through further digs to find the road followed by the Serer from the Upper Nile. The sacred city of Kaôn, which they founded on arrival in the Siné-Salum, seems to have been a replica of a city of the same name in ancient Egypt. We know that there are even Egyptian hieroglyphic texts called "from Kaôn," because they came from that city. The Serer heavenly god, whose voice was the thunder, was called Rôg, which is often complemented by Sen, a national epithet, typically Serer. Rôg suggests Ra. Sar is also a widely used Serer name: it designated the nobility of ancient Egypt. A linguistic variant of the same word, San, designated the nobility of the Sudan, whence San-Koré, which was the neighborhood of the nobles in the city of Timbuktu, where the famous university-mosque of Sankoré was built. We know that some Pharaohs of the Third Dynasty had the name of Sar, whereas Per-ib-Sen and Osorta-Sen (Senwart = Sesostris) were Pharaohs respectively of the First and Sixteenth Dynasties. The Egyptians did not have family names in the present-day sense: all the added names they assumed could thus be translated, such as Sen[14] meaning brother. But we know that modern names also derive from similar expressions which have been more or less disguised: thus, the French Dupont (du-pont) is the man from the bridge, Duval (du-val) the one from the valley.

ORIGIN OF THE AGNI (AÑI)

The name of this people as a whole is reminiscent of *Anu* or *Oni*, which was the title of Osiris in *The Book of the Dead*, the epithet constantly applied to him. Almost all Agni kings have the title or surname of Amon, the Egyptian god of humidity, which is found everywhere in West Africa, whence the significant title of Marcel Griaule's book, *Amma, Dieu d'Eau des Dogons* (Amma, Water-God of the Dogons).

Thus, there was Ammon Azenia in the sixteenth century, Ammon Tifu in the seventeenth. A son of this king was brought before Louis XIV, who treated him with distinction. Ammon Aguire, who reigned in the nineteenth century, signed a treaty of alliance with King Louis-Philippe of France. One is therefore inclined to believe that the Agni as well were originally from the Nile basin.[15]

ORIGIN OF THE FANG AND BAMUM

D.P. de Pédrals, in an article published in December 1951, relates that Fr. Trilles, after a series of studies, came to the conclusion that the Fang had had some contact with Ethiopian Christianity during their early migration: in the last century, they had not yet gotten as far as the Atlantic coast. So, their migration must have been relatively recent.

Similar studies by M.D.W. Jeffreys point to a connection between the Bamum and the Egyptians, Pédrals writes:

> Having noted in several books on Egypt the vulture-pharaoh and serpent-pharaoh relationships, and especially the fact pointed out by Diodorus: that the Ethiopian and Egyptian priests kept an asp curled up in their hats; having also noted various examples of zoomorphic two-headed representations, particularly in *The Book of the Dead (Añi papyrus)*, folio 7, M.D.W. Jeffreys declared himself convinced that "the Bamum cult of the king derives from a similar Egyptian cult."[16]

These facts also bear some resemblance to the existence of the royal vulture of Cayor, called Geb, which was also the Egyptian name for Earth, the reclining god.

FORMATION OF THE WOLOF PEOPLE

In Africa, totemic clan names are, to an extent, an ethnic indication; thus, the totemic names of Fall, Diagne, Diouf, Faye, Sar, and so on, are typically Serer. If a Serer has a totemic name other than one of these, his foreign extraction leaves no doubt in the minds of his fellow Serer.

The Tuculor, although crossbred, have equally characteristic totemic names: Wane, Kane, Diallo, Sy, Ly, and so on. Peul names are essentially Ka and Ba; where Sow is more likely to be Laobé. Touré is a Songhai name; Cissé, a Sarakolé name, and so on. Yet the Wolofs have no other totemic names than these, while recognizing that they are clanic names typical of the abovementioned peoples. Beyond these names, there are other Wolof names which are of Sara or Congolese origin.

Southern Congo	Senegal: Wolof
Balla	Balla: a man's proper name
Dia	Dia
Mbengue	Mbengue
N'Goma	N'Goma
N'Gom	N'Gom
Bemba	Bamba: a man's proper name
Ngumbu	Ngumb
Chila	Silla
Lua	Lo
Suku	Sugu
Bas	Bas
Chil	Syll
Hog	Sôg
M'Backé	M'Backé

Northern Congo	*Senegal: Wolof*
M'Backa-Waka	M'Backé-Waké
Bassa	Bassa
Mbo	Mbow
Maka	Make: name of a city
Rama	Rama: woman's proper name
Ndumbé	Mandumbé: man's proper name
Kandé	Kandé
Nguma	Ngumba: name of a city

Eastern Sudan	*Senegal: Wolof*
Wadda	Wadd
	Wadda: man's proper name
Gabu	Ngabu: name of a Baol village
M'Baï	M'Baï
N'Dam	N'Dam: village name recalling a clanic name
Busso	Busso
Guirmi	Guermi: a noble, a member of the ruling dynasty
Banda	Banda: man's proper name
Gulaï	Gulaï: man's proper name

Sara	*Senegal: Wolof*
M'Baï	M'Baï
Laï	Laï
N'Dam	N'Dam
Kaba	Kaba
Bua	Ba
Busso	Busso
Babuas	Babu
M'Backa-Waka	M'Backé-Waké

Central Sudan	Senegal: Wolof
Keba	Kebé
Mandara	Mangara
Falli	Fall
M'Bum	M'Bub
Karé	Karé
Kano: name of a city	Kane
Dukon	Djuk
Dien	Dieng

Chad	Senegal: Wolof
So: legendary people of the Sao	Sow (Laobé)

Ivory Coast	Senegal: Wolof
Lo	Lo

Sierra Leone	Senegal: Wolof
Mende	Mendi

The original habitat from which these clans emigrated was the Nile basin. Indeed, we can find there the same proper names as quoted above: these totemic names are taken from the book, *African System of Kinship and Marriage,* edited by A.R. Radcliff-Brown and Daryll Forde (International African Institute, Oxford University Press).

Totemic Clan Names of the Nuer	Senegal: Wolof and Others
Duai	N'Diaye (which would seem to question the authenticity of the legend of N'Diadian N'Diaye)
Tiop/Duob	Diop (N'Diaye and Diop would seem to be the only authentic Wolof names before intermarriage [17])

Nyang	Nyang	
Yan	Yan	
Lam	Lam	
Gik	Gik	All Wolof
Puok		totemic
Poic	Puy	proper names
Tai	Taï	
Nyanyali	Nyangyali	
Mar	Mar	
Lu	Lo	
Gom	N'Gom	Totemic names
Deng	Dieng	common to Sara,
Gak	Djak/Gak	Congolese, and
Gai	Gaï	Wolofs
Bath	Bâs	
Totemic Clan names of the Nuer	*Senegal: Wolof and others*	
Banyge	M'Banygue: Wolof man's proper name	
Ngony	Ngoné: Wolof woman's proper name	
Garang	Garang: Wolof man's proper name	
Lath	Lât: Wolof totemic name	
Fajok	Fay: Serer and Lebou totemic name	
Lathjor	Latjor: Wolor man's proper name	
Thiep	Thier: Baol village name	
Tul	Tul: Wolof village name	
Nyagen	Nyangen: Nyang village	
Dar	N'Dar: city name	
Thon	Thiun: Wolof totemic name	
Kan	Kane	
Ci	Sy	Tuculor totemic
Wan	Wann	names
Lith	Ly	

We must remember that the Nuer live in the Nilotic Sudan, in the very basin of the Upper Nile.

These two lists of comparative proper names are more instructive than many pages of literature; while very incomplete, they give an idea of how the African continent was peopled. Starting from the Nile basin in successive waves, the populations radiated in all directions. Some peoples, such as the Serer and the Tuculor, seem to have gone directly to the

Atlantic Ocean, while others stopped in the Congo Basin and the region of the Chad, with the Zulus going as far as the Cape.

The Congolese populations, Sara and Sara-kolé (who would seem to be only a crossbred tribe of Sara), would then later migrate toward the West, flowing down into the Cayor and Baol plains occupied by the Serer, and especially into the Djoloff.

The fact that in what was once French West Africa the name of the primitive totemic clan should still be borne by isolated individuals lost in a heterogeneous mass, corresponds to a relative emancipation of the individual from the primitive community. In fact, successive migrations finally disintegrated that fraction of the clan which had broken away from the mother branch.

The *Tarikh es Sudan* mentions the tribe of the Wolofs (Djolfs) and describes their virtues; it also mentions the existence of a tribe called Adior (Adjor).[18]

But Sâdi must certainly have related these facts on the basis of hearsay, for the Wolofs, despite what he thought, were not Peuls: the review of ethnic names proves that; so do their languages.

Likewise, the Adiors (inhabitants of the Cayor) were not Berbers: Adior and Wolof are one and the same thing, which Sâdi had no idea of. The Adior are one of the blackest peoples of Africa. Their language, Wolof, has no connection whatever with Berber.

According to the *Tarikh el Fettach*, an Israelite minority also lived in the bend of the Niger (region of Tendirma), and had made a specialty of cultivating vegetables watered with fresh well water instead of river water. This event must have been within the first millennium of the Hegira, but the date cannot be determined with precision.[19]

The Askias and Sonnis are of the same origin. They are neither Berbers nor Yemenites, but originate in the Upper Senegal, according to the investigation made by Kâti at the time.

The father of Askia Mohammed was named Arlum Silla and came from the city of Silla on the Upper Senegal. His mother, Kassaï, was also an autochthon.[20] Sonni Ali also came from the Upper Senegal. Ber—his surname reminds one of M'Ber (champion) in Wolof—was the first emperor to take the title of Dali, which is the equivalent of Caesar in the African tradition.[21]

NOTES

1. The Carthaginians deliberately falsified their travel narratives so as to mislead competitors; they scuttled their ships rather than yield their maritime secrets to the Romans.
2. D.P. de Pédrals, *op. cit.*, ch. X.
3. Budge, *Egyptian Sudan* (London, 1907).
4. Al Bakri, *op, cit.*, pp. 342-343.
5. J. Olumide Lucas, *The Religion of the Yorubas* (Lagos: C.M.S. Bookshop, 1948).
6. Pédrals, *op. cit.*, p. 107 (cf. map of Africa made by Coronelli in 1689).
7. Delafosse, *Les Noirs d'Afrique, op. cit.*
8. Moret, *Le Nile et la Civilisation égyptienne*, p. 212.
9. *T. F.*, ch. V, pp. 83–84.
10. *T. S.*, ch. XII, pp. 109–110.
11. A. R. Radcliff-Brown and Daryll Forde, *African System of Kinship and Marriage* (International African Institute, Oxford University Press).
12. Dr. Maes, *Pierres levées de Toundi-Dar* (Bul. Com. Et. A.O.F., 1924), p. 31.
13. *T. S.*, ch. XII, p. 116.
14. *Hedj ak i sen* meant "favorites and brothers" in Wolof originally; with evolution, it now means "his favorites and others." *Sen* has now become the opposite of brother, a secondary character.
15. *Encyclopédie mensuelle d'outre-mer*, April 1952, vol. 1, sect. 20.
16. *Idem.*, December 1951, pp. 347–349.
17. This conforms to the fact that N'Diaye and Diop are the only *gamu* or *kol*; that has to do with the kinship resulting from marriages contracted over long periods of time between two exogamic clans.
18. *T. S.*, pp. 38, 127–129.
19. *T. F.*, p. 119.
20. *T. F.*, pp. 17, 94, 114, and 151.
21. *T. F.*, ch. V, pp. 83–84.

Postface

The French edition of this book contains an eleventh chapter entitled "Linguistic Appendix," that has been eliminated from the present edition as being far too technical to interest the general reader. The Appendix is devoted to a presentation, without the application of any hypotheses, of certain grammatical facts. Were the formation of abstract nouns, diminutives, plurals, and so on in French not already fully studied, it would be necessary to carry out just such a study in order to complete our understanding of French grammar and elicit the genius of the language.

If, as a result of that study, it were found that the rules established recurred almost without change in other Indo-European languages in a systematic fashion, this would lead to the conclusion that there was a fundamental kinship within the language group. Such a conclusion would have been reached without requiring debatable linguistic hypotheses, simply on the basis of presentation without comment on the linguistic elements. A mere glance at the results would have been sufficient to show that we were on solid ground.

We have undertaken a similar study concerning Wolof, Serer, Peul-Tuculor, and Sara.

In attempting to complete the Wolof grammar beyond what had already been done (Fr. Guy Grand's *Grammaire* which is apparently the most complete treatment of the subject to date), we were able to establish rules for the formations of substantives, abstract nouns, diminutives, and plurals, as by the change of an initial consonant.

We also made a very complete study of the lingering question of "class languages" and their verb forms. We found that the same laws recurred in Serer, Peul (and Tuculor). Whence, rules which permit the passage from one of these languages to the others in a systematic fashion.

But it is the study of these "class languages" that truly led to the revelation of the genius of African languages of this type. The conclusions drawn therefrom then have sociological and ethnological significance, to the extent that they allow us to use the language as a basis for understanding the mentality of the people.

Those readers wishing to delve further into this aspect of the subject are advised to refer to the revised French edition, *L'Afrique Noire précoloniale,* published by Présence Africaine, 25 bis rue des Ecoles, 75005 Paris, France.

Note: The author had proposed the holding of five colloquia, within the framework of the UNESCO project of *General History of Africa,* to carry forward African research:

1. "The Peopling of Egypt"
2. "Deciphering of Meroitic Writing"
3. "Migrations, Toponyms, and Ethnonyms"
4. "Specific Causes of the Detachment of the Iberian Peninsula at the Dawn of Modern Times" and
5. "Air Cover of Africa."

The first four of these have been held.

BIBLIOGRAPHY

ABULFEDA. *Géographie*, translated by Reinaud. Paris, 1848.

ALVAREZ D'ALMADA. *Traité succinct sur les rivières de Guinée et du Cap Vert . . . , 1584.* Oporto, 1841.

BAKRI, Al. See Bekri, El.

BARBOT. *Histoire de la Guinée.* Paris, 1660.

BARTH, H. *Travels and Discoveries in Northern and Central Africa,* 5 vols. London, 1855.

BASSET, R. *Essai sur l'histoire et la langue de Tombouctou et des Royaumes Songhaï et Melli.* Louvain, 1889.

BAUMANN, A. & WESTERMANN, D. *Les Peuples et les Civilisations de l'Afrique,* translated by L. Homburger. Paris: Ed. Payot, 1947.

BEKRI, EL. *Description de l'Afrique septentrionale,* trans. Slane. Algiers: Typographie Adolphe Jourdan, 1913.

——. *Notes sur le pays des Noirs.*

BONNEL DE MÉZIÈRES, A. "Recherches de l'emplacement de Ghana," in *Mémoires présentés par divers savants à l'Académie des Inscriptions et Belles Lettres,* vol. XIII. Paris, 1920.

BUDGE, E.A.W. *Egyptian Sudan.* London, 1907.

CAILLÉ, René. *Journal d'un voyage à Tombouctou,* 3 vols. Paris, 1830.

CAILLIAUD, F. *Voyage à Méroé, au Fleuve blanc, au-delà de Fâzoql, dans le Midi du Royaume de Sénnâr.* Paris: Imprimerie Royale, 1826.

CHERUBINI, S. *La Nubie.* Paris, 1878.

CORONELLI. *Map of Africa.* 1689.

DAN FODIO, Cheikh Otmane. *Nour el-Eulbab.* Algiers, 1898.

DELAFOSSE, M. *Haut-Sénégal–Niger,* 3 vols. Paris: Larose, 1913.

————. *Les Noirs de l'Afrique*. Paris: Payot, 1922.

DESCHAMPS, Gov. H. *Les Religions africaines*. Paris: P.U.F., 1950.

DESPLAGNES, Louis. *Le Plateau Central nigérien*. Paris: Larose, 1907.

DEVIC, L.M. *Le Pays des Zendjs ou la Côte orientale d'Afrique au Moyen-Age, d'après les écrivains arabes*. Paris, 1883.

DIETERLEN, G. *Religion des Bambara*. Paris: Payot, 1949.

DIODORUS SICULUS. *Histoire universelle*, trans. Abbé Terrasson. Paris, 1758.

EDRISSI. *Description de l'Afrique et de l'Espagne*. Leiden, 1866. (See Idrisi.)

Encyclopédie mensuelle d'Outre-Mer. December 1951; April 1952.

FROBENIUS, Leo. *Histoire de la civilisation africaine*, trans. Dr. H. Back & D. Ermont. Paris: Gallimard, 1938.

————. *Mythologie de l'Atlantide*, trans. Gidon. Paris: Payot, 1947.

FUSTEL DE COULANGES, Numa Denis. *The Ancient City*, trans. Willard Small, 1873. New York: Doubleday Anchor reprint, n.d.

GAFFAREL, P. *Eudoxe de Cyzique et le périple de l'Afrique dans l'Antiquité*. Paris, 1872.

GHARNATI. *Route de Carthage*, trans. Beaumier. Paris, 1860.

GHYKA, Matila. *Le Nombre d'Or. Rites et rythmes pythagoriciens dans le développement de la civilisation occidentale*. Paris: Gallimard, 1976 reprint edition.

GRENIER, A. *Les Religions étrusque et romaine*. Paris: P.U.F., Mana collection, vol. 3, 1948.

GRIAULE, M. *Dieu d'eau*. Paris: Ed. du Chêne, 1948.

HACQUARD, A. *Monographie de Tombouctou*. Paris, 1900.

HAMIDULLAH, M. "L'Afrique découvre l'Amérique avant Christophe Colomb" in *Présence Africaine*. Paris, Feb.–May 1958, No. XVIII–XIX.

HERODOTUS. *The Histories of Herodotus*, trans. Henry Cary. New York: Appleton, 1899.

HOMBURGER, L. *Les Langues négro-africaines et les peuples qui les parlent*. Paris: Payot, 1947.

IBN BATTUTA. *Voyage au Soudan*, trans. Slane. Paris, 1843.

IBN HAUKAL. *Routes et Royaumes (Description de l'Afrique)*, trans. Slane. Paris, 1842.

IBN KHALDUN. *Histoire des Berbères et des dynasties mus-*

ulmanes de l'Afrique Septentrionale, trans. Slane. Algiers: Government Printshop, 1854, 4 vols.

————. *Prolégomènes historiques,* trans. Slane, 3 vols. Paris, 1868.

IDRISI. *Idrissi géographe,* trans. A. Jaubert. Paris: Royal Printshop, 1836. (See also Edrissi.)

JASPAN, M.A. "Negro Culture in Southern Africa Before European Conquest," *Science and Society,* vol. XIX, no. 3, Summer 1955.

JEANNEQUIN DE ROCHEFORT. *Voyage de Libye au Royaume de Sénégal.* Paris, 1642.

JOSEPHUS. *OEuvres complètes.* trans. Buchon. Paris, 1843.

JOUENNE, Dr. "Les Monuments mégalithiques du Sénégal," in *Annuaire et Mémoires du comité d'études historiques et scientifiques de l'A.O.F.* Gorée, 1916–1917.

KÂTI, Mahmûd. *Tarikh el-Fettach,* trans. O. Goudas & M. Delafosse. Paris, 1913 (republished, Paris: A. Maisonneuve, 1981).

LABAT. *Nouvelle relation de l'Afrique Occidentale,* 5 vols. Paris, 1728.

LABOURET. "Le Mystère des ruines du Lobi," in *Revue d'ethnographie et des traditions populaires.* Paris, 1920.

LE CHATELIER, A. *L'Islam en A.O.F.* Paris, 1899.

LE HÉRISSÉ. *L'Ancien Royaume du Dahomey.* Paris, 1911.

LENORMANT, F. *Histoire ancienne de l'Egypte.*

————. *Histoire ancienne des Phéniciens.* Paris, Ed. Lévy, 1890.

LEO AFRICANUS. *Description de l'Afrique,* trans. Temporal, 3 vols. Paris, 1896–1898.

LEROI-GOURHAN, André. *Milieu et Techniques, Evolution et Techniques.* Paris, Albin Michel, 1945.

————. *L'Homme et la Matière.* Paris: Albin Michel, 1943.

————. *Archéologie du Pacifique Nord.* Paris, 1946.

———— & POIRIER, Jean. *Ethnologie de l'Union française,* vol. I, "Afrique." Paris: P.U.F., 1953.

LUCAS, J. Olumide. *The Religion of the Yorubas.* Lagos: CMS Bookshop, 1948.

MAES, Dr. J. "Pierres levées de Toundi-Dar," in *Bull. Com. Et. A.O.F.,* 1924.

MANU. *The Laws of Manu,* trans. from the Sanskrit by George Bühler. Oxford: Clarendon Press, 1866 (reprinted, New York: Dover Publications, 1969).

MARX, Karl. *Capital: A Critique of Political Economy,* trans. by

Samuel Moore & Edward Aveling, ed. by Frederick Engels, reviewed and amplified according to the Fourth German Edition by Ernest Untermann. Chicago: Kerr, 1915.

MEVIL. *Samory.* Paris, 1899.

MONTEIL, Ch. *Monographie de Djenné.* Tulle, 1903.

MORET, A. *Le Nil et la Civilisation égyptienne.*

MUNGO PARK. Travel in the Interior of Africa (1795–1797). London, 1799.

PÉDRALS, D.P. de. *Archéologie de l'Afrique Noire.* Paris: Payot, 1949.

PLINY THE ELDER. *Histoire naturelle,* trans. E. Littré, 2 vols. Paris, 1860.

RADCLIFF-BROWN, Alfred R., ed. *African Systems of Kinship and Marriage.* New York: Oxford University Press, 1950.

RIBARD, André. *La Prodigieuse Histoire de l'Humanité.* Paris: Ed. du Myrte, Collection "Pour comprendre l'histoire," 1947.

SÂDI, Abderrahman es-. *Tarikh es-Soudan,* trans. O. Houdas. Paris: Ernest Leroux, 1900 (republished, Paris: A Maisonneuve, 1981).

STRABO. *The Geography of Strabo,* trans. Horace Leonard Jones. Cambridge: Harvard University Press.

TAUXIER. *Etudes soudainaises: Le Noir du Yatanga.* Paris: E. Larose, 1927.

TEMPELS, Fr. *Philosophie bantoue.* Paris: Présense Africaine, 1948.

VAN SERTIMA, Ivan. *They Came Before Columbus.* New York: Random House, 1976.

VIGNAUX, Paul. *Le Pensée au Moyen Age.* Paris: Armand Colim, 1938.

VIGONDY, Robert. Map of Africa, 1795.